AUSTRALIA'S PIVOT TO INDIA

Andrew Charlton is a member of the Australian Parliament. He serves as the chair of the Parliamentary Friends of India and represents the division of Parramatta, which includes one of the largest Indian diaspora communities in Australia. Before entering Parliament, he was a managing director at Accenture, founder of AlphaBeta, senior economic advisor to Prime Minister Kevin Rudd and an academic at the London School of Economics. He has a PhD in economics from Oxford University, where he studied as a Rhodes Scholar. Andrew is the author of two previous books – *Ozonomics* and *Fair Trade for All*, written with Nobel laureate Joseph Stiglitz – and two Quarterly Essays.

'It is a powerful declaration for the shared future between Australia and India that an emerging leader like Andrew Charlton has produced such a passionate tribute to the relationship between our countries. He reminds us how much we have to be grateful for – and proud of – in his recognition of the rich contribution of the Indian diaspora.'
—PENNY WONG

AUSTRALIA'S PIVOT TO INDIA

ANDREW CHARLTON

Published by Black Inc.,
an imprint of Schwartz Books Pty Ltd
Wurundjeri Country
22–24 Northumberland Street
Collingwood VIC 3066, Australia
enquiries@blackincbooks.com
www.blackincbooks.com

Copyright © Andrew Charlton 2023
Andrew Charlton asserts his right to be known as the author of this work.

ALL RIGHTS RESERVED
No part of this publication may be reproduced, stored in a retrieval system, or transmitted in any form by any means electronic, mechanical, photocopying, recording or otherwise without the prior consent of the publishers.

9781760644772 (paperback)
9781743823316 (ebook)

A catalogue record for this book is available from the National Library of Australia

Cover design by Alex Ross
Text design and typesetting by Aira Pimping
Cover photograph by Robert Cianflone / Getty Images Sport
Charts by Alan Laver
Index by Belinda Nemec

*Dedicated to the people of Parramatta and
the Indian diaspora across Australia*

CONTENTS

Preface   ix

1. Little India, Big India   1

Part I. Acquaintances

2. False Dawns and First Dates   15
3. Listless Leadership   22
4. Setbacks and Squalls   40
5. Divergent Economies   48
6. Strategic Misalignment   80

Part II. Friends

7. Pivot: Three 'C's' and Four 'D's'   99
8. Cricket   102
9. Cuisine   107
10. Commonwealth   111
11. Commerce   114
12. Democracy   121
13. Defence and Security   128

Part III. Family

14.	Diaspora	139
15.	Business	145
16.	Politics	153
17.	Education	163
18.	Media	169
19.	Culture	174
20.	Faith	179
21.	Health and Community Services	189

Part IV. Partners

22.	Investment	197

Notes — 203
Recommended Reading — 225
Index — 229

PREFACE

Shortly after his appointment as Australia's high commissioner to India in 1965, Arthur Tange sent an agitated note to Foreign Minister Paul Hasluck. Arriving to find a listless diplomatic relationship, Tange wrote to his boss that while there was fertile ground between the two countries, 'no one seems to know what seed to plant'.

This quote was given to me shortly after I became the chair of the Parliamentary Friends of India by my colleague Tim Watts, one of the great authorities on the Australia–India relationship in the Australian parliament. 'Andrew,' Tim said to me emphatically, 'we finally know, after more than fifty years, what seeds to plant in that fertile ground: the diaspora!'

The Indian diaspora has animated Australia's relationship with India and built a human bridge between our two nations. Much of what I know about Australia's relationship with India, I've learnt from members of the diaspora, and this book is dedicated to all those who have shared their stories and taught me about the history of India and Indian Australians.

My first trip to India, twenty years ago, was to launch a book I'd written about global economics. As a young economist, I was struck by the audacity of India's post-independence project to simultaneously build a modern industrial economy and an egalitarian democracy – without possessing much basis for either. Each time I went back to India, I became more fascinated by its quixotic national journey from medieval powerhouse to colonial vassal to impecunious republic to its present incarnation as emerging superpower.

For all its twists and turns, India's journey has brought it to a point of extraordinary promise. Just as the twentieth century was said to be the American Century, and the nineteenth century was the Age of Empire, we may well end the twenty-first century with India on top. India is already the largest nation in the world by population. And it's growing so quickly that by 2070 its population should rival that of China, the United States and the European Union combined. India also has the fastest economic growth of any major nation. It has the second-largest armed forces and the fastest growing military capability in the world.[1]

India's inexorable superpower trajectory isn't just evident in the numbers; it's also palpable in the streets. There is a sense of anticipation among the people of India: driving, running, selling, begging, cooking, shouting and sitting. In every city and village, you can feel the fast-dawning realisation that what happens here will change the world.

India's rise will also change Australia. Today the Indian diaspora has blossomed into an extraordinary community, numbering more than one million Australians – nearly one in twenty-five Australians has Indian heritage. And Indian Australians are by far the fastest growing ethnic group. The Indian diaspora is making an enormous contribution to Australia and helping to cultivate a fruitful relationship with one of the world's emerging superpowers.

Acknowledgements

I owe a debt to many people who have assisted, directly and indirectly, in the production of this book. I acknowledge fellow members of the Parliamentary Friends of India, in particular former chairs Michelle Rowland and Julian Leeser, who have done much to bring the parliament and the Indian people closer together, as well as fellow members Zaneta Mascarenhas, Chris Bowen, Jerome Laxale, Sally Sitou, Rob Mitchell and Julian Hill. Foreign Minister Penny Wong has re-established Australia's standing in the region and helped to bring Australia and India closer than they have ever been. The Minister for Immigration and Multiculturalism, Andrew Giles, has provided enormous support to the Indian diaspora.[2] Thank you to Dimity Paul, Sravya Abbineni and Kun Huang for being the kind of unflappable staffers who keep the wheels of government moving. Kevin Rudd taught me many things about Australia's foreign relations, sometimes conscientiously, often via osmosis.

This book draws on the scholarship of many experts in the foreign policy community, including Meg Gurry, Peter Varghese, Ian Hall, Roy MacLeod, Eric Meadows, Michael Wesley, Shashi Tharoor, Surjeet Dogra Dhanji, Aarti Betigeri, Harsh V. Pant, David Lowe, Auriol Wiegold, Hugh White, Lisa Singh, Jodi McKay, Peter Hartcher, Sarah Storey, Harinder Sidhu, Patrick Suckling, Barry O'Farrell, Rory Medcalf, David Brewster, Andrea Bevenuti, David Martin Jones, Gregory Pemberton, Gareth Evans, Matt Wade and many others. Janet Hay and Ian Stephenson from the National Trust kindly gave me access to some of the materials from the 'Tales from the East: India and New South Wales' exhibition held at Old Government House in 2018. The Australian Parliamentary Library gave me assistance with facts and figures.

Many Indian officials and diplomats were generous with their time in interviews and conversations. Dr Bibek Debroy, chair of Prime Minister Modi's Economic Advisory Council, helped me understand the contemporary Indian economy during his recent visit to Australia. Shaurya Doval, who leads the India Foundation, gave me a perspective on India's investment outlook and security environment. Dr Vijay Chauthaiwale, head of the Foreign Affairs Department of the Bharatiya Janata Party (BJP), and Ram Madhav, former National General Secretary of the BJP, gave me many insights into Indian politics. Montek Singh Ahluwalia taught me much about India's economic history while we worked together as G20 sherpa colleagues some years ago. I acknowledge the Indian Consul General in Sydney, Manish Gupta, and High Commissioner, Manpreet Vohra – their service to India and Australia has been extraordinary and I have learnt much from them.

So many friends have shaped my understanding of the bilateral relationship, and I acknowledge the Indian diaspora in Australia and especially the Indian community in Parramatta that I have the honour to represent. I thank them for their support and friendship, especially Harish Velji, Aisha Amjad, Priyan Rajaram, Renga Rajan, Parag Shah, Gurmeet Tuli, Jay Raman, Harmohan Singh Walia, Glen Maberly, Yogesh Kattar, Sanjay Deshwal, Darshan Desai, Maytrik Thaker, Bhavik Kapadia, Manoj Doshi, Kunal Mehta, Parul Mehta, Vaibhavi Joshi, Prasanth Kadaparthi, Ketan Patel, Jagvinder Singh Virk, Anagan Babu, Nitin Setia, Michael Thangavelu, Samiksha Sanghvi, Udeni Manamperi, Vipin Punia, Satyan Patel, Arunesh Seth, Sheba Nandkeolyar, Kunal Patel, Rishi Rishikesan, Ajoy Ghosh, Irfan Malik, Ramesh Sharma, Parminder Sharma, Sheba Nandkeolyar, Immanuel Selveraj, Kamaldeep Singh, Ritesh Duggal, Neeraj Duggal, Thiru Arumugam, Sonia Gandhi, Dr Naveen Shukla, Chetan Kusumgar, Bimal Joshi, Ankur Patel, Anusha Pranatharthihran, Kumar Jha, Jon Hillman, Sandip Hor and Jitesh Rao. Satwant Singh Calais has taught me much about Sikh history and the contemporary Sikh community in Australia. Nathan Rees, Julia Finn, Laurie Ferguson and Jodi McKay are current and former politicians with deep connections in the Indian community from whom I have learnt a lot. Bob Easton and Scott Wharton are two of Australia's most experienced businesspeople with deep connections to India. I acknowledge the political leaders in Australia with Indian heritage, including Daniel Mookhey, Sameer Pandey, Charishma Kaliyanda, Susai Benjamin, Raj Datta and Moninder Singh. I also thank all the people who have guided the Little India project, including councillors Patricia Prociv, Ange Humphries, Pierre Esber, Paul Noack and Dan Siviero.

I'm grateful to all the friends and colleagues who read sections of the book and gave me valuable comments and suggestions, including Jim Chalmers, Tim Watts, Aman Gaur, Zaneta Mascarenhas, Sravya Abbineni, Ranji Luthra, Priyan Rajaram, Natasha Kassam, and Susai and Anne Benjamin.

I am an avid follower of the Indian Australian media and this book has benefited from its high-quality journalism. I acknowledge publishers and journalists, including Minu and Rajesh Sharma, Rajni and Pawan Luthra, Pallavi Jain, Navneet Anand, Bhavya Pandey, Manpreet Kaur Singh, Jai Bharadwaj, Natasha Kaul, Anita Barar, Amit Sarwal and many others.

While the primary focus of this book is India, many people have given me perspectives on the South Asian region, including friends with Nepalese heritage, Goba Katuwal and Deepak Khadka, friends with ancestry in Bangladesh, Prabir Maitra and Rizwanul Chowdhury, friends with Sri Lankan heritage, including my parliamentary colleague Cassandra Fernando, and friends from Pakistan, including Syed Asim Raza.

Many old friends have encouraged me along the journey of writing this book and built my understanding of Australia's relationship with India. Shaun Star invited me to join the Australia–India Youth Dialogue many years ago. Dom Knight and Divya Rajagopalan gave me the wonderful experience of attending their wedding in Chennai. Sanushka Mudaliar is always on hand to gently correct my poor pronunciation and fill in my cultural lacunae. Udai Bakshi and Shane Watson taught me a thing or two about cricket in India. Lachlan Harris spurred me to start writing the book, and Amit Singh convinced me not to give up halfway through.

Thank you to my electorate office team – Launa Jabour, Kai He, Paul Murphy, Maryam Noorhabib, Jackie Bou Melhem and Julian Alley – for your support while I wrote this book and for your tireless service to our community.

Chris Feik published, edited and brought the book to life. Thank you to my parents, who created a multicultural family and fostered an interest in the world around us, and to my brother Kim and his family for their love and support. And finally, to my wife, Phoebe, and our children, Angus, Ruth and Ingrid, you are my whole world.

1

LITTLE INDIA, BIG INDIA

Little India

An old photograph in a wonky frame hangs on a wall in my office. It's a picture of one of Australia's oldest standing dwellings. The house is rather ordinary – a free-standing single-storey bungalow elevated on a platform, surrounded by a semi-enclosed verandah and shuttered windows, all underneath a pitched roof. The building isn't more than a kilometre from my office in Parramatta, but it seems a world away. 'The past is a foreign country,' goes the opening line of L.P. Hartley's famous novel *The Go-Between*. But the photograph calls on me to upend this notion. It reminds me that the present is tightly tethered to the past in ways we only hazily comprehend.

As I write this book, I'm studying another photo, of another house much further away. It's an almost identical bungalow in West Bengal, India. It has the same pitched roof, shutters, raised-platform floor and wrap-around verandah with parts semi-enclosed for privacy and shade.

The similarities between these two homes, it turns out, are not coincidental. The builder of the Parramatta house was a British Navy surgeon by the name of John Harris. Before arriving in Australia in 1790 as part of the Second Fleet, Harris had spent a decade posted to India, where he had resided for a time at the matching bungalow in West Bengal.[1] When he landed in New South Wales, Harris found the climate in Sydney not unlike the intense heat and throbbing rain of India. So the farmstead he built for himself in Parramatta had more in common with the colonial homes he'd experienced in Bengal than with the tightly enclosed houses of his youth in County Londonderry, Ireland.

John Harris's house is built on land that was once called Experiment Farm, where European crops were first successfully cultivated in Australia by convict farmer James Ruse in 1789. The harvest that sprang from this soil saved the fledgling settlement from starvation and established the viability of the British colony.[2]

The farm stayed in the Harris family until 1921, when the land was subdivided and the suburb of Harris Park was established. Many of the original cottages from this period are still standing, and the streets retain a consistency of development, with narrow lots, back lanes and simple-form timber and brick bungalows built close together.

In the decades of post-war migration, Harris Park became a landing point for successive generations of migrants to Sydney. The colonial link with India is meaningful because today more than half of the residents of Harris Park were born in India and almost all the old timber dwellings on the two main streets have been converted into Indian restaurants, sari stores and jewellery shops.

Now known as 'Little India', these streets are the epicentre of South Asian culture in Australia: a drawcard for both tourists and locals, who come to dine at the restaurants, visit the street vendors and take in the nightly festive atmosphere. Vibrant smells emanate from the most whitebread of timber bungalows. Juxtapositions like this give the suburb its unique character, rich in distinctive architecture and street life.

Each day from about noon, the streets begin to fill with people like a thermometer fills with mercury. Friendly shopkeepers and business owners emerge from their premises at a jog to say hello to a neighbour or passing friend. The people throw themselves into casual encounters, talking quickly and exuding an instant charm.

The transformation of Harris Park is a microcosm of the broader Australian migration story, in which the Indian diaspora is now the fastest-growing migrant community. Australia is home to more than one million people with Indian heritage – nearly one in every twenty-five Australians. Indian-born Australians are now the second-largest group of first-generation migrants in Australia. They recently overtook Chinese-born Australians and New Zealand-born Australians and, on current growth rates, will overtake the number of Australians born in the United Kingdom in the next decade to become the largest migrant group.

Like previous generations of migrants, Indian Australians are having a profound impact on Australia, contributing their energy, enterprise and values to our multicultural tapestry. Like all migrants, the Indian Australians in Harris Park straddle two cultures. Within weeks of each other they will arrange a Diwali festival with lights and Bollywood dancing and a Christmas celebration with a brass band and carol singing. On 26 January – coincidentally both Australia's national day and Indian Republic Day – they flip from one celebration to another with equal jubilation.

The community is coming together to build a ceremonial gate at the entrance to Little India as a symbol of the melding of cultures in the old suburb that was once the experimental farm of James Ruse. When Indian prime minister Narendra Modi visited Sydney in 2023 he unveiled a plaque to commemorate the Little India gate in front of an ecstatic crowd of more than twenty thousand people. Addressing the Australian diaspora, he urged them to show their support for Little India as well as their pride for 'Mother India', which he called a 'force for global good'.

Modi is a softly spoken man, but his words have impact, partly because he is giving voice to the great roar of the Indian people, who have emerged over recent decades from several hundred years of subjugation.

Big India

The gate in Little India is a nod to the larger India Gate in New Delhi. This monumental war memorial stands atop Delhi's grand ceremonial boulevard, which stretches for 3 kilometres between rows of jamun trees, red granite pathways and manicured lawns towards the palatial residence of India's president. This jugular artery is the axis around which the city was originally planned by Edwin Lutyens, the Edwardian architect who designed New Delhi nearly a century ago as a grand imperial capital within the British Empire. Lutyens forged a new style of architecture for the city, combining neoclassical motifs with accents borrowed from India's Mughal and Buddhist past.

Like other global cities with long histories, New Delhi has become an ornate palimpsest of architectural styles. Successive emperors and sultans demolished the fortresses and temples of their predecessors in order to glorify their own regimes, using architecture to demonstrate their political and cultural dominance.

Today, a new administration in Delhi is stamping its own mark on the city. Prime Minister Modi expunged the colonial name of the grand avenue that flows away from India Gate by changing it from Rajpath (Kings Path) to Kartavya Path (Duty Path).[3] Another small but significant transfiguration occurred in 2022 when a 9-metre-high statue of Netaji Subhas Chandra Bose, a nationalist hero from the Hindu wing of the independence movement, was installed under a canopy opposite India Gate that had once held a statue of King George V. 'At the time of slavery, there was a statue of the representative of the British Raj,' Modi said at the unveiling of the massive new effigy. 'Today, the country has also brought to life a modern, strong India by establishing the statue of Netaji at the same place.'

These mnemonic gestures will all be dwarfed by Modi's grand project: a rebuilding of the centre of Delhi. Modi declared the capital 'is not just a city, but ... a symbol of a country's ideas, promises, capability, and culture.' India's global emergence warrants a new capital to house the new *aatma* or 'national consciousness' that is being born. Modi has little interest in colonial architecture, which he believes is an insult to Indian sovereignty. Instead, his mega-project is to rebuild Lutyens' colonial-era buildings and replace them with an entirely new civic core linking India Gate to the Akshardham Hindu temple that will reflect an emerging power shedding its *ghulami ki mansikta*, a colonial mindset that Modi wants banished from the national psyche.

Modi's vision for Delhi reflects his broader vision, which is to connect India's proud history with its destiny as a first-rank nation. India was the richest and most sophisticated nation in the world for most of the first thousand years of the current era. Modi wants to use the energising force of nationalism to restore India's role as a global superpower.

In the streets of India, especially in the capital, you can feel the energy of anticipation for the nation's future. It springs from a universal sense that India's stature in the world is growing inexorably. Just as the twentieth century was said to be the American Century, and the nineteenth century was Pax Britannica, we may well end the twenty-first century with India's rise marking a new era.

India has already become the biggest country in the world by population. More people live in India than the combined population of the 150 smallest countries in the world. As noted, India has the fastest-growing economy of any major nation. It has overtaken the United Kingdom, its former colonial master, as the world's fifth-largest economy. Looking ahead, India appears set to continue its march up the global rankings, overtaking Germany and Japan within the next decade to become the third-largest economy in the world. At that point, India's demand for capital and materials will drive the world's financial markets and commodity prices.

India has the second-largest active-duty military in the world. It has the fourth-highest military spending of any country and now possesses the world's fourth-strongest military, according to the Global Firepower Index, which ranks countries based on the size and capability of their defence forces. India is one of nine countries with nuclear weapons and has successfully developed long-range nuclear-capable ballistic and cruise missiles.

Modi is calling on the Indian people to recognise *aitihasik kshan*, a historic and transformational moment in the nation's history. Indians have traditionally valued humility and deference. 'It is the fruit-laden tree whose branches bend,' reads the Sanskrit proverb. But Modi, who places great stock in his own humble background, believes that this is not a moment for national deference. He wants to galvanise his people around the ambition to make India a great nation by the year 2047 – the centenary of independence.

The spectacular growth of India, and the blossoming of the Indian diaspora, will thoroughly change Australia inside and out. Just as the new Little India Gate that sits on John Harris's old farm represents the contribution of Indian migrants to Australia, so the grand reshaping of Lutyens' magnificent colonial capital around India Gate in New Delhi is a sign of India's emerging influence on the world.

Australia and India
The Darling Ranges behind Perth in Western Australia shares a common history with the Nilgiri Mountains in South India. These two ancient geological discontinuities were formed from the same magma that began gradually cooling as it rose towards the Earth's surface nearly three billion years ago. The slow cooling process enabled the atoms within the rock to align into large white, black and pink crystals that today form the granite promontories, cliffs and escarpments that create a dramatic visual contrast with the surrounding grasslands and forests.

These rocky hills are now 6000 kilometres apart, but they were once the hinge that joined Australia and India in ancient Gondwanaland. It was from here that Australia and India began to drift away from each other 130 million years ago as the ocean floor broke apart.

Scientists have searched for early human links between India and Australia. As early as 1623, Dutch explorers likened the physical appearance of Indigenous Australians to that of 'Indians'.[4] Two centuries later, Thomas Henry Huxley, president of the Royal Society in the United Kingdom, asserted that Indigenous Australians were closely related to the people of South Asia, claiming that 'the only people out of Australia who present the chief characteristics of the Australians in a well-marked form are the so-called hill-tribes who inhabit the interior of the Dekhan, in Hindostan'.[5]

All this was mere colonial-era speculation, but it would later be backed by evidence from geneticists Alan Redd and Mark Stoneking, who found a strong genetic connection between Australia and India.[6] Their study of Indigenous Australian DNA suggested a migration from India to Australia about four thousand years ago, although their results are controversial and other genetic studies have reported different findings.[7]

That genetic evidence may be complemented by features of the archaeological record. The earliest fossils of the dingo in Australia also date back a similar length of time, suggesting that it was an introduced species around the same period. Bulu Imam, from the Indian National Trust for Art and Cultural Heritage, believes the dingo is the direct descendant of the Indian Santal hounds, known as Pariahs, which Indian hunters and gatherers brought to Australia four thousand years ago.

The proposed timing of Indian migration also coincides with the use of more sophisticated tools across Australia. Around that time, flint and chert rock tools began to be used for tasks including hunting, butchering animals, working wood and preparing animal hides.[8]

'The date that we get for when this gene flow from India occurs – roughly around 4000 years ago – does coincide remarkably well with the first appearance of microliths – the small stone tool technology – in the archaeological record for Australia and with the first appearance of the dingo,' Dr Stoneking said. 'It does at least raise the suggestion that all of these events might all be connected.'[9]

Anthropological observers have also perceived Indo–Australian connections in art and culture. The Gond people from the Gondwana region of India paint in a style of dots and dashes and use striking yellow, red, black and white hues in their art, which has been likened to the art of the first Australians. Other parallels in symbols, rituals and language have been identified. These similarities might be caused by a wave of prehistoric migration, or just be reflections of common geographic features and human characteristics. Perhaps they spring from some Jungian collective unconsciousness that throws up universal creative instincts and practices.

Australia's connections with India were vital to the new British colony after the arrival of the First Fleet. India was Australia's first trading partner. In the early years, emergency supplies from India saved the colony from calamity when its stores of food dwindled to just a few months' worth, and its people were 'nearly naked and [there were] great numbers without bed or blanket to lie upon'.[10] In subsequent decades, more than a third of all ships arriving in New South Wales came from the Indian ports of Bombay, Madras and especially Calcutta. Garole sheep were imported into Australia from Bengal in 1792 and bred their wondrous fecundity gene into Australia's wool industry. Much of the imported rum, which became a de facto currency in the colony, was Indian spirits made from molasses, cane sugar and palm sugar, shipped from Calcutta. By 1817, two out of every three ships that left Sydney went to India and goods from Bengal nourished the Australian colonies.

In the next century, Australian and Indian soldiers fought together on the battlefield as part of the British Empire. More than fifteen thousand Indians served beside Australians at Gallipoli.[11] Some sixteen hundred of them lost their lives in actions at Gurkha Bluff, Gully Ravine and in the climactic attempt to seize the summit of Sari Bair.[12] In total, more Indians than Australians died fighting for the Empire in World War I.

In World War II, Australian and Indian soldiers were brothers in arms once again, fighting together in defence of freedom in Italy, Singapore and Malaya. Towards the end of the war, in 1944, Australia became the first nation in the world to grant India diplomatic recognition.

Emerging into the radically changed post-war world, our two countries had much in common. We were relatively new nations. We shared a region, we shared history and we shared a language, democratic values and even sporting passions.

With so many similarities, Australia and India should have been close friends. But behind the well-worn diplomatic platitudes about 'Commonwealth, cricket and curry', the truth is that Australia's relationship with India has been poor for most of the past seventy-five years. For two countries with so much in common, our trade was too low, our investment was practically negligible and our cooperation in defence and global politics produced few achievements of substance.

As India is on the cusp of becoming a global superpower, and Indian Australians head towards becoming Australia's largest migrant group, the purpose of this book is to analyse Australia's modern relationship with India in the period since its independence. *Australia's Pivot to India* isn't a hagiography of the bilateral relationship, and it isn't a starry-eyed attempt at painting a rosy picture of the future.

The first part of the book, 'Acquaintances', describes the disappointing relationship in the decades after India's independence. Several explanations have been offered for why our relationship languished for so long. Many diplomatic factors may have played a part, but the compelling observation is simply that the relationship lacked a 'central core': we just didn't have the essential economic interests and strategic alignment for a deep and resilient relationship. After independence, India's early administrations took fateful decisions to build an 'inward-looking' economy protected by tariffs and investment restrictions. This stymied the development of a strong trading relationship with Australia. We did not develop the strong commercial links that emerged with our East Asian neighbours, who had pursued an outward-looking economic strategy based on export growth. Similarly, India took a geopolitical stance of non-alignment, which was at odds with the web of Western alliances Australia built to guarantee its security.

The second part of this book, 'Friends', describes the events in the 1990s that would radically change Australia–India relations, including the Soviet Union's collapse, India's economic restructuring and the gathering pace of Indian migration to Australia. None of these things in isolation created breakthrough bilateral moments. But over time they created the conditions for the relationship to blossom.

Australia and India were able to move past tired references to the 'Three C's' of Commonwealth, curry and cricket, which belied an absence of deep connections in trade, culture, security and diplomacy. We added ballast to the relationship through the 'Four D's' of democracy, defence, *dosti* (friendship) and the diaspora.

The third part of the book, 'Families', gives an account of the most important element of Australia's relationship with India: the diaspora. Now numbering more than a million people, the Indian diaspora in Australia is a vibrant, diverse and growing community. Indian Australians contribute significantly to the economic, social and cultural landscape of Australia. But the Indian diaspora also faces challenges in Australia, and we have work to do to ensure that this latest and greatest wave of migration from India is supported as strongly as most previous waves of migration from around the world in our modern history. The Indian diaspora is the essential element to promote cultural exchange, commercial relationships and strong bilateral relations. As this community continues to grow and flourish, the bonds between India and Australia are likely to strengthen further.

The final part of the book, 'Partners', explains that successfully executing the 'pivot to India' will come down to mutual investment. Both India and Australia need to invest more in our relationship. Australian businesses and investors need to allocate more capital to India, to support and share in its economic growth, and to give Australians a tangible pecuniary stake in India's success. Australia also needs to invest more in the success of the Indian diaspora to overcome barriers to full participation in Australian economic and social life. And both countries must continue to invest in regional diplomatic and defence initiatives.

If we make these investments, the partnership between Australia and India will be a powerful inspiration to the world. As one of the world's most multicultural success stories, Australia is proof that liberal democracy can accommodate harmonious pluralism. As an emerging economy rapidly achieving prosperity, India is proof that democracy can foster economic growth. Australia and India have always shared common values and institutions, but in an increasingly contested world, where alternative systems of government are in a global 'competition of efficacy', it has never been more important for us to join together as free societies.

The pivot to India is a national imperative that will recast Australia's perception of itself and our place in the world. If we support the continued flourishing of the Indian diaspora, we will add another chapter to our domestic multicultural success story. And if we build a genuine partnership with our region's emerging superpower, we will assure our future prosperity and security in the world.

PART I

ACQUAINTANCES

2

FALSE DAWNS AND FIRST DATES

'Long years ago we made a tryst with destiny, and now the time comes when we shall redeem our pledge,' said Jawaharlal Nehru just before midnight on 14 August 1947, on the eve of becoming prime minister of a newly independent nation. In what is now considered to be one of the greatest speeches of the twentieth century, Nehru welcomed the rebirth of India as a remarkable moment in history, 'when the soul of a nation, long suppressed, finds utterance'.[1]

Hours later, in the light of the morning sun, India's national flag was formally raised at the Durbar Hall in New Delhi. Shortly after eight-thirty, the saffron, white and green tricolour flag fluttered in the sky above independent India for the first time.

But Australians will be interested to note that the ceremony in Delhi wasn't the first official outdoor hoisting of the new national flag. By a quirk of time zones, the Indian flag had been officially raised about an hour earlier at the Indian high commissioner's residence in Canberra, at a ceremony attended by over three hundred guests at midday local time. Thus, it may be claimed that the first official outdoor raising of independent India's national flag occurred in Australia.[2]

However premature, the celebration in Canberra reflected Australia's long-held enthusiasm to forge strong bilateral ties with our newly independent neighbour.[3] Australia had been the first country in the world with which India established a full diplomatic relationship in

1944, before it had even established its sovereignty.⁴ When India finally gained independence in 1947, Australians responded warmly because, as Australia's foreign minister, Herbert Vere 'Doc' Evatt, noted, 'Our geographical proximity and our common interest in the affairs of the Indian Ocean and South-East Asia naturally throw our lots closely together.'⁵

In the ensuing eight decades, the desirability of a warm friendship with India has been affirmed and reaffirmed by every Australian prime minister from Chifley to Albanese. Motivated by strategic logic and fuelled with cultural enthusiasm, successive Australian governments have sought to build a deep relationship with India.

Yet, in the words of Ian Hall, one of Australia's foremost India analysts, these attempts have been 'fitful [but] they have not always borne fruit.'⁶ Indeed, for nearly six decades, bilateral relations were characterised by misperception, lack of trust, neglect, missed opportunities and even hostility.

In the 1950s, the relationship had sunk so low that Paul Hasluck, who later served as Minister for External Affairs, described Australia's relations with India as worse than those with any other country, including Russia. In the 1960s, we clashed over apartheid in South Africa and the war in Vietnam. In the 1970s, Prime Minister Gough Whitlam felt compelled to admit that there was 'something missing in ... the relationship',⁷ and the Department of Foreign Affairs concurred that India's importance to Australia was recognised 'perhaps more in the breach than the observance'.⁸ In the 1980s, Australian diplomats described a 'sense of drift' in Australia's relationship with India. And a Senate report in the 1990s concluded that the two countries were 'unusually distant in their relations'.⁹

For many decades, our bilateral diplomacy was rife with opportunities squandered and potential unrealised. Too often the relationship seems to have comprised what former diplomat Mark Pierce calls a series of 'false dawns and first dates'.¹⁰

Prime Minister Anthony Albanese's trip in September 2023 was his second visit to India in a year. Narendra Modi's trip in the same year was his second visit to Australia during his prime ministership. The genuine bilateral friendship on display when Albanese was embraced by Modi on his visit to Sydney shows that Australia's relationship with India today is as strong as it has ever been in the three-quarters of a century since the establishment of formal diplomatic ties. But despite this improvement, there is still significant room for growth.

Each year, the Lowy Institute captures the affinity between nations through its 'feelings thermometer', a measurement of Australians' perceptions about other countries on a scale of 0° (coldest feelings) to 100° (warmest feelings). In 2022, India scored a tepid 57°, well below New Zealand (86°), Canada (80°), the United Kingdom (77°), Japan (74°), the United States (65°), Taiwan (64°), Vietnam (64°), South Korea (63°), Europe (62°) and Papua New Guinea (61°). Of the twenty nations ranked, India was favoured only above Russia, China, Myanmar and Afghanistan – all nations with which Australia has distinctly complicated relations.

Indeed, despite the headline progress in Australia's bilateral relationship with India, the Lowy Institute poll has recorded a relative decline in Australians' feelings towards India (see Figure 2.1). In 2006, Australians ranked India sixth out of twenty in the poll. By 2022, India had fallen to sixteenth out of twenty – a surprising decline given the steadily improving bilateral relations and growing people-to-people links.

Figure 2.1 Lowy Institute poll of Australians' feelings towards other countries and territories, 2022

Respondents were given the following instructions: 'Please rate your feelings towards some countries and territories, with one hundred meaning a very warm, favourable feeling, zero meaning a very cold, unfavourable feeling, and fifty meaning not particularly warm or cold. You can use any number from zero to one hundred: the higher the number, the more favourable your feelings are towards that country or territory. If you have no opinion or have never heard of that country or territory, please say so.'

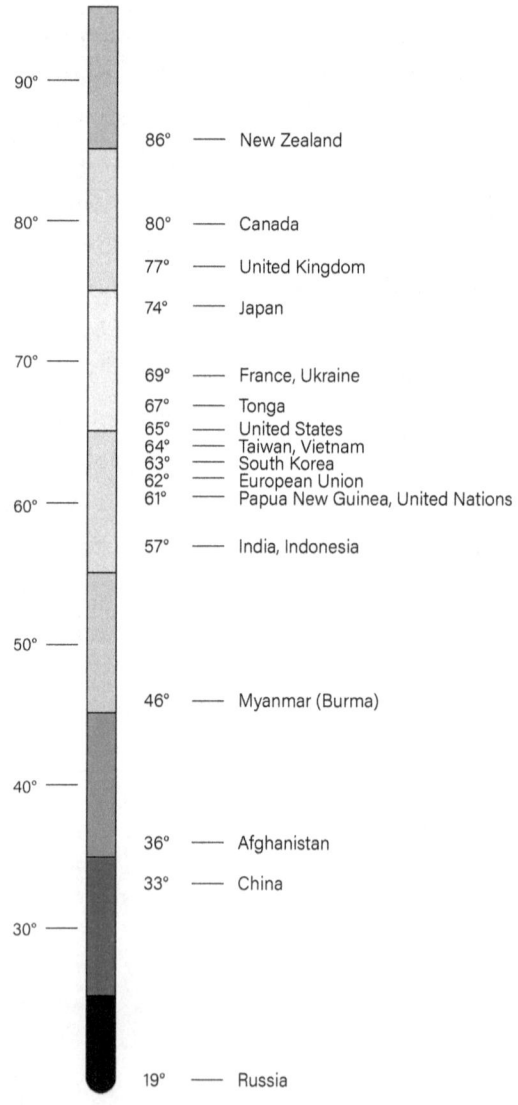

Figure 2.2 Ranking of India in the Lowy Institute 'feelings thermometer' poll

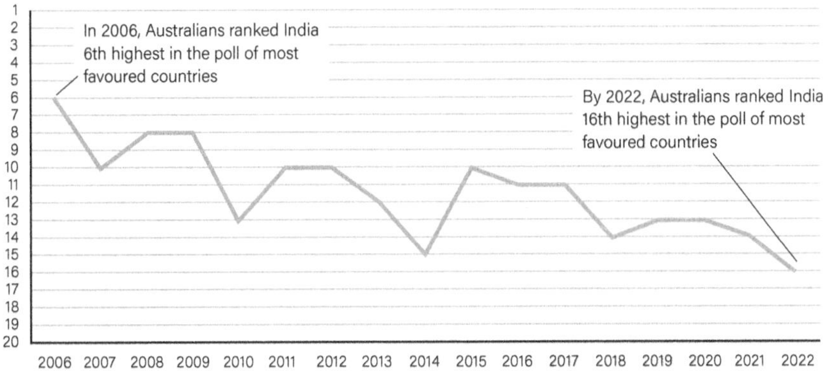

[Chart showing India's ranking from 2006 to 2022. In 2006, Australians ranked India 6th highest in the poll of most favoured countries. By 2022, Australians ranked India 16th highest in the poll of most favoured countries.]

Note: The countries ranked vary from year to year, but there are a number of countries (including India) that are consistently ranked each year. The number of countries ranked varies from seventeen to two.

Commercial relations between Australia and India are relatively weak. Australia's trade with India has grown over the years, but remains modest compared to the size of India's economy. Our $251-billion two-way trade with China is ten times larger than our trade with India. We trade $81 billion with the United States, $80 billion with Japan and $39 billion with South Korea. Our trade with India is just $26 billion.[11]

Figure 2.3 Bilateral trade in goods and services, 1987–2021

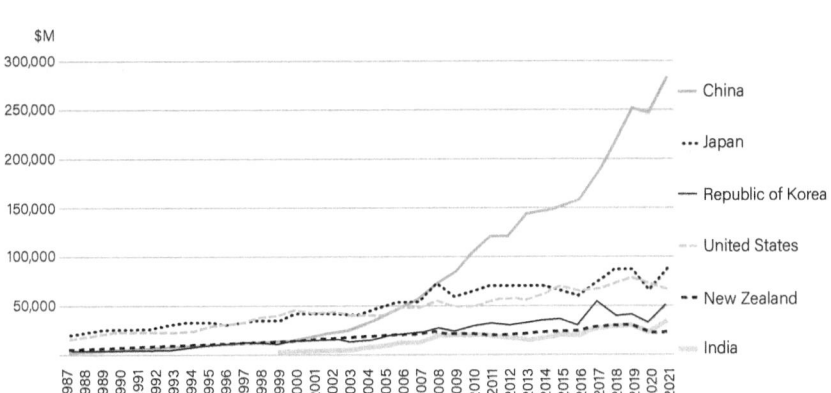

Source: DFAT

Australian investment in India is also very low. At the end of 2021, Australian investments in India totalled just $19 billion.[12] This is a fraction of the $1.1 trillion Australians invested in the United States and the $538 billion invested in the United Kingdom. And Indians don't invest much in Australia either. There is more than $4 trillion of foreign capital invested in Australia, but India accounts for less than 1 per cent of this. The level of investment between two countries is a barometer of the strength and nature of their economic relationship. A high level of investment indicates strong ties and cooperation, while a low level indicates weak economic alignment.

The obvious inference to draw from these diplomatic and commercial facts is that there is much room for growth. Many Australian governments have recognised the value of Australia's relationship with India and made sincere attempts to realise its potential. But notwithstanding recent improvements, our achievements have fallen short of our aspirations.

The important question is: why? By diagnosing the reasons for these failures, we can hope to lock in recent bilateral progress and build a plan for the future. There is no shortage of introspection on this question within Australia's foreign policy establishment. Much has been written by eminent academics and researchers.[13] In the next four chapters, I canvass four explanations for Australia's historically weak relationship with India.

The first is that the bilateral relationship was held back by failures of leadership, including inconsistent political attention and limited bureaucratic follow-through. Chapter 3, 'Listless Leadership', explores the extent to which failures of leadership and diplomacy prevented us from achieving a closer relationship.

The second explanation is that the relationship was constantly chipped away at by bilateral frictions which undid any goodwill. These frictions gave the relationship a 'two steps forward, one step back' quality that prevented it from taking off. Chapter 4, 'Setbacks and Squalls', explores some of the disputes and altercations between Australia and India.

The third and fourth explanations relate to deeper forces affecting the relationship and raise the possibility that Australia and India lacked fundamental common interests for most of our history.

Chapter 5, 'Divergent Economies', looks at the lack of structural complementarity between the two economies. India chose an economic development strategy which, unlike its East Asian neighbours, had remarkably few complementarities with Australia's economy. Australia was a trading nation, an exporter of resources and importer of manufactured goods, while India focused on economic self-reliance.

The final chapter in this section, 'Strategic Misalignment', details the two countries' fundamentally different geopolitical outlooks. Australia was a multilateralist and an enthusiast for alliances, while India believed in neutrality and strategic autonomy. Australia locked itself into alliances with other global powers, which restricted its scope to engage with India on issues of security and geopolitics.

Of course these explanations are not mutually exclusive. These and other factors may have all played a part in shaping the relationship for better or worse. But my bias is towards the more fundamental factors. I believe that, for a long time, the relationship lacked a 'central core': we just didn't have the essential economic interests and strategic alignment that form the ballast for a deep and resilient relationship.

3

LISTLESS LEADERSHIP

India has been called Australia's 'neglected neighbour',[1] but the neglect has been on both sides. For Australians, India often seemed too far away, too underdeveloped and too hard to do business with. For Indians, Australia was for a long time seen as an 'insignificant power', too small, too insular and too often in the pocket of the United States.[2]

Successive Australian administrations have recognised the value of India, and made sincere, vigorous – if sporadic – attempts to realise its potential. But most attempts have fallen short of expectations. The role of individual leaders in building strong bilateral relations is important. While it's true that nations build relationships based on their fundamental national interests, it's also true that these national interests are subjectively interpreted through the prism of a leader's own values and interests. This makes leadership, and the personal rapport between leaders, crucial to building positive relations.

At several points in our history, Australia's relationship with India has been held back by inconsistent political leadership and weak follow-through. As foreign policy expert Allan Gyngell once quipped, 'Every Australian government discovers India once, and then promptly forgets about it.'

Chifley to Menzies

Notwithstanding the challenges to come, the bilateral relationship got off to a good start. From the moment of Indian independence, there were high hopes on both sides for a strong friendship.

The early relationship was buoyed by Jawaharlal Nehru's positive impression of Doc Evatt. The two first met in 1938 at the London home of British Labour MP Stafford Cripps, when Evatt was a High Court Justice.[3] Nehru kept in touch as Evatt became Australia's Minister for External Affairs and was impressed by Evatt's role in the early years of the United Nations. Nehru was struck by Evatt's independent thinking and focus on the Asia-Pacific. Evatt's view, which found favour with Nehru, was that Australia's future security would be tied to a 'close friendship with India'.[4] Evatt mooted a defence alliance with India in 1944 and received early support from Indian officials who saw 'great scope for closer relations between Australia and India, especially for security and defence and in industrial and agricultural matters, in scientific research and in the expansion of commerce'.[5]

After the war, Evatt formed the view that Australia's 'security in the future will go hand in hand with close friendship with India'. In public, he emphasised the importance of India to the new regional order: 'In any approach to the problem of organising security in the Pacific, Australia naturally recognises the special position of India.'[6] Likewise, Nehru praised Evatt's determination to break with the past to 'create a more activist and forceful style of foreign policy for Australia' in its own region.[7]

Nehru enthusiastically encouraged Australia's participation in India's first attempt at regionalism, the Asian Relations Conference in New Delhi in 1947. Nehru wanted to use the conference to establish Asian solidarity, led by India, 'the pivot and fulcrum' for newly independent countries. Nehru's opening words to the conference set a stirring tone: 'We stand at the end of an era and on the threshold of a new period of history.' Nehru specifically welcomed Australians at the conference, 'because we have many problems in common, especially in Pacific and South-East regions, and we have to co-operate together to find a solution'.[8]

Australian Labor prime minister Ben Chifley also built a strong personal bond with Nehru. Chifley would call his Indian counterpart one of the great men of the world, while India's leader described the Australian as an 'outstanding personality' who was 'very helpful'.[9] The two leaders were in broad sympathy on many of the major issues of the day. The two countries worked together to assist Indonesia to achieve independence, demonstrating Australia's support for the decolonisation of Asia.

Bilateral relations deteriorated significantly with the change of government in Australia in December 1949, when Chifley was defeated by the Liberal–Country coalition under Robert Menzies. Menzies was Anglocentric and focused Australian foreign policy on imperial rather than regional concerns. He showed a casual indifference to Asia.[10] High commissioner to India Walter Crocker wrote in his diary in 1955 that 'Menzies is anti-Asian; particularly anti-Indian. He just can't help it.'[11] Senior Australian diplomat Keith Shann said that Menzies had 'no great interest' in Asia: 'he flew through it and over it to London'.[12] Alan Watt, secretary of the Department of External Affairs from 1950 to 1954, observed: 'the philosophy and religion of Asia were almost closed books to a man of his temperament, just as tropical climates oppressed his massive physical frame.'[13]

From the outset, Menzies had not fully supported India's independence, describing it as a country that had 'not yet reached the stage at which the majority of its people are by education, outlook and training, fit for self-government'.[14] He was also sceptical of India's desire to become a republic and retain membership of the Commonwealth. These positions were deeply offensive to Indians.

Menzies saw Australia as a European nation. He pointedly decided not to participate in the first, large-scale meeting of newly independent Asian and African states, the Bandung Conference in April 1955. The conference aimed to promote regional cooperation and build solidarity against colonialism. Menzies was unwilling to associate Australia with the summit's anti-imperialist theme.

Despite Australia's non-attendance at the conference, Nehru sought to encourage Australia's role in Asia. In his remarks at Bandung, the

Indian prime minister sent his greetings: 'Australia and New Zealand are almost in our region. They certainly do not belong to Europe, much less to America. They are next to us and I should like Australia and New Zealand to come nearer to Asia.'[15]

But as Nehru kept Asia's door open to Australia, Menzies walked past it. By declining to participate in this historic meeting of Asian states, Australia confirmed its status as, in David Walker's words, a 'stranded nation' – a country in Asia, but not of Asia.[16]

Australia and India differed on the major foreign policy issues of the era. There were frequent clashes over approaches to the Cold War. Menzies thought Nehru's policy of non-alignment was 'foolish' and believed that India was shirking the great responsibility to resist communism. India had an equally dim view of Australia's position. Indian leaders came to see Australia as a powerless adjunct to the United States and Britain, psychologically and diplomatically isolated from its neighbours in Asia. High Commissioner Peter Heydon told Canberra that a key factor keeping Australia and India apart was the Indian view that 'we have no real national personality of our own: we are copies of the UK domestically and of the U.S. in foreign affairs'.[17]

Australia and India also clashed over racial issues. Apartheid in South Africa was an affront to Nehru's values and conception of the modern world. He claimed a condition of the Commonwealth's survival was 'a strict adherence to … racial equality [and] the policy of the South African government was not compatible with it'.[18] But Menzies believed that the Commonwealth 'would break up in disorder' if domestic issues were discussed by members. Any suggestion, he said, of using the Commonwealth to influence South Africa 'misconceived the nature of our association'.[19]

Australia's stature in India was diminished by Menzies' stance on apartheid. 'Menzies was looked on as South Africa's staunchest champion at Commonwealth gatherings,' says journalist and editor Sunanda Datta-Ray, 'favouring an inner club of the older white dominions, leaving new Asian and African members out in the cold.'[20]

India strongly opposed Australia's restrictive immigration regime, the White Australia policy. The policy was seen as discriminatory and racist, and it was a source of tension in the relationship. In 1949, Nehru criticised the policy in the Indian parliament, stating that a 'racial policy was wrong and was to be deprecated'.[21] Indian high commissioner Major-General K.M. Cariappa said in 1954 that the White Australia policy was offending 440 million people in India and Pakistan and 'driving them away from the Commonwealth'.[22] An Indian newspaper called Australia's immigration regime 'an affront to Asian self-respect' and an abiding handbrake on good bilateral relations.[23]

Australia publicly justified the White Australia policy on economic rather than racial grounds, claiming its aim was to protect the wages and employment of Australian workers. But this disingenuous fig leaf further grated with Asian leaders. As the Australian high commissioner to India Iven Mackay said: 'There is no other way to explain why Australia would refuse to take ... [even] ... a small number of Westernised Indian professionals.'[24]

The policy's inherent racism and discrimination were an affront to the principles of equality and human dignity that India embraced after gaining independence. It associated Australia in the minds of many Indians with the period of colonialism and the exploitative legacy of British rule. 'The first thing that an Indian thinks about Australia, and probably the last, is the White Australia policy,' Australian journalist Neil McInnes wrote in 1960.[25]

Menzies and Nehru never developed a strong personal relationship. They were unable to overcome the differences in their political ideologies, with Menzies being a conservative and Nehru a socialist. They met at least twelve times between 1951 and 1962, including on three occasions when Menzies travelled to India; but – tellingly – Nehru never visited Australia.

Nehru was widely known to regard Menzies with 'wry amusement' and to believe him more suited to a Victorian museum than twentieth-century statecraft.[26] He thought Menzies' views were outdated, stuck in the colonial era, that he hadn't kept up with the post-war world of independent nations. On his visits to New Delhi, Menzies bored Nehru with cricket stories and seemed to show little interest in Indian affairs. Walter Crocker noted of Menzies' short visit in 1959 that, 'He didn't ask a single question about India ... He wanted to see none of the sights and he had no curiosity about and no interest in India or Indians.'[27]

It is difficult to disagree with the assessment of foreign policy scholar Meg Gurry that we can 'trace the origins of today's lacklustre [bilateral relationship] to [Menzies'] lack of interest in India.'[28] Historian Frank Bongiorno agrees that the 'imaginative and emotional deficiency in Menzies' engagement with Asia' had a chilling effect on regional relationships.[29] Indeed, that was also the contemporary view. The Labor Opposition accused the Menzies government of having 'missed the opportunity to interpret the new nations to the old world and the old world to the new nations'.[30]

Menzies and Nehru failed to establish a strong bilateral relationship during this important post-war era and the early days of India's independence. The two men had contrasting ideologies and styles and recognised few points of common national interest. Consequently, Australia and India remained culturally, strategically and diplomatically distant. It would take a new generation of leaders, and a new mindset in Australia, to begin to repair the damage.

Whitlam to Howard

On his first day as prime minister, Gough Whitlam articulated a new foreign policy direction for Australia, containing three elements calculated to appeal to India. First, Australia would move towards a 'more independent' stance in international affairs; second, we would wind back our role as deputy sheriff to the United States and be 'less militarily oriented' in the region; and third, we would eliminate 'racism' from our domestic policies. Whitlam declared that never again would Asian nations find Australia 'siding with Britain, France, Portugal, South Africa and the US, while all our neighbours are on the other side'.[31]

This was a welcome change of mood for the bilateral relationship. The new direction was backed by concrete action, including formal recognition of the People's Republic of China, accelerating Papua New Guinea's path to independence, removing the last remnants of the White Australia policy and beginning work on the *Racial Discrimination Act*.

The Indian government responded positively to Australia's newly 'independent' foreign policy and duly issued an invitation for Whitlam to visit New Delhi. In June 1973, Whitlam became the first Australian prime minister to visit India since 1959.[32] During the trip, Whitlam was at pains to point out that his government's new direction for Australian foreign policy brought Australia in line with India on 'a great range of issues facing the world on race discrimination, on de-colonisation, on Southern Africa, on human rights, on the need to keep this region free of great power rivalries'.[33] Acknowledging the historical weakness of the relationship, Whitlam declared that 'our relations with India have not been given the attention they should have. If this has been so, I intend to amend it and amend it thoroughly.'

To begin making amends, Whitlam appointed Bruce Grant as high commissioner, with clear instructions to communicate to the Indian government that '[Australia] will look to Asia as the crucible of an independent foreign policy. Our relations with the nations of Asia are primary. They necessarily underpin the structure of Australian foreign policy ... we regard India as one of the great nations of Asia, with whom we would like a relationship no less essential to an independent foreign policy than those we have with China and Japan.'[34]

While Whitlam's rhetoric was well received in Delhi, Australia soon discovered that it takes more than enthusiasm to build a strong bilateral relationship. Former high commissioner Patrick Shaw warned that, while Whitlam had established excellent relations with top-level Indian policymakers, Australia still had to add substance to sentiment: 'India ... is not simply the "pitiful helpless giant" ... we [must] strengthen our influence here [with] a modest investment of attention.'[35]

As the Whitlam government became distracted by domestic controversies, the new momentum began to fall away. Peter Curtis, who became high commissioner in Delhi in 1976, complained political sentiment was not being backed by resources and commitments: 'If we continue to be unable to match action to words we will increasingly lose opportunities to improve our relationship with an important regional neighbour ... It is ironic ... that as opportunities for expanding the relationship have increased ... resources have dwindled.'[36]

In Whitlam's case, and not for the last time in the relationship, prime ministerial rhetoric was not backed up by substance. Lack of follow-through was a regular subject of commentary in diplomatic dispatches from Delhi. Graham Feakes, Australian high commissioner to India from 1984 to 1990, grumbled about the Department of Foreign Affairs and Trade: 'there is no one in the Department who has a sense of what is going on in the relations between Australia and India across the board ... I imagine there could be no more than two or three people working there on the whole of the sub-continent.'[37]

Over the next twenty-five years, India's relationship with Australia lost the animus that characterised the Nehru–Menzies era, but never took off. There was progress, there were steps forward, there were setbacks, but the elements of substance that matter in bilateral relationships were missing.

After taking office four years earlier, Malcolm Fraser visited India as prime minister in 1979 and essentially repeated Whitlam's message that 'the relationship between India and Australia ... has been taken a little too much for granted' and promised that he would 'work positively to promote a better, a closer and a warmer relationship than had existed in the past'.[38] As with Whitlam, Fraser's words were well received on the Indian side but the visit resulted in few enduring outcomes. By 1983, foreign affairs department secretary Peter Henderson lamented that: 'the bilateral relationship lacks real depth. Neither side looms large in the thinking of the other and we have few illusions about our capacity to influence Indian views where we differ.'[39]

The experience of Bob Hawke's Labor government underlines the importance of both political leadership and the personal relationship between leaders in building strong ties. Hawke declared himself cautious about investing too much time in India, after his first interactions with Prime Minister Indira Gandhi at Commonwealth meetings were 'marked by a number of very bitter exchanges' which sapped his zeal for the relationship.[40]

Hawke's lack of interest in India was of great concern to the foreign policy establishment, who saw 'unassailable reasons of national self-interest' to build a closer relationship with our Indian Ocean neighbour.[41] Foreign Minister Bill Hayden was anxious to point out that 'the relatively low level of priority we have given our relationship with India has not been to our advantage ... it cannot be argued that we have done ourselves or anybody else any good by it.'[42]

Fortunately, prime ministerial interest in India grew substantially when Indira Gandhi, who thought Hawke was 'boorish',[43] was replaced by her son Rajiv, who found him 'delightful'.[44] Hawke met Rajiv Gandhi in October 1985, and, as Hawke would recount, 'we just clicked': 'there's no other leader I have met for whom I have developed such an immediate, deep and abiding affection.'[45] *The Australian Financial Review* reported on 'a charismatic appeal – which both men seem to share', which they felt 'bodes well for new rapport'.[46] Australia and India began cooperating on a range of international issues.

Hawke would later describe Gandhi as his 'great mate' – a sentiment the high commissioner Graham Feakes validated as genuine and 'for once not political exaggeration'.[47] Hawke invited Gandhi to visit Australia, and he came in October 1986, the first Indian prime minister to make a formal visit since Indira Gandhi in 1968.

Rajiv Gandhi's visit to Australia came with the considerable expectations that prime ministerial visits engender. Both leaders were interviewed by newspapers in the other's country; each referred to a new bilateral momentum. Gandhi praised Hawke's 'honest, straightforward manner' in press interviews. Hawke enthused about a 'dramatic new vitality' between the two countries, evidenced by plans to work jointly on arms control and apartheid in South Africa.[48]

When Gareth Evans took over as foreign minister, he worked to establish an extensive array of forums designed to promote the economic relationship, including the Australia India Business Council. But still the substantive relationship progressed slowly. In November 1986, Gandhi had candidly admitted that India's relations with Australia and New Zealand were friendly, 'but with little interaction in political or economic terms'. He conceded that India looked 'more to the West and elsewhere' than to the region.[49]

Following his election in 1996, John Howard recognised that there was much room for improvement in the relationship. A cabinet submission in October 1996 by the new foreign minister, Alexander Downer, and the trade minister, Tim Fischer, noted: 'In the past, Australia–India relations have been sporadic and insubstantial.'[50] The new government was keen to build stronger ties.

Unfortunately, efforts to improve relations under the Howard government suffered a major setback when India conducted five nuclear tests on 11 and 13 May 1998 at the Pokhran range in the Rajasthan desert. Downer called in the Indian high commissioner to convey the Australian government's 'condemnation of the tests in the strongest possible terms'.[51] Australia recalled its own high commissioner from New Delhi for consultations, suspended bilateral defence relations and expelled three Indian defence personnel then serving at defence colleges in Australia. In a stinging move, Australia also suspended all non-humanitarian aid to India and substantially increased Australia's development assistance program to Pakistan. Howard referred to India's soon-to-be constructed nuclear weapons as a 'grotesque status symbol'.[52]

Australia's strong reaction was not well received in Delhi. Indian officials denounced Australia's reaction as unreasonable, disrespectful and hypocritical, noting that Australia benefited from the United States' extended nuclear deterrence. Bilateral relations were effectively put into deep freeze for several years.[53]

In an attempt to repair the relationship, Howard travelled to India in July 2000. He sought a fresh diplomatic start, telling the media during a press conference that 'we then felt strongly about [nuclear explosions]. But you don't allow one issue to contaminate the entire relationship.'[54] During the trip, Howard tried to shift diplomatic gears into areas of potential economic cooperation. A Joint Ministerial Commission was announced to facilitate expanded trade and investment.

Howard didn't visit India again until the last year of his prime ministership. By this time, India's economic growth and strategic significance were unmistakable. 'I think India's certainly getting stronger,' said Howard, as he embarked upon the four-day trip in March 2006. 'We need to put more energy into the relationship for general strategic reasons.'[55]

The Howard government had realised, perhaps a little late, that India could no longer be ignored. Its economy had tripled in size since 1990 and had posted a spectacular 8 per cent rate of growth in GDP that year. 'We are living through this extraordinary transformation in the centre of gravity of the world's middle class,' Howard acknowledged, 'away from its overwhelming concentration in Europe and North America, to a situation where it will be predominantly, not exclusively, concentrated in the nations of Asia.'[56]

Howard's trip to India in 2006 was Australia's first acknowledgement that India was becoming a first-rank power in the world. He expressed unqualified enthusiasm for India's fast-growing economy and promised to change the language of engagement from neglect to partnership. A Memorandum of Understanding on defence cooperation was signed, covering counterterrorism, maritime security and peacekeeping. Howard also moved to take the heat out of the nuclear issue by emphasising the importance of nuclear energy for India's economic growth and energy security.

But John Howard's epiphany in 2006 was, according to Meg Gurry, 'too little, and for him, too late'.[57] Ten years into an eleven-year premiership is no time to finally 'get India'. This was not lost on New Delhi, whose foreign policy establishment recognised that Howard saw

Australia first and foremost as a member of the 'Anglosphere' and his international focus had rested primarily on relations with the United States and Britain. His interest in Asia was piqued principally by its growing economic strength, rather than any passion for Asian cultures, politics and people.

By leaving its efforts at deep engagement until after India had emerged as an economic and strategic force, the Howard government seemed opportunistic rather than genuinely eager about the bilateral relationship. As India grew in status, Australia's high commissioner, Robert Laurie, noted that Australia was 'going to have to compete for India's attention' and lamented that Australia had failed to establish any special position in the queue of countries seeking to build relations with the growing regional power.[58]

Rudd to Morrison

From the mid-2000s Australia's relationship with India began slowly to improve. The collapse of the Soviet Union brought India closer to Australia's alliance partner, the United States. A period of economic reform in India in the 1990s opened new opportunities for business engagement. The rapid growth in numbers of Indian students and migrants created many people-to-people links. Together these developments gradually brought Australia and India closer together.

Unlike some of his predecessors, Kevin Rudd had a genuine fascination with Asia that stretched back thirty years to his time as a student of Asian Studies at the Australian National University. The Rudd government brought new energy to the relationship. Foreign Minister Stephen Smith used a sporting analogy to draw a line under the past and point the way for the future. 'Australia's past approach to India has been like a 20/20 cricket match: short bursts of enthusiasm followed by lengthy periods of inactivity,' Smith said, before declaring that the 'period of fits and starts is over'.[59] In 2008 and 2009, there were a record twenty bilateral visits between Australia and India (ten Indian ministers visiting Australia and ten Australian ministers visiting

India). On his trip to Australia in 2009, External Affairs Minister S.M. Krishna spoke of the 'forward-oriented' thrust in the relationship.[60]

Rudd appointed one of Australia's most senior diplomats, Peter Varghese (later secretary of DFAT), to New Delhi as high commissioner, communicating the importance of the relationship to Australia. Rudd also supported India's participation in key forums, including the East Asia Summit and the ASEAN Regional Forum, and India's membership of APEC. He cast India as central to his personal proposal for an Asia-Pacific community by 2020, which would expand and modernise the regional diplomatic architecture.

By this time, the growth in India's economy was being matched by the growth in its military capability. In the 2009 Defence White Paper, the Rudd government recognised the changing security dynamics in the Indo-Pacific and signalled its intent to strengthen Australia's defence ties with regional powers, including India. There was a significant step up in defence cooperation, including strengthened intelligence and counter-terrorism activities, more than fifty joint exercises and other defence interactions occurring in 2009, as well as the inauguration of regular talks between the chiefs of defence forces.

Soon after the White Paper was released, Rudd travelled to Delhi in November 2009 to sign a Joint Declaration on Security Cooperation. He also used the visit to propose a free-trade agreement between the two countries. 'I firmly believe that a comprehensive, commercially meaningful FTA [free-trade agreement] between Australia and India could deliver substantial new market access for exporters and investors, and open up job opportunities in both countries,' Rudd said. Prime Minister Manmohan Singh was provisionally receptive and the two leaders 'agreed to take the relationship to the next level'.[61] This partnership laid the foundations for a broader free-trade agreement, the Comprehensive Economic Cooperation Agreement (CECA), intended to commence in 2011.

Prime Minister Julia Gillard achieved several major steps forward in the relationship, including an end to the ban on uranium sales, the start of negotiations for the CECA deal, and the 'Australia in the Asian

Century' White Paper, which highlighted the importance of India's regional leadership.

Australia's ban on uranium sales to India had been a longstanding sore point in the relationship. The ban was based on the assumption that Australia could use its position as one of the world's largest uranium suppliers (Australia has more than 25 per cent of global deposits) as a diplomatic lever to encourage other nations into non-proliferation. Malcolm Fraser, who introduced the policy in 1977, said that access to Australia's uranium deposits should be a 'tangible reward' for countries that signed up to the Nuclear Non-Proliferation Treaty.[62]

But the original logic of the ban had been long since undermined. India was able to purchase more uranium than it needed from Canada and Kazakhstan; and the United States had signed a nuclear deal with India that made Australia's ban pointless.[63] Gillard decided to cut Australia's losses and focus on promoting the bilateral relationship.[64] After securing her party's support to overturn the uranium ban, Gillard visited India in 2012 to share the good news in person.[65]

Two weeks after her visit to Delhi, Gillard launched the 'Australia in the Asian Century' White Paper. India's significance was highlighted – India was mentioned over a hundred times in the text – and it was identified as one of five regional nations most important to Australia, along with China, Japan, South Korea and Indonesia. This was music to the ears of many on the Indian side, who felt that Australia gave priority to China and many other Asian countries over India. The paper proposed making Hindi one of four priority languages for Australian schools, along with Chinese, Japanese and Indonesian.

All this political attention certainly improved relations. Yet many observers noticed that the effort put into building the partnership was not reciprocal. Canberra had done most of the running, with seven trips by Australian foreign ministers to New Delhi and three by Australian prime ministers during the ten years of the Singh government. In the same period, India's external affairs ministers visited Australia just three times and the prime minister not at all. This imbalance generated doubts about whether India saw Australia as a partner worthy of sustained attention.[66]

Tony Abbott's election as Australian prime minister in September 2013 occurred just eight months before Narendra Modi swept to power in India in May 2014. Within a year of each other, both Australia and India had elected new centre-right governments. The election of the Bharatiya Janata Party (BJP) raised hopes that New Delhi might invest more than earlier Indian administrations in the relationship with Australia.

These hopes were boosted in September 2014, when Abbott visited India and met with Modi, who accepted an invitation to visit Australia in November that year. Modi's trip was the first Indian prime ministerial visit since Rajiv Gandhi's twenty-eight years earlier. During this visit, Modi declared that Australia was no longer on the 'periphery' of New Delhi's 'vision', but now 'at the centre of our thoughts'.[67]

When Malcolm Turnbull took over from Abbott in 2015, he repeated his predecessors' pleas to overcome the torpor of the past: 'It's time for us to take our relationship to a new level. One in which Canberra and New Delhi are able to see eye to eye on the major issues confronting our region and the world.' Turnbull leant into some of the newer themes in the relationship, specifically higher education and the diaspora. By 2015 there were sixty thousand Indian students studying in Australia, and the Indian diaspora in Australia numbered more than half a million. 'Our nations are bound together not just by centuries of history but by millions of people-to-people links,' Turnbull said.[68]

A four-day visit to Delhi in 2017 was a public relations success for Turnbull. Perhaps for the first time, the agenda for an Australian prime minister's visit to India was calculated to achieve domestic electoral objectives as well as foreign policy goals. Turnbull played up to the growing community of voters in Australia with Indian heritage by visiting the iconic Swaminarayan Akshardham temple in east Delhi. The visit had particular resonance back in Australia because of the growing Swaminarayan community in many Australian cities. Turnbull was keen to show off his personal rapport with Modi, who was as popular among many parts of the diaspora in Australia as he was in India. The leaders travelled together to the Akshardham temple by public transport — a fifteen-minute trip by train. They chatted, clicked selfies and uploaded the pictures to social media during the journey. Commuters cheered and chanted 'Modi, Modi!' as they travelled together.

In addition to their telegenic public appearances, both leaders used the visit to discuss economic cooperation, defence and energy. Turnbull acknowledged that the CECA, which aimed to reduce trade barriers and increase investment opportunities between the two countries, had stalled. This was due to New Delhi's commitment to *Atmanirbhar Bharat*, its objective to achieve economic self-reliance. *Atmanirbhar Bharat* implied a doubling down on efforts to boost local manufacturing, while protecting key sectors such as agriculture from cheap imports.

Turnbull decided to pursue other avenues. He asked Peter Varghese, the former high commissioner to India, to identify possibilities for greater trade and investment that did not require a bilateral trade agreement. Varghese's report, 'An India Economic Strategy to 2035: Navigating from Potential to Delivery', was submitted in July 2018. It made the case that no other market offered more opportunity to Australia over the next twenty years and laid out a set of pragmatic steps to realise this opportunity.[69]

Scott Morrison, who replaced Turnbull in August 2018, said the Varghese report 'provides a roadmap for our economic future with India.'[70] On a personal level, Morrison was very focused on India for both strategic and political reasons. He embarked on a charm offensive, lavishing praise on what he called a 'land of durable institutions and shared values', and a 'natural partner' for Australia. At the G20 meeting in Japan in 2019, he posted a selfie of himself with the Indian prime minister to social media with the caption 'How good is Modi?' rendered in Hindi.

In June 2020, Morrison and Modi held a virtual summit, where they discussed ways to strengthen the two countries' relationship.[71] There was also concrete progress in defence and cybersecurity initiatives.

As I will discuss later, the Royal Australian Navy was extended a long-anticipated invitation to re-engage in the Malabar exercise with India, the United States and Japan. Following a gathering of the foreign ministers of these four countries on the sidelines of the UN General Assembly in September 2019, there was a ministerial-level meeting between the same four nations in Tokyo.

Morrison's approach to India was briefly criticised during the COVID-19 pandemic when, at the height of the crisis in India in April 2021, the Australian government announced that travellers from India – including Australian citizens – were barred from entering Australia. Anyone who tried to come home would face up to five years in jail and a $50,000 fine. At a time when India was suffering so severely, the travel ban seemed callous. The Australian Medical Association's president, Dr Omar Khorshid, called it 'mean-spirited'. Former Australian cricketer Michael Slater, who was in India as a broadcaster for the Indian Premier League, accused Morrison of having 'blood on his hands' and said the ban was a 'disgrace'.[72] Indian Australians who had travelled to look after sick relatives were shocked to discover they couldn't return. 'It's immoral, unjustifiable and completely un-Australian,' said Ara Sharma Marar, who was unable to come home after travelling to India to look after her father.[73]

One of Morrison's major diplomatic achievements was bringing India back to the table to negotiate and partially conclude the CECA. Australia and India had begun talks on this back in 2011, but discussions became bogged down and were suspended in 2015. In what turned out to be a masterstroke, Morrison appointed one of his predecessors, Tony Abbott, as Special Trade Envoy for India. Abbott leveraged his close relationship with Modi and popularity in India to achieve rapid progress.

The Australia-India Economic Cooperation and Trade Agreement was signed on 2 April 2022. The deal cut tariffs on goods including sheep, coal, lobsters and rare earths. It also includes a phased reduction of tariffs on wine and a host of other agricultural products, including nuts, avocados, cherries, blueberries, almonds, oranges and strawberries. Scott Morrison said of the deal: 'We are opening the biggest door of one of the biggest economies in the world in India.'[74] He acknowledged that this deal was an interim step, short of a full trade deal, but claimed it set out 'the road map to further and further economic cooperation into the future'.

The signing of the free-trade agreement in 2022, Modi's second visit to Australia in May 2023 and Anthony Albanese's visits to India in March and September 2023 represent strong progress in the two countries' relationship. Yet notwithstanding this recent engagement, relations between Australia and India over the previous seventy-five years have often suffered from listless political leadership. While there have been moments of political enthusiasm, and genuine personal chemistry between leaders at different times, the bond has more commonly been characterised by 'missed opportunities, mutual incomprehension, and benign neglect'.[75]

The consequence of this neglect was that the relationship was shallow, in the sense that it didn't have the depth and maturity to overcome inevitable obstacles and setbacks. Too often in our history, domestic and foreign-policy distractions were able to throw the relationship off course and thwart the expressed ambition for a strong friendship.

4

SETBACKS AND SQUALLS

On 9 May 2009, a closed-circuit security camera on a Melbourne train recorded graphic images of a twenty-one-year-old Indian student, Sourabh Sharma, being brutally bashed as he travelled along the Werribee line. The chilling images were soon broadcast by news outlets, causing outrage in India.[1] While there had been several earlier reports of attacks on Indian students in Australia, Sharma's case caught the headlines. The footage showed the young student being repeatedly punched and kicked by a gang of five hooded youths. One attacker rifled through his bag, taking a phone and a significant amount of cash. He appeared to laugh after kicking the victim. Television channels broadcast the frightening imagery for many days after its release. Several Indian newspapers put the pictures on their front pages.

Just a few days later, another Indian student was brutally assaulted. Shravan Kumar, from Andhra Pradesh, was stabbed with a screwdriver by gatecrashing thugs at a house party. Images of the young man lying in hospital on life support soon appeared in the Indian media. The story only grew when, while he was in a coma in Royal Melbourne Hospital, the home Shravan Kumar shared with other Indian students was burgled.

A few days later, on 25 May, Baljinder Singh, another Indian studying in Melbourne, was leaving Carnegie railway station when he was approached by two armed men demanding cash. While Singh rifled through his bag to hand over his wallet, he was stabbed in the abdomen. As he screamed for his life, his attackers laughed and fled the scene. Singh told the media he had once believed Melbourne was a safe place to live, but now thought Indian nationals were being targeted. 'I thought it was safe here, that's why I came to Australia. But we're not safe here now.'[2]

The spate of attacks, which stretched over many months, triggered a rally of more than four thousand Indian students protesting on the steps of the Victorian parliament. The Indian media's coverage of the rally got the attention of Indian politicians and let the world know of Australia's reputation for 'curry bashing'.

A few days later, Indian prime minister Manmohan Singh phoned Australian prime minister Kevin Rudd to express his concern about the violence. The following week he addressed the issue in the Indian parliament, saying 'he was "appalled" by the senseless violence and crime, some of which [were] racist in nature'.[3]

The attacks on Indian students received much more coverage in Indian media than in the Australian press. They became one of the biggest news stories in India for the whole year, with months of front-page stories and high-rotation segments on television news channels. The weekly Indian news magazine *Outlook* published a ten-page cover story on the attacks called 'Why the Aussies Hate Us'.

Many Australians couldn't understand why there was such a media firestorm in India. Rudd condemned the violence but called for the incidents to be seen in perspective. 'The truth is, in our cities right across the country, there are acts of violence every day. That's just a regrettable fact of urban life.'[4]

The Victorian Police pushed back on the suggestion that the attacks were racist acts: 'I don't think it's racially motivated', said Detective Senior Constable Darrell Allen, 'It's opportunistic crime.'[5]

One academic report suggested the incidence of Indian assaults in Melbourne was not demonstrably larger than for other groups and concluded that 'the global media has propagated and fostered claims about crimes and racism that are well outside the evidence'.[6]

But the outrage on the Indian side only grew. 'You had to live in

India to see what a big deal it was,' said Australia's high commissioner, John McCarthy. 'I don't think it's ever quite sunk in for people in Australia how much this issue caught the public imagination.'[7] *Outlook*'s editor-in-chief, Vinod Mehta, concurred: 'There is tremendous outrage in this country. I don't think the Australians realise that.'[8]

The dramatic images of violence were tailormade for India's influential cable news channels. Indian cultural historian Nalin Mehta said the story resonated with the country's growing urban middle class, who are the main target audience for India's news media: 'It had an element of middle-class students being victimised, it also had elements of racial and national pride. That's what made the story so sexy for channels targeting India's primary viewing audience.'[9] Australian journalist Matt Wade explained: 'Millions of middle-class families in India either have a relative studying abroad or aspire to send a family member to study overseas. As a result, media reports about Indian students being mistreated struck a chord with a key audience for India's burgeoning television market.'[10]

The spate of attacks on Indian students had a massive effect on the bilateral relationship. Political, economic and cultural ties were strained. Bollywood's largest labour union declared that its members would refuse to work in Australia until attacks on Indian students there stopped.[11] There was a 46 per cent drop in Indians applying for student visas for Australia in 2009 compared to 2008.[12] The crisis even inspired a Bollywood film, *Crook*, which was set in Melbourne against the backdrop of attacks on Indian students.[13]

The attacks on Indian students are just one example of the frictions that have periodically damaged Australia's relations with India. These historical issues and incidents have slowed diplomatic progress and introduced difficulties, delays or reversals. Over the decades, these frictions tended to relate to two themes: race and international security.

Just a few years before the student attacks, another racial issue dogged the relationship. On 29 June 2007, two car bombs had been discovered in London and disabled before they could be detonated. Fear swept across the United Kingdom, as the government raised its terrorism threat alert to its highest level. On the following day, 30 June, a terrorist rammed a Jeep Cherokee loaded with propane canisters into the glass doors of the main terminal at Glasgow Airport. Both attacks were planned and executed by Kafeel Ahmed, an Indian Muslim born in Bangalore and raised in Saudi Arabia. Ahmed was taken into custody by Scottish police after sustaining burns to 90 per cent of his body when the Jeep burst into flames.

Two days later, Kafeel Ahmed's second cousin once removed, Dr Mohamed Haneef, was arrested by Australian authorities at Brisbane Airport following a tip from British police, who linked him to a mobile phone SIM card used in the attacks in Britain. Haneef was the first person arrested and detained under the Australian government's 2005 *Australian Anti-Terrorism Act*, which contained sweeping powers for terror suspects to be detained for extended periods without being charged with a crime. An official report into the case would subsequently find that Australian authorities wrongfully arrested and held Haneef, ignored evidence and botched the investigation. A judicial inquiry into this case also found the evidence against Haneef 'totally deficient'.[14]

The case triggered outrage in India and Australia because of the way Haneef was treated. His twelve-day detention was the longest without charge in recent Australian history. When he was ultimately charged, a judge deemed him eligible for release on bail. In a response calculated to prolong Haneef's incarceration, Immigration Minister Kevin Andrews then announced that Haneef's visa had been cancelled immediately on 'character grounds' and that if he was released on bail, he would be taken into immigration detention.

In India, the local media covered the story prominently, with front-page headlines such as 'Delhi Summons Australian Envoy' when India's Ministry of External Affairs summoned the Australian high commissioner, John McCarthy, and expressed 'concern to the Australian government that [Haneef] should be treated fairly and justly under

Australian law'. Several commentators criticised the racial element of the new terrorism laws. Haneef believed his race and religion had been a factor in his harsh treatment: 'It might be just because I am an Asian Muslim,' he said.[15]

A little over a year later, accusations of racism were flung in the other direction during one of the biggest on-field controversies in Australia and India's cricket history. The 2008 Border–Gavaskar Test cricket series was marred by controversy in the second Test at Sydney when Australian all-rounder Andrew Symonds (who has Afro-Caribbean heritage) accused Harbhajan Singh of calling him a monkey during a tense exchange on day three. Singh was subsequently charged for making a racist comment and banned for three Tests.

Indian media accused the Australians of 'pulling out the race card' and noted the Australians' own long history of sledging.[16] The Indian team reportedly considered pulling out of the series and decided to appeal the decision. Singh claimed that he hadn't intended to say 'monkey' but had instead used the Punjabi slur *teri maa ki*, which, like the Australian curse 'bastard', is offensive but not racial. The appeal was heard by New Zealand High Court judge John Hansen, who found the racism charge was 'not proven' and lifted the ban.

Racial issues in the modern bilateral relationship occur in the long historical shadow of Australia's policy of restricting non-European immigration, in place from 1901 until the mid-1960s. The treatment of Mohamed Haneef, the violence against Indian students, and the Morrison government's Indian travel ban during the COVID-19 pandemic are all the more sensitive against the backdrop of the White Australia policy.

If racial issues were one sphere of friction between Australia and India, another area that regularly sapped momentum was international security. For decades, India and Australia have been tussling over nuclear weapons. The disagreements began in 1974 when India shocked Australia (and the world) by detonating a nuclear weapon near Pokhran in the Thar Desert in Rajasthan. The response in Australia – here the public and the government were heavily invested in non-proliferation – was angry. *The Sydney Morning Herald* claimed that 'India's moral authority is gone'. As Meg Gurry explains, Whitlam was 'particularly upset because [he] had placed a great deal of faith in the Treaty'.[17]

In 1990, another military issue became a significant bilateral irritant. This time it was a decision by the Australian government. The early months of 1990 had seen tensions in Kashmir reach boiling point. Unrest and a wave of protests by Kashmiri Muslims began to ripple through the region in response to what they saw as a crackdown by Indian authorities. Young pro-Pakistan demonstrators were out on the streets shouting anti-India Islamic slogans. Mosques crackled with loud speakers, issuing inflammatory sermons and threats to Kashmiri Hindus.[18] *India Today* described the mood in the Kashmir Valley as one of open defiance: 'mobs challenged the gun, defying policemen to fire at them'. They chanted slogans: 'Indian dogs go back' and 'What is freedom, Allah is the only god'.[19]

In this period, India and Pakistan were close to war.[20] Some commentators described the situation as a 'subcontinental Cuban Missile Crisis'.[21]

As tensions rose and the subcontinent was on edge, Australian defence minister Robert Ray announced that Australia was to sell fifty Mirage fighter jets to Pakistan. Meg Gurry called it an 'act of puzzling insensitivity'.[22] The timing made it seem a tacit declaration of support for Pakistan in the conflict. In fact, the sale had been in the works for several years, and its announcement was poorly timed.[23]

These subtleties were lost on the Indian government, which was understandably incensed. The Indian Ministry of External Affairs released an acerbic statement expressing 'dismay and unhappiness' over the timing of the delivery. They said they had '[at] least expected that a friendly Australia would not take action which has the effect of further disturbing the stability of the region'.[24] High Commissioner Graham Feakes was summoned to India's foreign ministry and told of 'serious concern' over an 'unfortunate and regrettable decision'. For a while, the Pakistan arms deal paralysed bilateral contact between India and Australia, and in many ways undermined the goodwill that had been generated in the relationship during the early years of the Hawke government.[25]

Nuclear issues threatened to derail the relationship again during the Howard government, when – as noted in Chapter 3 – in May 1998 India conducted another five underground nuclear tests. The tests followed China's apparent willingness to help Pakistan develop nuclear weapons and India's increasing apprehension that it now bordered two unfriendly nuclear states. The Australian response was vociferous. Prime Minister Howard said the Indian government was playing 'fast and loose with international safety and security in the interests of a short-term political gain'.[26]

The Indian government felt that Australia's harsh condemnation was a little hypocritical given our criticisms of nuclear proliferation were sent from the safety of our position underneath the security blanket of the United States. India's Ministry of Foreign Affairs rationalised that their citizens, unlike Australians, needed reassurance that they could be protected: 'Succeeding generations of Indians would [rest] assured that contemporary technologies associated with nuclear option have been passed on to them in this the 50th year of our independence.'[27]

Following the Pokhran nuclear tests, Australia's reaction prompted India to retaliate with a virtual diplomatic boycott. 'Between 1998 and 2002 the Australian high commissioner had no access to any major politician or decision-maker in India. Even the deputy prime minister, Tim Fischer, who was a very well-meaning minister, was not granted access to India's PM,' recalled Gopalaswami Parthasarathy, high commissioner of India to Australia from 1995 to 1998. Australia's overreaction to the nuclear tests completely mired the already tenuous relationship between the countries. 'Foreign Minister Alexander Downer felt that India would collapse under the weight of sanctions. And I told him that we will not deal with Australia,' said Parthasarathy.[28] Australia's response caused India to see us as merely echoing the United States without an independent point of view. The disagreement over India's nuclear program cast a long shadow over the relationship and stymied various attempts at defence cooperation.

These various frictions over the decades – mainly concerning race and security – created a stop–start dynamic. Each setback contributed to the diplomatic history of 'false dawns and false starts'. But the ability of these frictions to distract and derail is evidence of a deeper weakness. The simplest description of this weakness is that the relationship never mattered enough to either party. Australia is a small country and didn't penetrate to the core of India's attention for most of the post-war period. The reverse is also true: India, until recently, didn't rank in the top echelon of Australia's economic or security partners because there were always other countries with whom we had a stronger relationship.

Former foreign minister Gareth Evans used to refer to the concept of 'ballast' in bilateral relationships. It is what is needed to maintain communication and continuity when policy agreement breaks down – or, as he put it, 'when squalls blow up'.[29] The negative impact of the frictions that arose between Australia and India speaks to a lack of 'ballast' – a hollowness at the core of the relationship.

5

DIVERGENT ECONOMIES

One of the quotidian experiences of a tourist visiting Delhi is stretching out on the springy backseat of a black-and-yellow taxi as it meanders through thick traffic with all the smoothness of an earthquake. Most of these taxis are Hindustan Ambassadors, or 'Ambys', the bowler-hat-shaped cars that have dominated India's roads for much of the last sixty years.

When the Amby was launched in 1957, it was the height of style and status. The Ambassador was based on the Morris Oxford Series III, first made in the United Kingdom in 1956. Despite its British origins, the locally manufactured Amby was considered a definitively Indian car, a symbol of the newly independent nation. It was standard issue to senior bureaucrats and business executives and its possession bestowed a certain status on its owner.

Until the early 1980s, Ambassadors – often called the 'King of Indian Roads' – accounted for more than three-quarters of all the cars sold in India. Its dominant position was protected by government policies that kept out competing foreign cars, including high tariffs (as much as 150 per cent on imported vehicles) and restrictions on foreign car makers establishing factories in India.

Sheltered from international competition, the Amby became omnipresent on Indian roads. The plain-vanilla white version was the 'People's Car', its be-curtained version the 'Politician's Car', its red version the 'Celebration Car' and its black-and-yellow version the 'Kaali Peeli Taxi'.

There is a joke that any street vendor can fix a broken-down Amby and spare parts are available in any pan shop.

For its manufacturer, Hindustan Motors, this near monopoly was perhaps too much of a good thing. Lack of competition led to corporate lethargy, poor quality and limited innovation. Customers waited years between ordering and delivery of a new Ambassador. When the car did arrive, its doors were often ill-fitting, mechanical problems were regular and fuel efficiency was poor. Drivers would complain that pedals broke off after a few thousand kilometres and the air-conditioners wilted faster than lotus flowers. Drivers were known to use turmeric to clog holes in the exhaust and carry water bottles to cool off radiators that frequently overheated.

These days there are fewer old Ambassadors circulating in the traffic. The days of the ungainly Amby, once woven into the fabric of Delhi streets, appear numbered.

As the Indian economy opened up in the 1990s, the Ambassador became less popular. Consumers started to prefer smaller and more efficient vehicles. As the economy was liberalised, a plethora of foreign car brands poured into the country. By the turn of the century, Hindustan Motors had been pushed out by more innovative Indian car companies, including Mahindra & Mahindra, Maruti Suzuki and Tata Motors, which flourished in global markets. From a sheltered monopolistic industry producing second-rate vehicles, India now has one of the largest passenger car manufacturers in the world. In 2008 Tata bought Jaguar and Land Rover, bringing the most famous British automotive brands under Indian ownership.

The rise and fall of the Amby is an allegory for the Indian economy: the optimism of its launch after independence, the sheltered years of protectionism, the loss of competitiveness and then the renaissance in the liberalisation era, which saw a new generation of Indian automakers become global innovation leaders.

This chapter will argue that the structure of the Indian economy has been a major hindrance to its bilateral relationship with Australia.

Unlike many other Asian countries, India went down an inward-looking path of economic self-reliance rather than an outward-looking path of export-led growth. In the second half of the twentieth century, the East Asian 'Tiger economies' were importing Australian minerals by the boatload to fuel their construction booms and provide the raw materials for booming manufacturing exports; and Australia was importing billions of dollars of manufactured goods from them in return. Burgeoning trade and investment became the building blocks of strong diplomatic relationships between Australia and its Asian commercial partners.

The Indian economy grew orthogonally to the Australian economy as a result of colonialism stripping its industrial capacity, and post-independence protectionist policies sapping its global competitiveness. Unlike East Asian countries, India's economy was much less complementary to Australia, as evidenced by dismal two-way trade and investment flows.

While Australian motorists were driving Toyotas, Hyundais, Hondas, Nissans, Mazdas and Mitsubishis (many of which had been manufactured by our East Asian trading partners using Australian raw materials), there were scarcely any imports of Indian cars to Australia in the twentieth century. And Indians were driving their own Ambassadors that embodied essentially no Australian raw materials.

Medieval India: The Golden Bird

The vast Indian subcontinent is densely packed with remarkable architectural monuments, from sandstone forts to marble palaces, which stand as memorials to the wealth and power of their builders.

At the House of Jagat Seth in Murshidabad, West Bengal, the status of the owners is reflected in the intricate carvings, frescos and paintings on the facade. But some of the more unusual features inside the building – including a mint, secret underground passages, fine jewellery, and hidden rooms for the storage of bullion – hint at the power and influence of the family that inhabited the palace during the seventeenth and eighteenth centuries.

The Jagat Seth family were not only the richest family in the world at that time, but possibly the richest family that has ever lived. Their wealth in today's money exceeded a trillion dollars – more than the value of Jeff Bezos and Elon Musk combined. Originally traders of fabrics, spices, jewels and saltpeter, the family set up offices in many cities and created extensive networks of messengers and translators which underpinned regional trading. What elevated the Jagat Seth from successful traders to stupendously wealthy plutocrats was the solution they created to one of the most difficult problems in the medieval financial system: the movement of money.

In the seventeenth century, trade and taxation involved physically moving money across great distances, often by horse or elephant. Convoys were slow and vulnerable to robbery, making the essential process of transferring money both lengthy and risky. The Jagat Seth family reduced this risk by receiving funds in one region, depositing the amount in their local treasury and forwarding a letter to their branch in another region to release the equal amount of money. This simple process essentially invented modern-day banking.

With this innovation, the Jagat Seth grew to control much of the financial system, from minting money and collecting tax revenues for the government, to controlling exchange rates and lending to emperors and zamindars. The House of Jagat Seth was no less than a central bank. Indeed, British officer Captain Fenwick, writing on the 'affairs of Bengal in 1747–48', referred to Mahtab Rai Jagat Seth as 'a greater Banker than all in [the City of London] joined together'.[1]

At their peak, according to some sources, the Jagat Seth owned about half of the total land in Bengal. Their family wealth was greater than the entire economy of England at the time. A contemporary Bengali poet wrote, 'As the Ganges pours its water into the sea by a hundred mouths, so wealth flowed into the treasury of the Seths.'[2]

In the late nineteenth and early twentieth centuries, the House of Jagat Seth in Murshidabad fell into disrepair and neglect as the family's financial power declined. In the late twentieth century, the palace was restored to its former glory and opened to the public as a museum. The restoration work has been carried out with great care, preserving the original architectural features and decor.

Most Australians think of India as a historically poor country, but the House of Jagat Seth serves as a reminder of a time when India was incredibly wealthy, with the most advanced financial and trade systems. For the best part of two thousand years, India's economy was the largest in the world, and for several centuries it was the richest country in the world, known as the Golden Bird.

Going back as early as 500 BC, the Mahajanapadas had sophisticated economies, well-developed trading networks and their own punch-marked silver coins.[3] Economic growth was strong in the high medieval era, coinciding with the Delhi Sultanate in the north and the Vijayanagara Empire in the south. The prosperity of these empires is evident in their still-standing monuments and the admiring journals of medieval travellers.

India's prosperity peaked during the Mughal period (1526–1858 CE), when India's economy accounted for around a quarter of the entire global economy. In the reign of Emperor Aurangzeb, the Mughal Empire included almost all of South Asia, had the strongest military in the world and developed an advanced economy including thriving trade, customs processes, taxation systems and world-leading manufacturing capabilities.

The Mughal court was prosperous and sophisticated. Their architecture was exceptional and they built some of the world's most magnificent monuments, including the Red Fort and the Taj Mahal. In 1700, Emperor Aurangzeb's bulging treasury reported an annual revenue of more than £100 million. By comparison, in the same period, under William of Orange and his successor, Queen Mary, revenues of the Exchequer of Great Britain never exceeded £5 million.

It wasn't just the emperors and the Jagat Seth who were wealthy. Even ordinary Indians living in cities were richer than their European counterparts. As late as 1757, Robert Clive, the British governor of Bengal, described the city of Murshidabad as being as 'rich as the city of London, with the difference that there are individuals in [Murshidabad] possessing infinitely greater property than [those in London]'.

During the Mughal Empire, India was at the centre of world trade routes, producing a staggering 25 per cent of the world's manufactured goods. Indian methods of production and of industrial and commercial organisation could stand comparison with those in any other part of the world.[4]

Bengal weavers created fabulous textiles including high-quality cottons and silks that were sold throughout the world. European fashion became increasingly dependent on Mughal Indian textiles. Indian cottons were the most in-demand products in the world in the eighteenth century, consumed in the Americas, Europe, Africa, China and Japan. Bengal also had a large ship-building industry during the sixteenth and seventeenth centuries, which produced 223,250 tons annually. Ship-building in Bengal was advanced compared to European ship-building at the time, with private Indian companies selling ships to European firms and the English Navy.[5]

For many people, the wealth and prestige of India before colonisation might seem like a distant memory. But it has enduring relevance for India's economy and global outlook. It serves as a powerful reminder of the latent strength of India and its potential for the future. The destruction of India's historic wealth at the hands of the British still shapes India's approach to international affairs today.

Colonial rule: The shaking of the Pagoda Tree

The enormous wealth, power and sophistication of the Mughal Empire makes its subjugation to the comparatively backward British Empire during the course of the eighteenth and nineteenth centuries something of an enigma. At the time, England was a diminutive, impecunious agricultural country of less than ten million people. India's population of 150 million accounted for one-fifth of the world's total and its economy was the world's leader in industry and trade.

What makes the takeover of India even more remarkable is that it was not the British government that seized India but a private company, employing no more than a handful of people in its small office – just five windows wide – in Leadenhall Street in the city of London. By the end of the eighteenth century, this dangerously unregulated private company had conquered the fabulously wealthy Mughal Empire. 'What honour is left to us,' asked a Mughal official named Narayan Singh after the East India Company had usurped the Peacock throne, 'when we have to take orders from a handful of traders who have not yet learned to wash their bottoms?'

The story of how the East India Company plundered India, in what has been described as 'the supreme act of corporate violence in world history', is a remarkable tale.[6] And the story is important for our purpose, because the shape of the Indian economy left behind after nearly three centuries of British influence and control has cast a long shadow over the economic relationship between Australia and India.

The British takeover of India was, in the immodest words of one of its principal architects, Robert Clive, 'a Revolution scarcely to be parallel'd in History'.[7] But like many historical atrocities, the plunder of India began innocuously. The first East India Company ship to arrive in India, the large merchant vessel *Hector*, landed in Surat in 1607, carrying 110 men and twenty-four guns. But the vessel's passengers arrived not as violent conquerors but as humble supplicants attempting to establish a toehold and negotiate commercial concessions alongside the already well-established Portuguese and Dutch traders.

For most of the next century, the operations of the company were generally commercial. British ships laden with gold and silver would depart from London, purchase tea, spices, silk, cotton, indigo dye and other goods from Indian artisans and producers, and return to England to sell the cargo at a profit. This trade was mutually beneficial, and the company would grease the wheels of power by ensuring that their eastward cargos included European luxuries for the Mughal emperors (a coach and coachman found particular favour with Emperor Jahangir in 1615) and their westward cargoes included exotic animals, birds or jewels to delight the English monarchs.

English traders were encouraged by the Mughal rulers. In 1634, Emperor Shah Jahan extended English trade concessions to the region of Bengal. In 1717, customs duties were completely waived for English traders. As the company grew, it built small bases, or factories, along India's eastern and western coasts in Madras, Bombay and Calcutta.

The British East India Company was fiercely competitive with the Dutch and French throughout the seventeenth and eighteenth centuries, with each nationality trying to establish commercial dominance in India. This tension escalated into a series of skirmishes, culminating in the Anglo–Dutch Wars, which began in the mid-seventeenth century. To strengthen the East India Company in these conflicts, the reigning English monarch, King Charles II, granted it military powers, including the rights to territorial acquisitions, and to command fortresses, hire troops, make war and exercise both civil and criminal jurisdiction over the acquired territories.

These new martial powers transformed the East India Company, during the period of the Anglo–Dutch Wars, from a commercial entity into a military and territorial organisation. So began a more sinister era in which the company would become, in the words of one of its directors, 'an empire within an empire', which would beat off its colonial rivals and establish vast military and administrative control over great chunks of the most prosperous provinces of India.

In the eighteenth century, the company exploited growing weakness within the Mughal Empire and divisions among provincial rulers, using its military forces to install puppet regimes under its control. In 1765, the company forced Emperor Shah Alam to hand over the power of taxation to the East India Company, giving the corporation astonishingly wide powers to run the local economy for its own profit. As the Riyaz-us-Salatin noted shortly afterwards: 'The English have now acquired dominion over the three subahs [provinces] and have appointed their own district officers, they make assessments and collections of revenue, administer justice, appoint and dismiss collectors and perform other functions of governance. The sway and authority of the English prevails … Heaven knows what will be the eventual upshot of this state of things.'[8]

Within fifty years, the British had extended their control over almost the entire subcontinent south of the Mughal capital of Delhi. This unleashed a period of unbounded pillaging and asset-stripping by the company, which the British themselves described as 'the shaking of the pagoda tree'.[9]

With puppet rulers under their control, and with the power of taxation, the East India Company's business model changed. In the first half of the eighteenth century, the company had paid for Indian goods with £6 million of bullion. But after 1757, there was no longer any need to bring silver from England to pay for the textiles, spices and saltpetre it wished to buy and export. Instead, Indian tax revenues would provide the finance for all the company's purchases. India would henceforth be treated as a vast treasure trove, to be milked and exploited, and all its profits drained away to London.

The apotheosis of this exploitation occurred during the Bengal famine of 1770–71. The start of the famine has been attributed to a failed monsoon in 1769 that caused widespread drought and two consecutive failed rice crops. But the exploitative tax policies of the East India Company made the situation much worse. Company officers exacted dues from a dying populace as diligently as they had from a healthy one. Tax evaders were publicly hanged. In Calcutta, 'one could not pass the streets without seeing multitudes in their last agonies', while 'numbers of dead were seen with dogs, jackalls, hogs, vultures and other birds and beasts of prey feeding on their carcasses'.[10] The company behaved appallingly, sending from its office in Calcutta a letter informing its Leadenhall Street headquarters that 'notwithstanding the great severity of the late famine … some increase [in revenue] has been made'.[11]

The company came under increasing scrutiny in England as employees arrived back in London with conspicuous fortunes. Reports emerged of some company employees enriching themselves by hoarding rice while millions of Bengalis were starving in the famine. One English publication called the company a 'scandalous confederacy to plunder and strip'.[12] And a member of parliament called for a public inquiry into the company since it had 'a revenue of two million pounds in India acquired God knows how, by unjust wars with the natives'.[13]

In the following decades, the company's financial instability and political interference came to be seen as a malevolent element back home in Britain. Politician Edmund Burke wrote that the company might 'like a mill-stone, drag [the government] down into an unfathomable abyss ... This cursed Company would, at last, like a viper, be the destruction of the country which fostered it at its bosom.'[14] Parliament curtailed the powers of the company in the *Regulating Act* of 1773, which introduced new controls and oversight, and reduced the company's political influence.

The First War of Independence was the final straw that ended company rule of the East India Company and transferred sovereignty over India to the British Crown in 1857, where it remained for ninety years until 1947. Through passage of the 1858 *Government of India Act*, the British established 'direct rule' and reorganised the army, the financial system and the administration in India.

Their new administrative and economic policies helped the British consolidate their control over the country. New taxation and land policies helped them keep the Indian farmers under control and amass huge sums of revenue to finance their administration. Their agricultural policies directed Indian farmers to focus on various cash crops and produce the raw materials for the industries in Britain. And they completely monopolised trade with India and excluded their foreign rivals.

The effects of the British on India's wealth and prosperity are dramatically visible in the data. In 1700, India accounted for a staggeringly high 25 per cent of the global economy (see Figure 5.1). By the time of independence, India accounted for an equally staggering (but this time staggeringly low) 4 per cent of the global economy. The British took India from being the wealthiest country in the world to being one of the poorest.

Figure 5.1 India's share of world GDP (%) over two millennia

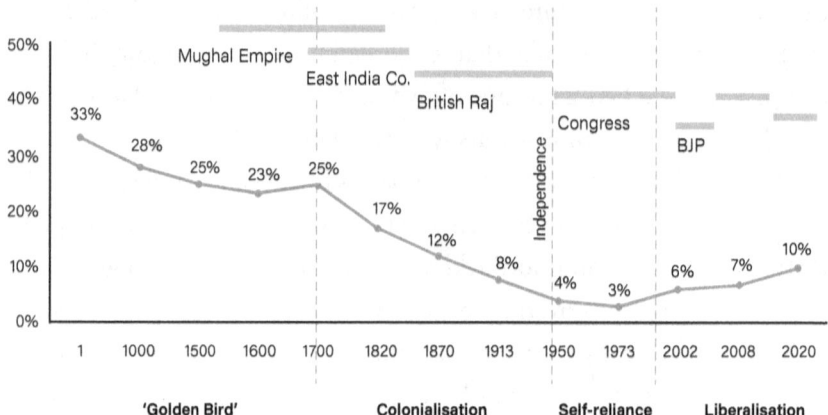

Source: Angus Maddison, World Bank data

As well as having a profound influence on the Indian economy, Britain's economic legacy would affect India's future interactions with other nations. Indeed, the deep roots of the modern relationship between Australia and India extend into the period of British colonial rule. Although Australia and India had different and separate relationships with Britain, we were both colonial dominions and our economies developed as part of the same imperial mercantilist system.

The concept of 'mercantilism' – coined by Adam Smith in 1776 – was the animating economic philosophy behind Britain's drive for colonial expansion in the period of New Imperialism in the latter part of the nineteenth century.[15] Mercantilism measured national wealth by the amount of gold and silver a nation possessed. Smith believed that the way to grow national wealth was to restrain imports and encourage exports, thereby producing a trade surplus with other countries which would generate an inflow of bullion. This system dominated British imperial economic policies and shaped the economies of all its colonies, including Australia and India.

Britain was not content to allow the economies of its colonies to develop in whatever manner was most convenient or beneficial for their own interests. Rather, Britain shaped the economies of its colonies to generate a trade surplus and enhance its industrial power. First, the colonies were designed to supply England (which had few natural resources of its own) with cheap raw materials for British industrial production. Second, the colonies were set up as export markets for British production, which increased jobs and industrial development at home.

Britain had for some time been using a range of mercantilist policies across its empire, including the *Navigation Act* of 1651 (requiring all of a colony's imports to be either bought from Britain or resold by British merchants in Britain), the *Staple Act* of 1663 (requiring colonial ships to unload their cargo once they were docked in England so that each item could be taxed to generate revenue for England) and the *Restraining Acts* of 1699 (which protected manufacturers in England and restricted manufacturing in the colonies). Over time different policies were introduced, but the central philosophy remained constant: that colonies existed to supply cheap raw materials to Britain and to purchase back British finished goods.

In other words, Britain did not set up its empire as an open network in which dominions could freely trade with one another. Instead, it operated the imperial economy as a web, with England the fat spider at the centre, generally discouraging interactions that it did not intermediate.

Britain discouraged direct trade between Australia and India in the nineteenth century. Indeed, the very first tariffs imposed in Australia by the British were implemented by Governor Philip Gidley King in 1802, just fourteen years into the life of the colony. These tariffs applied to goods imported from countries other than Britain and were levied for the explicit purpose of favouring British imports. In a letter to the Colonial Secretary, Governor King stated, 'My reasons for this measure are the necessity of encouraging English manufactures in preference to those which come from India [and other colonies].'[16]

Over the course of the nineteenth century, Britain shaped Australia into a pastoral and mining production economy to supply raw materials to Britain and import manufactured goods.[17] This exchange was accelerated through the large-scale transfer of labour and capital from Britain to Australia to finance and operate massive agricultural expansion. As a result, the nineteenth century was an era of land grants, voluntary mass migration and huge international capital flows. By 1850, Australia was already supplying well over half of the British market for imported wool.

The same mercantilist philosophy shaped the colonial economy of India in roughly the same era.[18] Britain wanted India to serve as a significant supplier of cheap raw materials to its industry and a large captive market for its manufactured goods.[19] To achieve this, British policies suppressed domestic Indian manufacturing and restricted export opportunities. In two centuries, colonial policies completely transformed India's economy from a relatively advanced industrial trading nation under the Mughal Empire into a supplier of basic agricultural commodities to the British Empire.

Nowhere was the deindustrialisation of India more evident than in its once flourishing textile industry. British policies imposed taxes on Indian cloth production, as well as restrictions to prevent them from being sold into the British market. At the same time, British manufacturers were able to sell cloth back to India without any tariffs. The centre of gravity of the global textile industry shifted from India to England. The vibrant Bengali textile industry fell into a slump, while the English city of Manchester was nicknamed 'Cottonopolis' as its production boomed.

These policies across many industries changed India from being an exporter of processed goods for which it received payment in bullion to being an exporter of raw materials and a buyer of manufactured goods.[20] In the words of India's first prime minister, the effect of British rule was that 'the classic type of modern colonial economy was built up, India becoming an agricultural colony of industrial England, supplying raw materials and providing markets for England's industrial goods'.[21]

As both India and Australia were shaped into colonial economies, their prospects for bilateral trade dwindled. Successive Australian politicians and foreign-policy observers have cited our shared British colonial history as a commonality that has strengthened the Australia–India relationship. But in our economic relations, the opposite is true. As former colonies, our economies have been shaped in ways that reduce our industrial complementarity and suppress mutual trade.

Post-independence: Self-reliance
India's first prime minister, Jawaharlal Nehru, inherited an overwhelmingly impoverished country after centuries of British rule. The average Indian had annual income of just US$550 (roughly one-twentieth of the US average), little education (literacy rates were just 18 per cent) and a life expectancy of just thirty years. Reflecting on the poor condition of his nation in 1947, Nehru wrote, 'There is no mystery about this poverty ... the present poverty of the Indian people is the ineluctable consequence of [British economic policy].'[22]

Nehru was determined to restore his country's economic fortunes by reversing the British legacy of deindustrialisation. But the question was *how* to achieve rapid industrialisation. Looking around the world, Nehru saw broadly two paths for economic development.

One path, which we refer to in this book as the outward-looking model of economic growth, was utilised by many East Asian nations. Using different versions of this outward-looking model, first Japan, then Taiwan, Korea, Hong Kong, Singapore and later China and some of the South-East Asian economies would deliver rapid growth through trade with other nations. The two key features of the outward-looking model were a focus on trade (particularly export competitiveness) and heavy domestic investment (particularly infrastructure and industry).

The first element of the outward-looking model was a strong export economy. A competitive manufacturing sector was built in part through strong state intervention to keep wages low, artificially suppress the exchange rate and reduce tariffs on imported intermediate goods (while maintaining tariffs on consumer goods). The combination of these policies ensured that local exporters were highly competitive in international markets. In the post-war period, cheap manufactured goods from East Asia have dominated global merchandise markets.

The second element of the outward-looking strategy, as practised by East Asian countries, was massive investment. Japan's success in automotive industries, Korea's success in electronics and shipbuilding, and China's dominance of consumer-goods manufacturing all came with huge state-directed (or at least state-facilitated) investment in factories and facilities. In Japan and Korea, powerful central bureaucracies supported private companies to become industrial behemoths; while China poured billions into state-owned companies with mandates to focus on export markets. Powerful governments ensured that national output was directed into public investment – roads, bridges, ports, railways and schools.

Both elements of the outward-looking growth model require a strong central government. The government needs to be powerful enough to overcome sectional and short-term domestic interests in favour of long-term growth. For example, the government needs to be powerful enough to resist calls from incumbent business interests that want protection to shield their domestic markets from competition. And the government needs to be powerful enough to divert scarce national resources from consumption (which benefits the current generation) to investment (which benefits future generations).

As Nehru looked out onto the world, he also saw an alternative to the outward-looking economic growth model. The inward-looking model of industrialisation was gaining popularity in countries in South America and the Soviet states after World War II.[23] The inward-looking model was based on the concept of 'import substitution', which goes back centuries but is commonly associated with the Argentine economist Raúl Prebisch, who popularised it in the 1950s.[24] The logic of import substitution is simple: countries can grow their local manufacturing industries by preventing the import of foreign manufactured goods. By restricting imports of clothing, metals, chemicals and cars, governments can force their citizens to purchase these goods from domestic firms, which have an opportunity to scale up their production. Where the outward-looking countries directed their manufacturing companies to find customers in global markets, the inward-looking countries focused their manufacturing companies on domestic consumers.

Whether a developing country chose the outward or inward model of economic development in the post-war period had a fundamental impact on its relationship with Australia. Those countries that pursued the outward-looking growth path (such as Japan, Taiwan, Hong Kong, Korea, Singapore and later China) developed strong economic relationships with Australia. The export and investment model required the import of commodities and export of manufactured goods, which was highly complementary to Australia's economy, which generally exported commodities and imported manufactured goods. Strong economic and trade ties laid the foundation for a meaningful bilateral relationship.

By contrast, those countries that pursued the inward-looking growth model (such as Argentina, Brazil, Mexico, Nigeria, Tanzania, Ghana and Russia) in the post-war period developed much weaker economic relationships with Australia. These countries (many of which already had their own natural resources) were much less focused on importing raw materials. And their choice of autarky rather than trade meant they never developed competitive manufacturing sectors to service Australia's demand for imported merchandise.

India initially chose the latter path, a version of the inward-looking model, which would limit its economic relationship with Australia in its first decades of independence. It made this choice for three reasons.

First, the nationalist leaders of India after independence were heavily affected by the hangover of colonial rule. India had suffered centuries of unequal trading relations dictated by colonial rulers, which led to deep cynicism about trade and openness among the founding fathers of India's development policy. Their mistrust was reinforced by new Marxist theories of development, particularly 'dependency theory', which contended that trade relationships between industrialised and developing nations are inherently disadvantageous to the poorer nations and inevitably perpetuate global inequalities.[25]

Economic self-reliance had deep roots in the nationalist movement. Mahatma Gandhi had long preached that India's ability to produce its own necessities without being dependent on imports was a prerequisite for independence, or in his words 'the soul of *swaraj* (self-rule)'. Indian nationalists valued 'Swadeshi', or self-reliance, as part of their pushback against colonialist dependency. They adopted a new flag in 1931, now the national flag of India, which contains the central *charkha* – the traditional hand-cranked cotton spinning wheel used in villages across the nation – symbolising the economic regeneration of India and the industriousness of its people. On India's first Independence Day, 15 August 1947, Prime Minister Nehru unfurled a hand-spun Indian flag at Princess Park near India Gate.

The nationalist impulse for self-reliance and the desire for freedom from colonial dependency naturally leant towards an inward-looking economic growth strategy that focused on domestic production and rejected foreign imports. But two other factors were influential on India's post-war decision to close its economy off from the world.

Jawaharlal Nehru's own education and ideals left their imprint on all facets of the post-independent Indian state. He exercised firm personal control over every element of the nation's government. He made every important administrative decision and many incidental ones. He was simultaneously prime minister and chairman of the top-level committees on economic planning and international affairs. The story of Nehru is therefore the story of post-independence India, which he in large part shaped. He was, in his own words, a 'queer mixture of East and West', having grown up in England and attended the privileged Harrow School and prestigious Cambridge University. Nehru was drawn to British socialist ideas, especially those of the Fabian Society, whose members, including prominent figures such as George Bernard Shaw, H.G. Wells, and Beatrice and Sidney Webb, were preaching socialisation of essential services and government control of basic industries – a so-called mixed economy – as the best means of eliminating poverty and generating sustained economic growth.

But it was really Nehru's study of the Soviet economy that sharpened his interest in the possibilities of socialism for economic development and social equality. In 1927, he travelled to the USSR, where he attended the tenth anniversary of the Bolshevik Revolution, which filled him with hope and optimism. Nehru saw the Russian Revolution, like the French Revolution, as the culmination of successful nationalist struggles which spoke to his own anti-colonial impulses and inspired India's own cry for freedom from British rule.[26] Nehru was so impressed he would write a book about his visit, which fawned over the industry, enterprise and administration of the Soviets. 'Russia thus interests us,' he wrote, 'because ... conditions there are not even now, very dissimilar to conditions in India. Both are vast agricultural countries with only the beginning of industrialisation, and both have to face poverty and illiteracy. If Russia finds a satisfactory solution for these, our work in India is made easier.'[27]

Inspired by Russia, Nehru put Soviet-style central economic planning at the heart of India's initial development strategy, based on a system of five-year plans.[28] These plans set the direction of a predominantly (but not wholly) inward-looking growth strategy. The initial focus was on growing domestic industries under state leadership to achieve self-reliance. Trade received very little attention: exports were benignly neglected and imports were restricted through quantitative restrictions, import duties and exchange controls.[29] For example, the import tariff for cars was around 125 per cent in 1960 and by 1985 India had the highest tariffs in the world.

The third factor influencing India's decision to follow an inward-looking development strategy was the power of domestic business interests. Nehru tried to implement Soviet state-led development but he tried to do it in a very different context, including democratic institutions and a strong business lobby. The powerful incumbent Indian business interests were uncomfortable with Nehru's desire for government ownership of major industries, but they reached a compromise in which the government implemented heavy regulatory control over the private sector, but those regulations generally favoured incumbent business interests to the exclusion of foreigners and new entrants.[30] Foreign goods were restricted through tariffs and quantitative restrictions on imports. Entrepreneurship was reduced through a complex system of licensing which gave special protection to existing businesses. Nehru accepted this compromise because he didn't have much faith in the prospects for Indian manufacturing exports, so instead focused on supporting domestic companies to replace imports.

Together these influences – post-colonial desire for self-reliance, Nehru's inclination towards socialism and the lobbying of domestic business interests – pushed India into a inward-looking import substitution model of economic growth, which lasted (in various forms) until the reform era that began in the early 1990s. The chart below shows that India, up until those reforms, maintained much higher tariff rates than Korea and China. As late as 1987, India had average applied tariffs of 93 per cent, while China's tariffs were half that level and Korea's were just a third.

Figure 5.2 India's applied tariff rate (%), 1987–2020

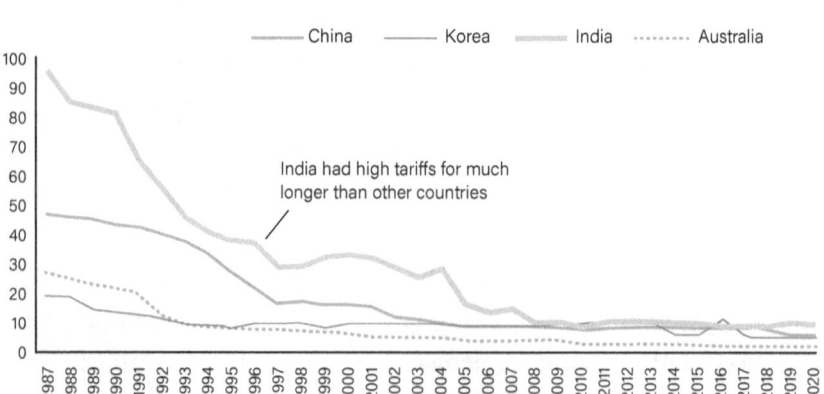

Note: Applied tariff rate is calculated as the simple mean of all products.
Source: World Bank data and author

This high level of protection was one of the essential policy elements of the inward-looking growth model, designed to ensure that the local market was reserved for local manufacturers, not dominated by imports from foreign countries. Figure 5.3 shows the effect of these policies on India's trade levels. Korea adopted an outward-looking strategy from the early 1960s, which saw its trade boom to nearly 60 per cent of its GDP by the early 1970s. China, like India, initially adopted an inward-looking strategy and saw low levels of trade through the 1960s and '70s. But Figure 5.3 shows China's trade accelerating after Deng Xiaoping's Open Door Policy in 1978 dramatically switched China from an inward-looking to an outward-looking growth strategy. Following those reforms, China's trade accelerates up to 62 per cent of GDP by 2005. By contrast, Figure 5.3 shows India's trade remaining low through the 1980s and only beginning to accelerate gradually after 1990.

Figure 5.3 India's merchandise trade as a share of GDP (%), 1960–2020

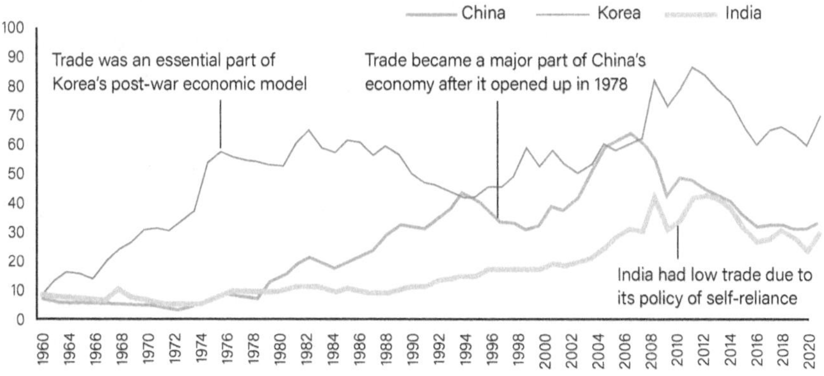

Source: World Bank data

The inward-looking investment strategy as implemented by the Indian government in the post-independence period faced a number of challenges. The heavy hand of government created a web of red tape – pejoratively referred to as the 'Permit Raj' – in which Indian companies had to seek approval from Delhi for any major move. Businesses were hemmed in at every turn by government monopolies, decrees, quotas, prohibitions and permits. A licence was required to start a new company. If they wanted to launch a new product, they needed further approval. If they wanted to expand production or lay off workers, they needed a permit from the Planning Commission. They even needed permission to go bankrupt!

Licence Raj: The sick man of Asia

The red-brick building in Connaught Place is in a ramshackle state. The upper-floor windows have been mostly smashed in and the ground-floor garage doors are rusting. If you look hard enough, you can still see the image of a big bottle on the wall. The logo beside the bottle has all but disappeared, leaving behind the faint grey footprints of a five-letter word: 'Campa'.

The dilapidated Connaught Place building is the fallen and forgotten seat of the Campa Cola soft-drink empire. Campa Cola was launched in the 1970s as a replacement beverage immediately after Coca-Cola left India. During its heyday, it was manufactured in over fifty factories across the country and became one of the beverages of choice across India.

The story of Campa Cola – its sudden rise, and complete fall – is emblematic of India's inward-looking economy in the post-independence era.

Indira Gandhi's government was even more hostile than her father had been to multinational companies operating in India. She accused foreign businesses of making large profits from Indian consumers, pushing out local Indian companies and damaging India's balance of trade. In 1974 she introduced the *Foreign Exchange Regulation Act*, which required the Indian subsidiaries of multinational corporations in many industries to become 'Indianised' by selling a majority of their shares to locals, or to enter into joint ventures with local controlling partners.

Coca-Cola – the American drink that is basically capitalism in a bottle – became a target for the socialists and nationalists in the Swadeshi movement. Critics saw Coca-Cola as a symbol of Western cultural imperialism and pointed out that while only 10 per cent of India's villages had safe drinking water, 90 per cent had access to Coca-Cola.

George Fernandes, industry minister under the Janata Party government elected in 1977, took a hardline approach. He accused Coca-Cola of profiteering from Indian consumers, with high margins that had helped them repatriate $12.5 million 'by way of imports, profits, home office and service charges' to their corporate parent at the expense of local soft-drink manufacturers. 'The activities of the Coca-Cola Company in India during the last twenty years,' he said, 'furnish a classic example of how a multinational corporation ... can trifle with the weaker indigenous industry.'[31]

Fernandes insisted that the Coca-Cola Company not only transfer 60 per cent of the shares of its Indian firm but also share the formula for its concentrate to Indian shareholders. The company agreed to give up most of the shares but not the formula, which it contended was a trade secret it had held close to its chest for over a century and a half. After a stand-off, Coke exited the Indian market.[32]

Fernandes believed Indian industry could produce soft drinks, employing people and bringing 'development' to 'backward' areas. Campa Cola was one of the local brands that emerged to capitalise on the vacuum left by Coca-Cola. Campa played to the Swadeshi sentiment, branding itself with the slogan 'The Great Indian Taste'.

The government also tried to fill the void with a government-owned soft drink. The Central Food Technological Research Institute was tasked with developing a formula for a new national cola. George Fernandes established a government-owned company, Modern Food Industries, to market the new drink under the brand 'Double Seven', which was chosen after a national competition. The local colas had mixed results, attracting devotees and detractors. Santosh Desai, a *Times of India* newspaper columnist, said, 'Double Seven was a government-produced cola, and it tasted like that.'[33] Nobel Prize–winning author Salman Rushdie dismissed the Indian sodas as 'disgusting local imitations'.[34]

Ultimately the local drinks were mostly pushed out of the market when economic policy shifted to become more friendly towards foreign companies in the 1990s. Riding a wave of economic liberalisation, Coca-Cola re-entered India in 1993 and quickly either absorbed or pushed out most of the homegrown brands. Today the Indian cola market is dominated by Coca-Cola and Pepsi and their associated brands, which together control around 90 per cent of the market.

Coca-Cola is just one example of the hostility to foreign capital in post-independence India, which saw many foreign companies leave the country, including Shell, IBM and Caltex.[35] Even the multinational companies that were allowed to stay faced many business constraints. The Indian currency, the rupee, was non-convertible, which made it difficult to move profits earned in India back to their home country. Companies had to go through several government departments before getting permission to begin production. In some instances, a firm would have to get the green light from up to eighty agencies before it was granted a licence to operate.[36] Even after getting a licence, the state interfered in matters such as the volume and pricing of the final product.[37]

Coca-Cola's experience was part of India's strategy to discourage foreign goods and encourage domestic companies. From refrigerators to razors, the focus of government policy was on Swadeshi products: made by Indians, bought by Indians. Nowhere was 'made in India' more eye-catching than on the streets, where tight restrictions on imported vehicles shielded the Ambassador and other local car makers from Toyotas, Volkswagons, Fords, Hyundais and other foreign competitors.

India's hostility to foreign capital was matched by its enthusiasm for public capital. In the 1950s, Nehru declared that progress could be achieved only if the government controlled the 'commanding heights' of the industrial economy. His first Industrial Policy Statement in 1948 reserved a swathe of industries for predominant state ownership, including energy, railways, coal, iron and steel, aircraft manufacture, ship building and telecommunications.[38] Over the decades, the government poured billions of dollars into projects that Nehru liked to call 'temples of concrete'.

The government also initiated a spate of nationalisations. In 1953, nine players in the airline industry were nationalised by Nehru and consolidated into two state-owned enterprises. Three years later, Nehru consolidated 245 private-sector insurers into a single government monopoly corporation, Life Insurance Corporation of India (LIC). Nehru called the nationalisation of life insurance 'an important step in our march towards a socialist society' and sought to extend life insurance to the whole population. In 1969, Indira Gandhi took over fourteen private banks. In the 1970s, she nationalised general insurance and coal, and grabbed the assets of foreign oil companies.

In 1960, the public sector accounted for 8 per cent of India's gross domestic product. By 1991, this had risen to 26 per cent. At its best, the public sector played an important role in closing industrial gaps and accelerating investment in critical areas of the economy. At its worst, the public-sector enterprises became catch basins of inefficiency and corruption, run as private fiefdoms by politicians and bureaucrats.

Over time, more and more state-owned enterprises became uncompetitive industries weighed down by outdated technologies. By the end of the 1980s, more than ninety of India's 244 enormous state-owned industries were completely bankrupt and burdening the budget with losses of more than $750 million each year.[39]

By the 1980s, in its quest for self-reliance, India had created one of the most closed and regulated economies in the world. Only the communist countries were more autarkic. The domestic economy was a sclerotic confection of state-owned industries; an array of debilitating tariffs; a system of controlled prices; filing cabinets full of regulations, and government buildings full of bureaucrats frustrating innovation and efficiency. The Indian economy became a 'license-permit-quota raj'.

Falling behind: The Hindu growth rate
In the 1990s, the Chinese government of Deng Xiaoping rushed ahead with its effort to free the country from the shackles of an over-bureaucratised economy. China was aggressively pursuing foreign investors by

allowing full foreign ownership of Chinese companies, offering big tax concessions and waiving import duties on capital goods. Cumbersome approvals from the central or provincial governments were eliminated.

Everything from Barbie dolls to McDonnell Douglas passenger jets was being made in China. China's ambitious young entrepreneurs, armed with brick-sized mobile phones, set out to conquer global merchandise markets.

The contrast with India was stark. In 1991, China was the world's thirteenth-largest exporter, with some $70.5 billion in exports. India, by contrast, ranked thirty-third, behind even tiny countries. China's gross domestic product was growing at more than 12 per cent annually; India's was growing at less than one third of that rate.

The economic comparison between India and the rapidly developing East Asian economies was unflattering. For many decades, India was unable to achieve the high growth rates seen in Japan, South Korea, Taiwan and later China, Thailand and Malaysia. Economic growth per capita in India was just 1.6 per cent per annum between 1947 and 1990, while it was much higher in Japan (5.6 per cent), Korea (8.2 per cent) and China (5.1 per cent). Indians mournfully referred to their relative stagnation as 'the Hindu rate of growth'.

Over a long period of time, the consequences of low growth are severe. Figure 5.4 shows that in 1960 South Korea, which was still emerging from its war, had broadly the same living standards as India. But sixty years later, South Korea's per capita income is now above $30,000, more than fifteen times higher than India's, which is around $2000. The chart shows that China, which had a very similar level of development to India until the 1990s, now has six times India's per capita income, having started at about the same level at the time of its revolution in 1949.

Figure 5.4 India's GDP per capita (US$), 1960–2020

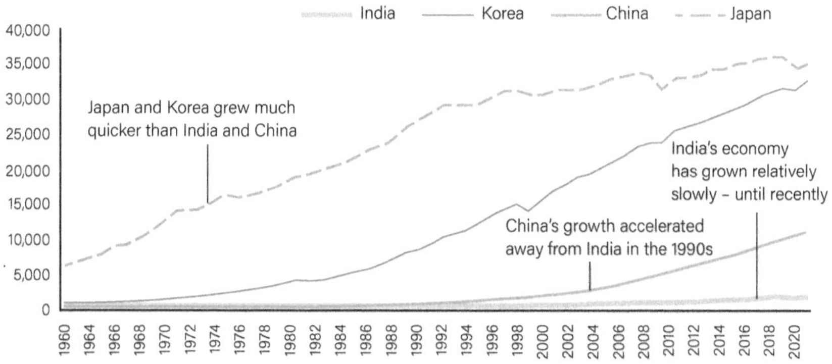

[Line chart showing GDP per capita from 1960 to 2020 for India, Korea, China, and Japan. Y-axis ranges from 0 to 40,000. Annotations: "Japan and Korea grew much quicker than India and China"; "China's growth accelerated away from India in the 1990s"; "India's economy has grown relatively slowly – until recently".]

Note: GDP is measured as annual per capita GDP in constant 2015 US$.
Source: World Bank data

Why did India's inward-looking policies deliver such poor outcomes for its economy and for people's living standards? It has become fashionable since liberalisation in the 1990s to write off Nehru's inward-looking policies as hopeless idealism that tied the country up in socialist red tape for forty years. Some of this criticism is fair. But in the late 1940s and 1950s, many elements of Nehru's economic strategy were perfectly in step with worldwide economic orthodoxy. And the inward-looking model wasn't without its benefits. The Indian economy was mostly insulated from global downturns and supported more equitable outcomes. Inequality increased much less in India than in other developing nations. Its Gini index, a measure of income inequality on a scale of 0 to 100, is 33, compared to 41 for the United States, 45 for China and 59 for Brazil.

Despite these benefits, India's economy suffered from slow growth caused by dark decades of low investment, low innovation and high corruption.

Investment plays a crucial role in driving economic growth by financing the creation of new factories, agricultural equipment, public infrastructure and technology. Investment was low in India for several reasons. Certainly the government's discouragement of foreign investors was one factor. Local investors were also held back by heavy government regulation that slowed down business decisions and restricted private-sector involvement in many parts of the economy. India's trade imbalance was also a drag on investment. Because of its lack of exports, India faced a shortage of foreign exchange, which meant it wasn't earning enough American dollars, German marks, Soviet rubles and other international currencies to pay for the import of materials, machinery and technology that it could use to create new factories and other investments.

Figure 5.5 shows that investment in India between 1960 and 1990 averaged just over 21 per cent of GDP, whereas it was nearly 40 per cent of GDP in Japan. If GDP is the amount of income a country has each year, then its investment ratio is the share of that income that is saved and put to work to generate even more income in the future. In general, the less a country invests in productive assets the slower its rate of future growth. In simple terms, India was putting away 20 cents from every dollar it earned into creating factories and other assets that would spur future growth, while Japan was putting away 40 cents in every dollar.

Figure 5.5 Gross fixed capital formation (% of GDP), 1960–1990

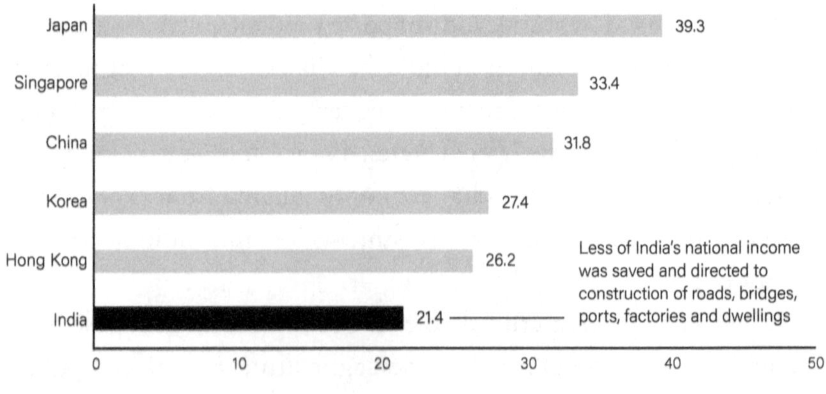

Country	% of GDP
Japan	39.3
Singapore	33.4
China	31.8
Korea	27.4
Hong Kong	26.2
India	21.4

Less of India's national income was saved and directed to construction of roads, bridges, ports, factories and dwellings

Source: World Bank data

Low innovation was another key factor in slowing India's growth. Nehru established an inefficient and monopolistic public sector and burdened the private sector with the most stringent price and production controls in the world. And by discouraging foreign investment, India lost the benefits of both foreign technology and foreign competition. The closed economy meant that the business sector rarely felt the pressure to promote industrial competitiveness. Rather than improve efficiency, businesses focused more on maintaining their monopolistic positions by lobbying for the maintenance of high tariffs and import restrictions.

The third factor that impacted India's growth was the corrosive corruption that became endemic in Indian commerce. The heavy role of government was initially designed to ensure that the wealth of the country was shared equally, but many of the regulations had the unintended consequence of creating a culture of 'gaming the system'. Businesspeople navigated complex government restrictions by soliciting favours from politicians and bureaucrats. The business sector became plagued by patronage, political interference, bureaucratic rigidity and a lack of economic incentives.

Overall, in comparison to other developing economies in Asia, the post-independence policy settlement served India poorly. The energies of the Indian people were shackled in a mixed economy that combined the worst features of capitalism and socialism. Their model was inward-looking and import-substituting rather than outward-looking and export-promoting. Ultimately, it denied India a share in the prosperity that a massive expansion in global trade brought in the post–World War II era.

Unhinged: Economic complementarity with Australia

India's economic policies in the decades after independence slowed its economic growth, but they had the ancillary effect of weakening its economic relationship with Australia. While Australia was building strong economic partnerships with many countries around the world, our trade with India languished.

Table 5.1 shows how Australia's trade relationships have changed over time. In the long period from 1885 to 1947, Australia's top trading partner was the United Kingdom. From 1947 to 1980, our top trading partner was the United States. From 1980 to 2000, Japan took the top spot, before that position went to China in the most recent data.

But the position of India through these periods is interesting. In the half-century or so before India's independence, Australia and India were strong trading partners in foodstuffs, fabrics and animals. India ranked third behind only the United Kingdom and the United States. But when India became independent and embarked on its development strategy of self-reliance, Australia's trade relationship with India began to deteriorate. Remarkably, from 1947 to 1980 India fell from Australia's third-most important trading partner to its nineteenth-most important. In the next two decades it fell again to twentieth position. Australia succeeded in exporting certain goods to India during this period – primarily wool, coal, lead and zinc – but these commodities never amounted to more than 1 or 2 per cent of our exports. Only in the twenty-first century did India's trade relationship with Australia improve, after India had adopted a new development strategy in the 1990s.

The weak economic relationship between Australia and India was the missing ballast in our bilateral relationship. All the goodwill, all the high-level visits, all the fine diplomatic rhetoric couldn't make up for the fundamental lack of mutual economic interests. Our strategy was focused on the 'three C's' of Commonwealth, curry and cricket, but we missed the fourth C: commerce.

Australians thought that our joint colonial history would be a point of diplomatic commonality. But as this chapter shows, the British shaped our two economies in ways that reduced complementarity and constrained our independent economic relationship. Australians also thought that our joint commitment to democracy would bring us closer together. In fact, India's democracy was one of the reasons it was unable to resist the power of the business lobby and other sectional interests to build a protectionist, inward-looking economy.

Table 5.1 Australia's top twenty trading partners (ranked by total value of trade), 1885–2017

1885-1947	1947-1980	1980-2000	2000-2020
1 United Kingdom	1 United States	1 Japan	1 China
2 United States	2 Japan	2 United Sates	2 Japan
3 India	3 United Kingdom	3 New Zealand	3 United States
4 France	4 Germany	4 United Kingdom	4 Korea
5 Japan	5 New Zealand	5 Korea	5 Singapore
6 New Zealand	6 Canada	6 China	6 New Zealand
7 Germany	7 France	7 Germany	7 United Kingdom
8 Belgium	8 Italy	8 Taiwan	8 Thailand
9 Canada	9 China	9 Singapore	9 Germany
10 Indonesia	10 Singapore	10 Hong Kong	10 India
11 Sri Lanka	11 Hong Kong	11 Indonesia	11 Malaysia
12 Italy	12 Malaysia	12 Italy	12 Taiwan
13 South Africa	13 Saudi Arabia	13 Malaysia	13 Indonesia
14 Malaysia	14 Papua New Guinea	14 France	14 Hong Kong
15 Egypt	15 Soviet Union	15 Canada	15 Italy
16 Papua New Guinea	16 Indonesia	16 Thailand	16 France
17 China	17 Thailand	17 Papua New Guinea	17 Vietnam
18 Norway	18 Netherlands	18 Netherlands	18 Papua New Guinea
19 India	19 India	19 Saudi Arabia	19 United Arab Emirates
20 Sweden	20 Belgium	20 India	20 Netherlands

Note: Rank is based on average total merchandi trade at current values over the period.
Source: Australian Bureau of Statistics, DFAT Australian trade historical series

Table 5.2 Australia's top twenty investment partners (ranked by total value of investment), 2021

Investment into Australia	% of total	Investment from Australia	% of total
1 United States	25.5	1 United States	33.5
2 United Kingdom	17.4	2 United Kingdom	16.2
3 Belgium	9.5	3 Japan	3.9
4 Japan	6.3	4 New Zealand	3.4
5 Hong Kong	3.1	5 Canada	2.9
6 Singapore	2.9	6 Cayman Islands	2.8
7 Luxembourg	2.2	7 Germany	2.3
8 China	2.2	8 China	2.2
9 Netherlands	2.1	9 Hong Kong	2
10 Canada	1.8	10 France	1.9
11 Switzerland	1.7	11 Singapore	1.9
12 New Zealand	1.7	12 Netherlands	1.6
13 Germany	1.2	13 Ireland	1.4
14 France	1	14 Bermuda	1.2
15 Bermuda	1	15 Switzerland	1
16 Ireland	1	16 Korea	0.8
17 Korea	0.7	17 Papua New Guinea	0.7
18 Norway	0.7	18 Luxembourg	0.6
19 India	0.7	19 India	0.6
20 Virgin Islands, British	0.6	20 Taiwan	0.6

Note: Measured as total direct, portfolio and other investment
Source: Australian Bureau of Statistics, DFAT Australian trade historical series

In 1990, an Australian newspaper lamented that 'nothing has succeeded in prising open the door to the Indian economy'.[40] Despite decades of attempts, our economic relationship seemed to be perennially in first gear.

This seemed like a puzzle: Why, among all our Asian neighbours, would Australia not be close to the one with which we have the most democratic parallels and historical connections? Counterintuitively, it was precisely these similarities that were keeping us apart. India's colonial history and democratic institutions forced it into an economic development model that had minimal complementarities with Australia's economy.

India's economy is a product, in part, of the development strategy it chose. Unlike other Asian countries, India chose an 'import substitution' strategy that focused on self-reliance and poverty reduction rather than trade and investment. This created an economy, which, unlike the 'export growth' models of East Asian countries, was much less complementary with Australia's.

East Asian governments were stronger, their business lobbies relatively weaker and civil society more compliant. These countries – such as Japan, Korea, China, Malaysia and Vietnam – used powerful central government direction to divert national resources into domestic infrastructure, competitive national industries and strong export sectors. Consequently these 'Asian Tiger' economies were importing Australian minerals by the boatload to fuel their construction and investment booms. And Australia was importing billions of dollars of manufactured goods from them in return.

India couldn't follow this path. The central government was, for most of the twentieth century, too weak to resist the protectionist pull of business. Civil society was too strong to allow national resources to be diverted from poverty reduction into national industrial competitiveness.

So while India's strong democratic traditions created some political synergy with Australia, they forced India into an economic model that pushed us apart. After decades of protectionism and import substitution, Australia would have to wait for the 1990s, when economic liberalisation arrived in India on the wheels of Japanese cars and a tide of American soda pop, for things to change.

6

STRATEGIC MISALIGNMENT

Colonial hangover

We live in the 'first empire-free millennium' in history, but the legacy of bygone empires still powerfully shapes our times.[1] Australia and India, both former British dominions, had different colonial experiences that shaped their respective paths to independence and cast a long shadow over their national journeys.

Australia was initially a penal colony, settled first by convicts, before an influx of British migrants occupied the land under the doctrine of terra nullius. Indigenous Australians, whose land was seized and culture was suppressed, were marginalised in the broader colonial project, which focused on developing a new British society in a distant land.

Australia achieved self-governance through a peaceful and gradual process, with the Australian colonies federating to form the Commonwealth of Australia in 1901. This was achieved through a series of constitutional conventions, leading to the development of a stable parliamentary democracy which maintained close ties with the Commonwealth and retained the British monarch as its head of state.

As we saw in Chapter 4, India was colonised for a different purpose. The Indian colonial project was designed to subjugate and exploit the resources of the Indian people rather than replace them with British migrants. The Indian people gained independence from British rule in 1947, after a long and arduous struggle that involved both peaceful and violent means. The colonial experience in India instilled a strong desire for self-determination. Unlike Australia, India severed most of its colonial ties and embarked on a path of self-reliance, establishing a secular, democratic republic with a new constitution and distinct cultural identity.

Australia and India's distinct colonial experiences have had profound effects on their approach to international affairs. The two countries entered the post-war world with remarkably different worldviews and they saw geopolitics through divergent lenses.

India's experience left it with a profound fear of ever again being dominated by another country. This anxiety drove India's distrust of global superpowers and its determination to pursue its interests without joining either of the two Cold War blocs. 'We do not intend to be a plaything of others,' declared Nehru, who would be the principal author of India's 'non-alignment' policy.

Australia's imperial history left it with a fundamentally different lesson of statecraft. Membership of the British Empire provided Australia with security and prosperity in the first century of European settlement. And our alliance with the United States continues to underpin our security today.

If Australia's motivating foreign policy anxiety is 'fear of abandonment', India's is 'fear of subjugation'.[2] These different perspectives, shaped by different colonial experiences, caused Australia and India to move in different geopolitical directions. India's centuries of oppression left it suspicious of superpowers and preferring non-hegemonic multilateralism, while Australia's more benign relationship with its colonial ruler made it more comfortable with great power geopolitics. For decades, the two countries operated in separate strategic spheres and their interactions were characterised by either indifference or discord.

Alliances versus non-alignment
When India gained independence in 1947, its immediate foreign policy priority was to defend its hard-won sovereignty. Its greatest fear was domination once again by a more powerful country. This drove India to

remain neutral in global affairs and stay away from the adversarial dynamics of the Cold War. India resisted aligning with either the United States or the USSR. Rather than join one of the superpower alliance blocs, India's goal was to become the leader of the new world and establish strong relations with the newly decolonised nations in Asia and Africa.

Like many aspects of its post-independence politics, India's approach to international affairs was deeply intertwined with the persona of Nehru, who retained the external affairs portfolio throughout his prime ministership and saw himself as a global statesman representing the new world. Nehru's ideology and idealism defined India's worldview and its approach to foreign affairs. Nehru had led India to independence in a uniquely Indian way through Gandhian nonviolence and sought to incorporate those principles in his approach to international affairs.

In 1947, Nehru convened the Asian Relations Conference in Delhi, which brought together the newly independent nations and marked the emergence of India as an important player in world affairs. Reading Nehru's speech at that conference, you can feel the optimism bubbling out of the idealistic global statesman standing in the glow of post-war independence. 'The old imperialisms are fading away,' he told representatives from Afghanistan, Myanmar, Sri Lanka, Turkey, Indonesia, China, Korea, Mongolia and Vietnam. 'Standing on this watershed which divides two epochs of human history and endeavour, we can look back on our long past and look forward to the future that is taking shape before our eyes.'[3]

In that speech, Nehru outlined principles that would later define the Non-Aligned Movement (NAM), the forum of countries that are not formally with (or against) any major power bloc. 'We have no designs against anybody; ours is the great design of promoting peace and progress all over the world,' Nehru declared. 'We propose to stand on our own feet and to co-operate with all others who are prepared to co-operate with us.'[4]

Australia was not attracted to the principle of non-alignment and saw the world differently. From Australia's perspective, the post-war world was an epic struggle between Western freedom and Soviet tyranny. In this struggle, all countries had to pick whether they were on the side of good or evil. Australia sided with its closest allies, the United States and Britain.

For Australian prime minister Robert Menzies, non-alignment was not an option. He feared international communism was bent on expansion through Asia, and believed the only means of protecting Australia was by forming anti-communist alliances. 'The simple English of this matter is that with our vast territory and our small population we cannot survive a surging Communist challenge from abroad except by the co-operation of powerful friends – the United States and the United Kingdom ... Similarly if the battle against communism is to be an effective one, it must be as far north of Australia as possible.'[5]

Thus, while India was articulating the principles of non-alignment and avoiding foreign military entanglements, Australia was busily doing the exact opposite. With the purpose of securing protection from the United States, the Menzies government committed Australian forces to Malaya in 1950 and 1955, Korea in 1950 and Vietnam in 1965.

And while India was avoiding foreign alliances, Australia was an enthusiastic joiner of all manner of pacts and treaties. Australia believed that as a small nation, we should seek protection through relations with bigger nations. Menzies described Australia's vulnerability, 'Situated as we are in the world, washed on our western and northern shores by potentially hostile seas, and numerically incapable [of] defending ourselves'. Australia's primary foreign policy objective was to ensure that if we are ever in a war, we should 'enter with great and powerful friends'.[6]

We joined the United States and New Zealand in the ANZUS Treaty of 1951. We joined New Zealand and British-ruled Malaya in an evolving Commonwealth defence plan known as ANZAM in 1953. We joined the Southeast Asia Treaty Organization (SEATO), formed in 1954 as a military alliance to defend South-East Asia against communist aggression.[7] We joined the Commonwealth Strategic Reserve in Malaya in 1955. We joined nine non-communist nations in the Asian and Pacific Council (ASPAC) in 1966. And we clubbed together with Malaysia, New Zealand, Singapore and the United Kingdom in the Five Power Defence Arrangements in 1971.

As Australia teamed up with the United States in a dizzying array of pacts and alliances, Indians came to see us as an appendage to American foreign policy that was hardly worth engaging with.[8] Indians described Australia as a backwater, and Australia's high commissioner to India, Arthur Tange, complained that one Indian minister would regularly greet him with: 'Well, Sir Arthur, so what has Australia done for the Americans today?'[9]

From idealism to realism

India's post-war idealism began to fracture in the face of material threats to its security and territorial integrity. By the 1960s, India was already being abandoned by its allies in the Non-Aligned Movement. The so-called 'Asian solidarity' that had been floated at the Asian Relations Conference was cracking under pressure from Cold War realities. Asian leaders were alarmed by the many conflicts in the region – including China's civil war, the guerrilla war in Malaya, the Korean War and the Vietnam War.

In the face of these threats, many Asian nations came to recognise the benefits of great power protection and the costs of non-alignment. Gradually, the continent polarised into aligned blocs. China, North Vietnam, North Korea and others leant towards the Soviet Union. Taiwan, South Korea, the Philippines, Pakistan, Singapore, Malaysia and Thailand gravitated towards the United States.

India found itself alone in the world. Having eschewed alliances since its independence, it was not part of any security bloc and had no superpower friends. The price of its isolation was suddenly and devastatingly apparent when India found itself in two wars early in the 1960s.

In a sudden and brutal invasion in 1962, China used overwhelming force to seize territory and decimate Indian defences. India was caught almost completely by surprise. Under the slogan 'Hindi Chini Bhai Bhai'

(India and China are brothers), India had sought to build friendly relations with China for a decade. It had supported China's takeover of Tibet and urged the United Nations to formally recognise Beijing.[10]

Despite India's efforts, China harboured resentment that its territory had been encroached upon by the borders drawn up in the process of partition. China tested the border by building a military road to connect Tibet with Xinjiang through the Aksai Chin, which India claimed was part of its Ladakh region. After a number of border skirmishes between 1959 and 1962, China forcefully attacked across the disputed boundaries in October 1962, killing and capturing seven thousand Indian soldiers. China's invasion left India humiliated. It put a spotlight on India's weak armed forces and military isolation.

Three years later, India found itself in another conflict, this time with Pakistan. In early 1965, Pakistani and Indian forces clashed over disputed territory along the border between the two nations. Hostilities intensified later that year when the Pakistani army attempted to seize the region of Kashmir. The ensuing seventeen-day war resulted in thousands of casualties before a ceasefire was declared.

The Indo–Pakistani War again exposed India's military isolation. Pakistan benefited from alliances it had built in the previous decade. Its army had been modernised with the help of $700 million of military aid from the United States through their mutual defence agreement of 1954. Pakistan also received military and diplomatic support from China, which repeatedly threatened to join the conflict on the Pakistani side.[11]

These two wars led to a significant change in India's foreign policy. Indira Gandhi, who became prime minister in 1966, believed that India's principled independence had been a mistake. The policy of idealism had left India isolated, in conflict with its neighbours and abandoned by great powers. Gandhi asserted that the problems of developing countries needed to be faced 'not merely by idealism, not merely by sentimentalism, but by very clear thinking and hard-headed analysis of the situation'.[12]

Gandhi turned to the Soviet Union in an attempt to attract a major-power ally in the confrontation with Pakistan. The Soviet Union became the dominant supplier of military hardware to India, accounting for more than 80 per cent of arms imports in the 1960s. In 1971, the two countries signed the Indo–Soviet Treaty of Peace, Friendship and Cooperation, specifying Soviet military support for India in the event of an attack by Pakistan.[13]

By signing this treaty, India shredded its independence, lost much of its manoeuvrability in foreign policy and took a step towards becoming an unofficial Soviet ally. But the treaty was popular among the Indian public, who felt betrayed by the United States and China. One member of parliament applauded the new 'realism' in India's policy, and saluted Gandhi for having 'put some meat in our vegetarian non-alignment'. Another member of parliament said: 'At a time when international relations are being forged for naked self-interest, it is absurd to talk of ideals.'[14]

Seen from Australia's perspective, India's foreign policy in this period had transitioned from naive to dangerous. Indira Gandhi had abandoned the idealist foreign policy of her father, which Australia disliked, and replaced it with close relations with the Soviet Union, which Australia feared.

At the same time, Australia was moving further into the orbit of the United States, with Menzies committing Australian troops to the war in Vietnam. Any doubt in India that Australia was a faithful and unquestioning American ally was quashed in 1967 when Harold Holt stood on the White House lawn to announce that Australia was 'All the way with L.B.J.'

India's frustration with Australia's American fealty was exacerbated by its concomitant friendship with Pakistan. Pakistan had become a key ally of the United States and a major recipient of American military aid through the Mutual Defence Agreement and its membership of SEATO. This association drew Australia and Pakistan closer together, much to India's chagrin. Australian diplomats reported that our associations with

Pakistan placed 'limits on the development of a closer relationship with India'.[15] Australia was regularly accused of 'ganging up' against India, including in 1957 when Australia supported pro-Pakistan resolutions on the Kashmir dispute.

Certainly, Australia and India seemed to occupy different geopolitical universes. India seemed under constant territorial threat, having suffered attacks from its two most powerful neighbours. And it was defending itself alone, without a firm superpower ally it could rely upon. In complete contrast, Australia had virtually no territorial disputes and benefited from a close military and cultural alliance with the regional hegemon.

Big Brother in South Asia
If the 1960s had seen India's foreign policy shift from idealism to realism, the next few decades saw India demonstrate greater assertiveness. India's leaders 'have seen that the non-aligned flag does not work anymore', wrote Australian analyst Samina Yasmeen. 'India needs to have the military behind it.'[16]

India's growing assertiveness was principally focused on South Asia, where it aimed to develop long-term primacy in its own neighbourhood. The Indo–China War and subsequent Indo–Pakistani War had shifted India to adopt security as the prime national interest. For Indira Gandhi, the establishment of subcontinental hegemony was a prerequisite for security and became the overriding goal of Indian foreign policy.

The Bengali independence movement presented India with an opportunity to strengthen its regional position. India defended its role in the Bangladesh Liberation War of 1971 on the grounds of its national security being threatened by the humanitarian crisis in East Pakistan. But its intervention decisively shaped the geopolitical landscape of South Asia to its advantage. Prime Minister Gandhi launched a lightning military strike which brought the Pakistani army to its knees, took ninety-three thousand Pakistani prisoners and gave seventy-five million people of Bangladesh their independence.[17]

The creation of Bangladesh changed the balance of power in South Asia. Previously, many countries had operated a doctrine of 'equivalence', giving similar diplomatic treatment to Pakistan and India. But with Pakistan losing half its population, India could legitimately claim primacy. Many countries began to diverge from the equivalence policy, including Australia, which began to consider going 'on the public record as recognising India's position as the dominant power on the sub-continent ... [as we are no longer] in the business of equating Pakistan and India'.[18]

India further asserted its strategic power in the region in May 1974, when it tested its first nuclear bomb successfully in Rajasthan's Pokhran desert. After the test, codenamed 'Smiling Buddha', India became the world's sixth nuclear power and the first nuclear state outside the five permanent members of the United Nations.

India's nuclear weapons program had started nine years earlier, in 1965, shortly after China's first nuclear test in 1964 and the 1965 war between India and Pakistan. Both events contributed to India's growing sense of national insecurity and swayed Indian public opinion in favour of developing a nuclear weapon. Entering the nuclear club appealed to India's sense of itself as a great nation. As an Australian parliamentary report noted, 'India is a great power with a burgeoning middle class – a middle class that is anxious to shed the image of beggar India which is so widely prevalent here. That middle class will applaud any expansion of Indian defence forces.'[19]

India characterised the test as a peaceful nuclear explosion, but it caused global outrage, including in Australia. Australian diplomats were perhaps less shocked than they made out. Australia had, after all, considered its own domestic nuclear options for some time.[20] Ultimately the government had decided the wisest option would be to support global non-proliferation from beneath the safety of the US nuclear umbrella. India did not have that choice. Without a web of military alliances or a superpower patron, India needed to guarantee its own security. China's nuclear tests in 1964 left India with little choice but to accelerate its own nuclear program. As we have seen, this would be a sore point again in the Australia–India relationship.

When he succeeded his mother as prime minister, Rajiv Gandhi gave fresh impetus to India's defence build-up. He turned India into a fully fledged military power by massively increasing the defence budget in the 1980s to nearly 20 per cent of government spending. India boosted its air force to nearly a thousand (mostly Soviet) aircraft and increased its armed forces beyond a million personnel to become the third-largest standing army in the world.

India's naval capability also expanded rapidly. India had always been seen as a continental power, with military capability designed to protect it from threats along its land borders to the north and west. But Indian strategists realised in the 1980s that their real potency would come from projecting maritime power across the Indian Ocean, including towards three of the world's most important arterial sea lanes: the entrance to the Gulf, the Suez Canal and the Malacca Strait. India's ability to choke these crucial thoroughfares that bring oil and gas from the gulf to Asia would be one of its most formidable points of leverage in any potential conflict. Rajiv Gandhi himself declared that, 'The defence of India requires our control over the sea approaches to India.'[21] He boosted India's naval capabilities through the acquisition of an aircraft carrier from Britain in 1986 and a leased nuclear submarine from the Soviet Union.

In what came to be known as the 'Rajiv Doctrine' in the 1980s, India flexed its muscles across an arc of interest from the Maldives to Nepal to Sri Lanka. India intervened in domestic conflicts in the Maldives and Sri Lanka in the 1980s, casting itself as a watchdog of security in South Asia.[22]

Not all of its neighbours appreciated India's growing regional assertiveness. Pakistan's most influential newspaper, *The Muslim*, editorialised after the Maldives intervention that India should not insert itself into domestic conflicts in the region. 'Does this mean that from now on India will be given a free hand to intervene in any South Asian country?', the paper asked.[23] The overbearing presence of India caused concerns among

India's smaller neighbours as well, some of whom came to view it as over-armed, supercilious and hegemonical.

Australia's approach to India's growing assertiveness and military build-up was lukewarm. While Australia didn't see India as a direct security threat, its changing posture was affecting the regional balance of power in ways that Australia did not necessarily welcome. Kim Beazley, defence minister in the Hawke government, accepted that India 'has never and does not threaten Australia'. But he did note that 'the Indian posture is nevertheless intriguing', and 'any development of a force projection capability in our general region must interest us'.[24]

In this period, Australia also increased its presence and assertiveness in Asia, through both military engagement and institution-building. Australia was primarily motivated by regional security concerns, particularly the rise of communism and our sense that we needed a strong ally to maintain stability in the region. Most of our efforts at regionalism were therefore attempts to increase the engagement of the United States and other Western powers in Asia through various defence, economic and regional pacts and treaties.

From India's perspective, Australia's approach was generally seen as at best unhelpful and at worst alienating. Almost every regional grouping Australia seemed to support had the unfortunate characteristic of both including the United States and excluding India. As noted above, Australia was a founding member of SEATO in 1954, alongside the United States, the United Kingdom, France, New Zealand, Thailand, Pakistan and the Philippines. India disliked SEATO, which it thought was antithetical to the independence of Asian countries. At the United Nations, India accused SEATO of being 'the modern version of a protectorate' dreamed up by imperialistic 'outsiders' who were trying to dictate to the peoples of Asia.[25] The inclusion of Pakistan exacerbated these concerns, as a move that could potentially tilt the regional balance of power in Pakistan's favour and deepen the security rivalry between the two countries.

The Whitlam government made several attempts at promoting Asian regionalism, but these efforts often excluded India. Whitlam formally recognised Beijing, established diplomatic relations and signed a trade deal, all in his first year in office. Whitlam's prioritisation of China alarmed India at a time when Sino–Indian relations were tense following their 1962 conflict and China's decision to side with Pakistan in its December 1971 war with India. Whitlam further provoked India by floating the idea of creating a new regional Asian grouping to replace ASPAC. Whitlam publicly mentioned Indonesia and Japan as potential members, but didn't refer to India, causing high commissioner Patrick Shaw to counsel the prime minister that 'it would not seem to be in the best interests of the region to isolate India'.[26]

Malcolm Fraser continued to build on Whitlam's approach of engaging with Asia, and his government took part in the formation of the ASEAN–Australia Forum in 1976. This forum aimed to foster cooperation between Australia and the member states of the Association of Southeast Asian Nations (ASEAN). Australia was an invitee to the forum, not the organiser, but this was just one more piece of regional architecture that did not include India. (India was granted full dialogue partner status by ASEAN in 1995 and admitted as a member of the ASEAN Regional Forum in July 1996.)

Bob Hawke's signature regional achievement was the establishment of the Asia-Pacific Economic Cooperation (APEC) forum, another body that excluded India. While the primary focus of APEC is economic cooperation, it also serves as a platform for broader regional engagement, including security and political issues. Australia became a founding member in 1989, with eleven other countries, including the United States. China was admitted in 1991. The forum was expanded in 1998, with the admission of Russia, Vietnam and Peru. For more than twenty years, India has sought APEC membership for strategic and economic reasons. In 2015, Indian prime minister Narendra Modi raised the issue of membership in APEC with the US president. Today APEC includes twenty-one countries that are home to more than 2.9 billion people. But India is still not a member.

At a meeting of ASEAN and other East Asian leaders in Brunei in 1995, Foreign Minister Gareth Evans presented participants with a new map which depicted a segment of the globe under the title 'East Asian Hemisphere'. Evans told the assembled group, 'Australians now accept enthusiastically that the East Asian hemisphere – within the wider Asia-Pacific region – is where we live ... and where we can best guarantee our prosperity.' Indians would have noted that the map was drawn to include latitudes from Russia to Antarctica, and longitudes from Burma to Samoa.[27] The map ended at Bangladesh – India was not in Australia's vision of Asia. To New Delhi, it may have seemed that every time Australia defined its neighbourhood, India was never in the picture.

Strategic autonomy

During the Cold War, India maintained close ties with the Soviet Union and Australia was a staunch ally of the United States. But when the Soviet Union fell, India and Australia were no longer constrained by these ideological differences. Both countries had now to reassess their strategic priorities.

India's 'Look East' policy, announced in 1991, sought to deepen engagement with the Asia-Pacific region by expanding trade, investment and infrastructure links. India lowered tariffs to Japan and South Korea and signed free-trade agreements (FTAs) with several ASEAN countries. It has also sought to develop connectivity with the region through various initiatives such as the India–Myanmar–Thailand Trilateral Highway, the Kaladan Multi-Modal Transit Transport Project and the India–CLMV (Cambodia, Laos, Myanmar and Vietnam) Business Conclave. The 'Look East' policy has been effective, with India's total trade growing more than sevenfold in the past thirty years.

India and Australia both recognised the importance of working together to promote regional stability.[28] India, in particular, has worked in recent decades towards improving its relationships with neighbouring countries such as Sri Lanka, Bangladesh and Nepal and reducing tensions with Pakistan. Indian leaders have emphasised the importance of maintaining a favourable regional environment for growth.

India's recent approach to international relations has been more pragmatic and proactive. It seeks to advance India's national interests and enhance its global influence by retaining autonomy to optimise ties with all major countries, and this will include 'cultivating America, steadying Russia, managing China, enthusing Japan and attending to Europe'.[29]

India has joined the United States, Japan and Australia in forming the Quadrilateral Security Dialogue (the Quad), a strategic partnership that seeks to promote 'a free and open Indo-Pacific'. Australia, as a long-term American ally, has benefited from India's growing relationship with the United States, enabling greater bilateral and multilateral cooperation. Narendra Modi now describes India and the United States as 'natural allies'.

The principle of strategic autonomy in Indian foreign policy has been a subtle but important departure from the principle of non-alignment, which by the 1990s was in a state of terminal fatigue and irrelevance. Autonomy gives India the flexibility to align pragmatically with partners in areas where their interests align. As Foreign Minister Subrahmanyam Jaishankar declared in 2020, 'India will engage in issue-based diplomacy' and build diversified partnerships as it grapples with an increasingly multipolar world.[30]

India's response to Russia's invasion of Ukraine in 2022 is a conspicuous example of its application of strategic autonomy to a difficult geopolitical issue. Australia, the United States, Canada, almost all of Europe, Japan, New Zealand, South Korea and Taiwan all condemned and sanctioned Russia for its invasion of Ukraine. India, by contrast, has remained cautiously neutral – making it something of an outlier among the world's democracies.

India's independent approach on Russia has allowed it to follow its own national interests. These include maintaining its military relationship with its 'steady and time-tested' friend.[31] Russia remains India's largest defence supplier. More than three-quarters of India's military hardware stock has Russian origins – and much of it is in need of repair and maintenance using Russian-made components.

India has also capitalised on the economic opportunity presented by the Ukraine crisis. As the West cut ties with Russia, India expanded its economic relationship. India doubled down on buying Russian energy – much to American annoyance – lifting its purchases of Russian oil and liquefied natural gas more than tenfold to take advantage of bargain prices.

Most importantly, India has been reluctant to criticise Russia for fear of driving it further into the arms of China. As the West isolates Russia, India fears Russia is already looking eastwards. 'You're already seeing a very close Russia–China relationship emerging, even in the last few years,' says Rajeswari Pillai Rajagopalan, a political scientist at the Observer Research Foundation in New Delhi. 'So the current Indian approach is, we don't want Russia to go completely into the Chinese fold.'[32]

As its stance on Ukraine indicates, India's modern foreign policy eschews the high-minded principles of Nehruvian idealism. In a symbolic break with the past, Modi became the first Indian leader since 1979 not to attend each annual summit of the Non-Aligned Movement. In the words of Foreign Minister Jaishankar, India will have to 'nimbly expand the space to pursue its interests and not be caught flat-footed by dogma'.[33]

India's foreign policy successes have by no means been categorical and it is occasionally criticised for 'free riding' on others. But there is no question that the country has made extraordinary strides in achieving its goals over the past three decades, amassing much more global prestige and many more friends than it had at the end of the Cold War.

Conclusion: Worlds apart

Until recently, the geopolitical divide between Australia and India was a chasm. Their colonial experience, their Cold War alignments, their security contexts, their regional focus and economic policies were a world apart. These differences led to contrasting approaches to regional and global issues, reflecting the different priorities and strategic interests of each country. While New Delhi's strategic approach traversed Nehruvian non-alignment, regional realism and military expansion, its interests rarely intersected with Canberra's focus on great-power allies.

In both the economic and strategic realm, Australia and India seemed to have little in common in the second half of the twentieth century. There was a hollowness at the core of our relationship that no amount of diplomatic effort could fill. Our economies lacked fundamental complementarity: Australia was a trading nation, India was interested in economic self-reliance. Our strategic outlooks were diametrically opposed: Australia was a multilateralist and enthusiast for alliances, while India believed in neutrality and strategic autonomy.

PART II
FRIENDS

7

PIVOT: THREE C'S AND FOUR D'S

John Button observed 'an unbridgeable gulf of time, distance and culture' between Australia and India when he visited Delhi in 1989. The industry minister felt a cool indifference in the senior Indian politicians and bureaucrats he met. He returned to Australia deflated, feeling that 'Australia was too far away, too small, and quite irrelevant to [India's] daily preoccupations'.[1] Button's sentiment more or less summarises the preceding four decades of unfulfilled promises and unrealised aspirations in Indo–Australian relations.

But slowly, over the next few years, the tide of history began to draw Australia and India together. Three events unfolding over the course of the 1990s would radically change bilateral relations.

The first event was the end of the Cold War and the dissolution of the USSR, which caused many countries to rethink their foreign policy. With the fall of the Soviet Union, India and Australia were no longer constrained by ideological differences and could focus on forging stronger bilateral ties based on shared values and mutual interests.

India's economic liberalisation was another crucial development in the 1990s that opened the door for better relations. Faced with a deep economic crisis in 1991, India introduced sweeping reforms to euthanise bankrupt state-owned industries, do away with an array of debilitating tariffs and slash regulation. India's liberalisation unleashed its economy, grew its middle class and enabled much stronger business engagement with Australia.

The changing pattern of Australia's migration was the third catalyst for stronger ties. Indian migration to Australia grew significantly as a result of a greater preference for skilled workers, growing mobility among India's middle class and rising educational opportunities. The chart below shows the rapid acceleration of Indian migration to Australia in the 1990s. Up to that point, migration from India was lower than from many other countries, including the United Kingdom, New Zealand and China. In the 1990s, it accelerated so that India became the largest country of birth for Australian migrants.

Figure 7.1 Country of birth of migrants by year of arrival

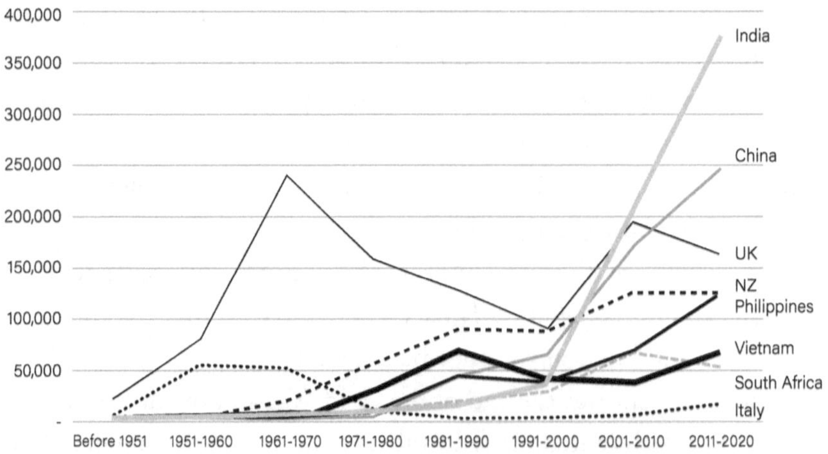

Source: ABS 2021 census (G10 country of birth of person by year of arrival in Australia, count of persons born overseas)

None of these developments – the end of the Cold War, India's economic reforms and the gathering pace of Indian migration to Australia – created breakthrough moments for the relationship. But over time, they profoundly changed the context, like a gradual blossoming of flowers and bearing of fruit from seeds planted many years earlier.

Within a few years of Button's visit, Australia and India found themselves in a radically different strategic and commercial climate, one far more conducive to closer ties.[2] Ideological barriers that had kept us apart were dissolved, economic incompatibilities that stifled trade disappeared and thousands of migrants arrived.

For many decades, Indian and Australian diplomats summarised the strengths of our relationship in the 'Three C's' of Commonwealth, curry and cricket. This overused cliché betrayed a shallow relationship. The 'Three C's' gave a semblance of familiarity but were a poor substitute for genuine connections in trade, investment, culture, security and diplomacy. As Australia's bond with India developed more substance, Australian diplomats began to describe the emerging dimensions of cooperation as the 'Four D's': democracy, defence, *dosti* (friendship) and the diaspora.[3]

The chapters in this section describe how cooperation has developed since the 1990s. Some of the 'Three C's' have deepened and grown to become genuine areas of cultural engagement, including cricket, where the Indian Premier League cricket has become an international success; and cuisine, where the increasing sophistication of Indian food here has outgrown the era of Anglicised curries. While the prestige and relevance of the Commonwealth has not grown substantially, Australia and India have developed a new 'C' in 'commerce' through our burgeoning business and trade relationship. At the same time, we have made great strides in many of the 'D's', including democracy, where our shared democratic heritage underpins growing political bonds; defence, where growing security cooperation reflects a joint commitment to maintaining a peaceful Indo-Pacific; and our flourishing diaspora (the subject of the final section of the book), which forms a human bridge between Australia and India.

8

CRICKET

The Australian cricket team was feeling confident when it won the toss at the start of the Kolkata Test match in March 2001. It was rated as the best team in the world and had just set a new record by winning sixteen Tests in a row. It had cruised to victory in the previous Test at Wankhede Stadium in Mumbai by ten wickets and now led the series 1–0. What the team didn't know was that this match would become one of the most famous cricket matches in history.[1]

Australian captain Steve Waugh chose to bat first. Australia posted a massive first innings total of 445, with Steve Waugh and Matthew Hayden as top scorers. In response, India's first innings was disastrous, as it was bowled out for just 171, with Harbhajan Singh the top scorer (notching just twenty-eight runs). Australian spinner Shane Warne and fast bowler Glenn McGrath dismantled the Indian batting line-up.

Following India's poor performance, the Australian captain Waugh enforced the follow-on, requiring India to bat again immediately. At this point, it seemed Australia was on the verge of another comfortable victory. However, Indian batsmen V.V.S. Laxman and Rahul Dravid stepped up and scripted one of the most memorable comebacks in cricket history.

Laxman, who was promoted to number 3, played a majestic innings of 281, the then-highest individual Test score by an Indian. Rahul Dravid supported him with an equally crucial knock of 180. Their partnership of 376 runs for the fifth wicket turned the match on its head. India eventually declared its second innings at 657/7, setting Australia a target of 384 runs to win.

Harbhajan Singh, the Indian off-spinner, played a pivotal role in the Australian second innings, taking six wickets for seventy-three runs. His hat-trick in the first innings made him the first Indian bowler to achieve this in Test cricket. Australia was bowled out for 212, and India won the match by 171 runs, becoming only the third team in Test cricket history to win a match after following on.

This victory not only levelled the series 1–1 but also marked the beginning of a new era of self-belief and competitiveness in Indian cricket. The Kolkata Test is still remembered as a testament to resilience, determination and the never-give-up spirit exhibited by the Indian team.

The cricketing relationship between Australia and India has evolved over the years into a highly competitive and intense rivalry. Both countries have a rich cricketing history, and matches have generated immense interest and excitement among fans. The rivalry has helped bring the people of India and Australia closer together, fostering camaraderie and respect between the two nations, both on and off the field.

Cricket matches between India and Australia have often resulted in unforgettable moments and thrilling encounters. Famous matches such as the 2001 Kolkata Test, the 2003 Adelaide Test and the 2020–21 Border–Gavaskar Trophy series have showcased the spirit and passion of both teams. These matches have not only reinforced the cricketing rivalry but also created a bond between the Indian and Australian people. Numerous Indian cricketers, such as Sachin Tendulkar, Rahul Dravid, V.V.S. Laxman and Virat Kohli, have earned respect and admiration from Australian cricket fans for their talent and sportsmanship. Similarly, Australian cricketers such as Shane Warne, Glenn McGrath, Ricky Ponting and Steve Smith have been appreciated and respected by Indian fans.

In recent years, the nature of our cricket relationship has changed. Previously, Australian cricketers would travel for Test series across the world, where the pitches were slow and soft, the food was risky and the weather was hot. Today more than a dozen of Australia's best male and female professional cricketers play alongside Indian players in the Indian Premier League (IPL), which has been instrumental in bringing cricketers from both countries together. Many Australian coaches and support staff have also participated in the IPL, creating friendships and collaborations that extend beyond the cricket field.

Former Australian cricketer Shane Watson joined the IPL's inaugural season in 2008 for the Rajasthan Royals. He was named the player of the tournament in the IPL twice (in 2008 and 2013) and won the tournament twice (in 2008 and 2018) and has become one of the league's best-loved overseas stars. 'I love India for the true passion for the game of cricket,' Watson says, 'It's something you don't experience anywhere else around the world.'[2]

Many Australian players, including Steve Waugh, Brett Lee and Adam Gilchrist, have played, travelled and lived in India during and after their careers. Brett Lee's post-playing career included acting in an Australian-Indian romantic comedy, *unINDIAN*, about an Indian single mom and an Aussie English teacher who fall in love. 'When the great Shane Warne passed away last year, millions of Indians mourned along with Australia. It was like we had lost someone,' said Prime Minister Modi. These cricket connections have helped strengthen the bond between the two nations and led to increased cooperation in other fields, such as trade, education and tourism.

Australians with Indian heritage have made a massive contribution to Australian cricket. Many Indian migrants have a great passion for the sport. Former Australian women's national cricket team captain Lisa Sthalekar is regarded as one of the finest female all-rounders in the game. Sthalekar was the first woman to complete the double of a thousand runs and a hundred wickets in one-day internationals (ODIs). She became only the fifth Australian woman to be inducted into the ICC Hall of Fame.

Indian Australians have also helped boost the ranks of local cricket teams across the country. 'Many Indians in Sydney and Australia run small clubs that play cricket day and night,' says Australian Indian Sports, Educational and Cultural Society founder Gurnam Singh. 'My friend has a cricket league and they have forty teams who play every Sunday.'

Cricket Australia data reveals that the most common surname of all registered cricket players in Australia is Singh. The second-most common surname is Smith, third is Patel, fourth is Jones and fifth is Brown.

But despite the high community sport participation numbers, very few Australians of Indian extraction have played for Australia or, indeed, at the Sheffield Shield level. Australia Test opener Usman Khawaja feels the biggest challenge throughout his career has been fitting in: 'When I came into Australian cricket, I was the young fella from a subcontinent background coming into a very white Australian cricket team.' Pakistani by descent, Khawaja has spoken at length about the reasons for the underwhelming representation and the challenges faced by subcontinental cricketers in Australia's overwhelmingly Anglo-Saxon cricket culture. Lawyer and political adviser Aman Gaur notes that 'while there are younger players coming through the system (e.g. Jason Sangha), it is not simply a rosy picture.' Khawaja wishes to see Australian cricket producing more role models for kids from different cultural backgrounds.

One of the newer role models in Australian cricket is Alana King, the Melbourne-born leg spinner whose sensational career has seen her rack up a catalogue of achievements, including wins in the Women's Big Bash League, the Women's Cricket World Cup and the Women's Ashes. King's parents moved to Victoria from Chennai in the late 1980s. 'Alana played with the boys initially, when she was about fifteen years old,' her mother, Sharon, says. 'At that time, there weren't many girls in cricket, and not many from the subcontinent. And I know she'd want more girls, and boys, from the subcontinent playing cricket at a higher level.'[3]

Through the growth of the Indian Premier League and the participation of Australian Indians, cricket has changed from being a game we play 'against' India into a game we share with India. In 2023,

Prime Minister Anthony Albanese was welcomed in Ahmedabad with a giant billboard at the Narendra Modi Stadium, where he attended an Australia–India Test match. The billboard pictured the two prime ministers beside the words '75 years of friendship through cricket'.

9

CUISINE

Sydney's Little India is a bustling streetscape of Indian restaurants, groceries and sweet shops. Amid the twenty-odd Indian restaurants and food stalls in the area, there are a handful specialising in hard-to-find varieties of Indian food that cater to in-the-know locals and venturesome food travellers.

Momozz, a busy restaurant on Wigram Street, cooks up Indian-Chinese food, which traces its origins back to Hakka Chinese traders who settled in the city of Kolkata in the late 1700s, when it was the capital of the British empire in India. At that time, Chinese immigrants were largely silk traders, cobblers, tanners and carpenters. Communities of Chinese people sprang up throughout the area, especially in Tiretta Bazaar and Tangra, the two Chinatowns in Kolkata.

Most Indians found the Chinese food bland, so the migrants created an 'amped up' version of Chinese food by adding chili, garlic and thick gravies that give the dishes the consistency of Indian curries. This adapted cuisine was a hit with locals and instigated what continues to be India's most successful food fad, spreading from Kolkata to Mumbai and all over India.

Michael, the owner of Momozz, serves Manchurian Chicken, a dish of red gravy with heavy notes of ginger, chillies and garlic. His chow mein is a stir-fry of Hakka noodles with capsicum, carrot, shallots and soy sauce. And his butter chicken dumplings are as delicious as they sound.

The traditions of Indian-Chinese food spread around the world as members of India's Chinese community moved abroad. Dragon House, a restaurant in Parramatta, was started by a Hakka Chinese family who migrated to Australia from India. The owner, Francis Li, worked in a Chinese restaurant in Mumbai before moving to Sydney, where he serves the kind of spicy Chinese food you get in the Chinese restaurants in India, including dishes such as chop suey, triple Szechuan, and hot and sour soup. 'Our Chinese food is modified to make it more suited to the Indian palate, because we use ginger, garlic, chilli and some other Indian spices,' said Francis's partner, Mary. It's not like the kind of mild spice you find in upscale fusion restaurants, but an authentic sweat-releasing heat you only find in a traditional home-cooked meal.

Li says most Dragon House customers are people from India, Pakistan, Bangladesh, Fiji and Sri Lanka who are looking for the Chinese-Indian cuisine they remember from back home. But the food is also popular among Australian, Korean, Japanese and Chinese people who are keen to try something new. 'They think it's really tasty and nice, it's different from the normal Chinese restaurants.'

Indian food, like the people themselves, is endlessly adaptive. Curry, which is thought to have originated thousands of years ago, has since evolved into a truly global food, having travelled the world through trade, colonisation and immigration. Today, curry is everywhere, from chicken tikka masala in the United Kingdom to fiery green curry in Thailand, katsu curry in Japan and bunny chow in South Africa.

For a long time, Indian food in Australia tended to be North Indian cuisine. 'People who have never been to India or know very little of India will only know north-western or Punjabi food. It's always some vegetable or protein floating in brown or orange or red sauce,' says Padma Lakshmi, the cookbook author and television personality who appeared in the Netflix food documentary series *Ugly Delicious*.

The Punjabi community were among the earliest Indian immigrants to Australia. The large influx influenced Australian understanding of Indian food and their thick tomato or dairy curries with bread dominated the menus of Indian restaurants. Indian food was often made bland for local palates, with a handful of dishes becoming ubiquitous. For most Australians, 'Indian food' meant butter chicken and chicken tikka masala – even though butter chicken is a modern dish first made in Delhi in the 1950s and tikka masala was invented in Britain.

In recent decades, Australians have come to appreciate more of the variety in Indian cuisine, which consists of many different regional traditions influenced by the diversity in soil, climate, culture and religion, and employs locally available spices, herbs and vegetables. And Indian restaurants in Australia today are less focused on offering a homogenised derivative of the northern Indian cuisines and more likely to be presenting authentic flavours.

Dosa Hut was one of the pioneers of traditional South Indian food culture in Australia. It was started by two telecommunications students at the Victoria University of Technology, Melbourne, Praveen Indukuri and Anil Kumar Karpurapu. 'We had to travel 60 kilometres for a half-decent dosa when we first came here, and we decided to change that,' says Anil. Their South Indian cuisine encompasses flavours from Tamil Nadu, Andhra Pradesh, Kerala and Karnataka and features regional ingredients such as coconut, lentils, tamarind, plantain and ginger. The first Dosa Hut opened in Footscray in 2007 and has grown to dozens of stores across Australia, serving over seven million customers annually.

Some of the largest Indian chain restaurants have started to open outlets in Australia to serve the growing diaspora. Saravanaa Bhavan is a vegetarian restaurant originally from Chennai which now operates 120 outlets across twenty-eight countries. It opened its first store in Australia in Parramatta in 2014. Company spokesperson Shekar Mani said Australia wasn't initially on their list. 'It took us a while to come,' Mani said, noting that they had waited to see the Indian population grow in Australia before they established a presence.

Saravanaa Bhavan isn't like the traditional Australian suburban Indian restaurants catering to Western tastes. It seeks to serve the Indian diaspora who want unadulterated South Indian flavours. Its goal is to take 'our Indian customers back to the village, to their hometown'. We chose Parramatta because of the 'steadily increasing Indian population', said Mani. 'Within Sydney, we plan to open a few more stores because the response here has been so big.'

Indian street food has also gained popularity in Australia. Newer Indian restaurants, such as Delhi Streets in Melbourne, are serving chaats, including bhel puri (puffed rice with assorted lentils and chutney) and pani puri (a ball-shaped crispy shell filled with a mixture of tamarind chutney, potato, onion or chickpea). Unlike traditional restaurant-style dishes that tend to be gravy-based and homogenous, chaat is colourful, multi-textured and contains many flavours in a single bite.

Rashmi Sharma, owner of Let's Chaat Food in Canberra, says Australians are embracing the Indian street food she remembers from her childhood. 'Being a pure vegetarian, I couldn't see anything I wanted in Canberra. I wanted to go back to my Indian roots and the authentic taste I had been missing.'

The flourishing food culture in Australia is a living allegory for the nation's diverse and evolving society. Indian restaurants have recently been recognised among Australia's best dining experiences. Five Indian restaurants – three from Melbourne and two from Sydney – featured in the Australian Good Food Guide (AGFG) Chef Hat Awards in 2022. These include Melbourne's Tonka, Atta and Ish restaurants and Sydney's Urban Tadka and Manjit's Wharf. These leading restaurants are popular across the community for combining modern interpretations with traditional favourites.[1] The mingling of ingredients and techniques from around the globe mirrors the blending of people, stories and traditions that has come to define the modern Australian identity. Amid this rich and dynamic melting pot, food emerges as a universal language, a bridge that connects communities and nourishes the nation's common identity.

10

COMMONWEALTH

When the Commonwealth was established in its modern form after World War II, India's participation seemed unlikely. Prominent Indian nationalist leaders, including Jawaharlal Nehru, rejected any idea of India joining the British Commonwealth after independence. At the Lahore session of the Indian National Congress in 1940, Nehru declared: 'India could never be an equal member of the Commonwealth unless imperialism and all that it implies is discarded.' He said he did not 'believe in reforming imperialism by entering into a partnership with [it]'.[1] At that time, the Commonwealth consisted mainly of countries that still recognised the British monarch as their head of state. India, however, declared itself a republic, with its president as the head of state, making its eligibility for membership of the Commonwealth a matter of debate.

Australia, as a key member of the Commonwealth, played a significant role in encouraging India's membership. Australian prime minister Ben Chifley favoured maintaining close ties with India and believed that its inclusion in the Commonwealth would be beneficial for the organisation and all its members.

Australian officials, along with other Commonwealth members, were instrumental in crafting the London Declaration in 1949 that allowed India to remain a part of the Commonwealth as a republic, without recognising the British monarch as its head of state. The declaration stated that independent nations within the Commonwealth were 'freely associated as members of the British Commonwealth of

Nations' and recognised King George VI as the 'symbol of their free association' and the head of the Commonwealth. This decision paved the way for other countries to join the Commonwealth as republics or with their indigenous monarchies, broadening the scope and diversity of the organisation.

Since 1950, Australia and India have engaged in various forms of cooperation through the Commonwealth. The Colombo Plan has operated to promote economic and social development in Asia and the Pacific region. Australia and India were among the founding members of the plan, working together to enhance technical cooperation and provide development assistance to less developed nations in the region. Over the years, both countries have sent experts and provided training under the plan.

Australia and India have also cooperated in the field of education and research within the framework of the Commonwealth. For instance, the Commonwealth Scholarship and Fellowship Plan (CSFP) has allowed students from both countries to study in each other's institutions, fostering academic collaboration and cross-cultural understanding. Both countries have participated in Commonwealth initiatives to strengthen security and counterterrorism measures. For example, Australia and India have collaborated on the Commonwealth's Countering Violent Extremism (CVE) Unit, which works to build resilience against radicalisation and support member countries in preventing and responding to terrorist threats.

While these examples speak to a history of cooperation, the Commonwealth's relevance and impact on world affairs has been modest. Despite its size and geographical reach, it has been unable to use its diversity to create global influence. It has often struggled to establish a unified stance on global issues or establish definitive consensus on its own agenda, with smaller island nations prioritising climate change, while larger, more industrialised countries focus on trade and economic growth.

The Commonwealth has faced criticism for perceived inaction in the face of human rights abuses within member states. For instance, the organisation was criticised for its slow response to systemic abuses in Sri Lanka during the country's civil war. Sri Lanka was even allowed to host the Commonwealth Heads of Government Meeting (CHOGM) in 2013, which sparked controversy.

In recent decades, India has shown relatively little interest in the Commonwealth, which is not highly rated in Indian strategic circles. Modi missed the CHOGM in Malta in 2015 and Rwanda in 2022, although he attended the summit in London in 2018. His predecessor, Singh, absented himself from the 2011 CHOGM summit in Australia and the 2013 meeting in Sri Lanka.

But as the scope for Australia and India to substantially cooperate in international affairs through the Commonwealth narrows, there are new opportunities and institutions emerging. Australia and India have cooperated through the G20 summits since 2008. G20 cooperation has focused on global economic growth, international trade and investment, and financial market regulation. The East Asia Summit has become a key forum for dialogue and cooperation on important strategic, political and economic issues facing the Indo-Pacific region. While India is not a member of APEC, it has expressed interest in joining, and Australia has supported India's bid. Both countries cooperate in the Indian Ocean Rim Association (IORA), a regional forum for strengthening economic and cooperative ties among Indian Ocean nations. And the Quad has become an important new institution for Indo-Pacific stability, cyber policy and counterterrorism.

11

COMMERCE

Coca-Cola made its official return to India after a seventeen-year absence with a celebration in the shadow of the Taj Mahal on 24 October 1993. A colourful procession of Coca-Cola trucks, vans and uniformed deliverers paraded through the streets of Agra to great fanfare, signalling to India that Coke was back in a big way.

The Indian government approved Coca-Cola's re-entry into the Indian market as part of its economic liberalisation drive which, among a swathe of other reforms, overturned the *Foreign Exchange Regulation Act* prohibiting foreign companies from owning more than 40 per cent of any business in India.

'I really think the Coca-Cola approval is a major signal that India is open for business,' said a Coca-Cola Company spokesperson who promised the company would invest $20 million to expand its beverage blending operation. 'I think the very visibility of Coca-Cola is a very clear message that the Indian market is entering the world economy.'[1]

As Coke popped open its first bottle in the city of Agra, it sounded the death knell for India's Swadeshi hopes. A new generation of Indian leaders were jettisoning the nation's foundational economic principles established by Jawaharlal Nehru and Mahatma Gandhi. Gone were the socialist beliefs that the state should determine the nature and pace of economic growth. Gone was the attitude that consumerism is a vice. Gone was the antipathy to foreign-controlled companies. Gone was the inward-looking economic development model that encapsulated the new nation's aspiration for *Atmanirbhar Bharat*, self-reliant India.

The two people responsible for breaking the tablets of Nehruvian socialism were Prime Minister P.V. Narasimha Rao and Dr Manmohan Singh, the fathers of India's economic reform. Rao had become prime minister unexpectedly in 1991, after the assassination of Rajiv Gandhi. He found himself almost immediately in the midst of a severe economic crisis.

The crisis emerged gradually because of India's weak inward-looking economy, which borrowed too much and exported too little. But the situation had become a crisis when the Soviet Union collapsed, crushing one of India's main export markets and a crucial supplier of oil. Suddenly India was all but bankrupt.

Prime Minister Rao told his new finance minister, Manmohan Singh, 'We must use this crisis and turn it into an opportunity to do all those things that we should have done before but were somehow prevented by history or other circumstances from doing.'[2] The two leaders realised the crisis was an opportunity to gain public support for sweeping reform. With Rao's backing, Singh introduced changes that marked a sharp break with India's past.

One of the early reforms, the 1991 New Industrial Policy, dismantled the so-called 'Licence Raj' – the stifling state-run socialist system widely blamed for shackling the Indian economy. The policy enabled businesses to operate more freely and spurred private sector growth. Industrial licencing and public sector monopolies were abolished in most sectors. The *Monopolies and Restrictive Trade Practices Act* was wound back to make it easier to do business.

Rao and Singh also reversed India's inward-looking trade policies. Import tariffs were significantly reduced and import quotas were slashed, promoting competition and opening India's economy to global trade. Average import tariffs dropped from 125 per cent in 1991 to around 35 per cent by 2000. Rules regarding foreign direct investment (FDI) were relaxed, inviting global capital into the country. FDI increased from $97 million in 1991 to $5.3 billion in 2000.

A complementary suite of financial sector reforms unleashed the power of private capital. The government deregulated interest rates, opened the banking sector to greater competition and shifted from a fixed exchange rate regime to a market-determined exchange rate system. The financial sector reforms aimed to create a more efficient, competitive and market-driven environment, which would support the growth of the Indian economy.

By lifting the dead hand of the state from the economy, the reforms revealed India's strong industrial base and human capital potential. India had an enormous pool of sophisticated scientists and technicians, and deep reservoirs of entrepreneurial talent.

The reforms led to a more open and market-oriented economy that propelled India onto the world stage as a major emerging market. India's GDP growth rate accelerated from 1.1 per cent in 1991 to 8.8 per cent by 2000, driven by the expansion of industries such as information technology, manufacturing and services. The percentage of the population living below the poverty line declined from 45.3 per cent in 1993 to 27.5 per cent in 2004. Millions of people were lifted into the middle class, creating a surge in consumer demand for goods and services.

India's sweeping economic reforms in the 1990s helped rescue the country from its financial crisis and set it on a path of rapid growth and development. But rapid economic change also brought some challenges. The economic reforms, particularly in sectors such as information technology and services, primarily benefited the urban middle class and skilled workers, leading to increased income inequality. By 2010, India's hundred wealthiest people had increased their combined worth to $300 billion, a quarter of the country's GDP. 'The bulk of India's aggregate growth,' the Cornell economist Kaushik Basu warned, 'is occurring through a disproportionate rise in the incomes at the upper end of the income ladder.'[3]

The growing consumerism and materialism in Indian society sparked debates about the impact of these changes on traditional values and cultural identity. Economic reform physically transformed India's cities. Gleaming new malls opened, where customers could select German washing machines, Korean air conditioners and Japanese televisions. Massive billboards dotted the streets promoting the products of Western multinationals. In his book about New Delhi's economic transformation, *Capital*, Rana Dasgupta mournfully describes the new urban streetscapes as 'a strobe-lit succession of unrelated glimpses'. Certainly, for better or for worse, the astonishing metamorphosis of India's cities signalled the nation's emergence from a bastion of socialism to the centre of the global economy.

India's liberalisation opened the door to much stronger commercial relationships with its trade partners. This period marked the beginning of a new era in Indo–Australian relations, characterised by greater economic ties and a more aligned vision for regional prosperity.

India's centrally planned economy had stifled trade between Australia and India. Australian exports were choked by tariff barriers and 'Permit Raj' licencing requirements. But now trade grew substantially, encompassing a diverse range of goods and services, including minerals and agricultural products. India's strong growth saw Australia's merchandise trade exports to India rise nearly twentyfold between 1990 and 2010.

India's economic liberalisation also boosted relations with Australia by expanding its educated consumer class, which in turn fuelled demand for quality education. Australia emerged as a popular destination for Indian students seeking tertiary study abroad. Education has grown to become Australia's largest service export to India, valued at $4.2 billion. Upwards of fifty thousand Indians are studying in Australia, generating valuable people-to-people links between the two countries.

India's reforms enabled both countries to work together more closely in diplomatic forums. One of the reasons for excluding India from APEC in the 1990s was that its high rates of protection and difficult business climate were antithetical to APEC's principles of open trade. India's liberalisation opened the door to its participation in the East

Asia Summit, the ASEAN Regional Forum and the Indian Ocean Rim Association. These collaborations further reinforced the diplomatic ties between India and Australia.

As India's economy grew and its global influence expanded, both countries recognised the potential benefits of a closer partnership. In 2009, India and Australia elevated their bilateral relationship to a strategic partnership, which included regular high-level dialogue on defence, regional security and economic cooperation. As we have seen, the negotiations for a Comprehensive Economic Cooperation Agreement (CECA) between India and Australia began in 2011.

Australia's back office
Since the 1970s, it's been all too common for manufacturing jobs in Australia to be relocated to developing countries. When factories close because the jobs have gone, whole communities are affected. In the last few decades, white-collar jobs have begun to be offshored in large numbers too. The movement of services roles has been harder to observe, because jobs axed are often scattered between offices in several locations and workers go unheard because they lack a collective voice.

Australia's ANZ bank established a hub in Bangalore with four hundred software programmers in 1989. Coles supermarkets offshored its credit-card processing operations to India in 1999. Hutchison Telecommunications moved two hundred customer support jobs to Mumbai in 2003. Telstra relocated 450 IT jobs, and Optus moved its call-centre jobs to India in 2004. Macquarie Group established its global services centre in Gurugram in 2011, where it handles various technology, operations and business support services.

The outsourcing of business processes by Australian companies to India is one of the strongest parts of Australia's economic relationship with India. But it is also one of the least discussed, because Australian companies are often reluctant to publicise the transfer of jobs offshore.

What began as a trickle has developed into a torrent of outsourced jobs, as Australian companies look for skills and cost savings in India.

Over time, Indian outsourcing has shifted from simple tasks, such as call centres and basic IT functions, to more complex and specialised services. Australian companies now offshore a dizzying array of activities, including payroll processing, tax compliance and planning, travel and expense processing, marketing, accounts receivables and collections, customer support, lead generation, administrative support, business processing, knowledge management, legal processes and IT systems management. The mantra of Australian businesses is 'do what you do best, and outsource the rest'.

Directly offshored jobs are just the tip of the iceberg. Most Indian workers engaged by Australian companies are employed indirectly through contracting giants such as HCL, TCS, DXC, Accenture, IBM, Capgemini, Cognizant, Infosys and Wipro, who collectively employ more than four million people in India and have a staggering collective revenue of nearly $300 billion. Just one of these companies, Tata Consultancy Services (TCS), employs more than half a million people in India, fulfilling outsourced tasks for companies around the world.

Through these companies, Australian businesses have quietly outsourced hundreds of thousands of jobs. Figures on the total number of workers in India engaged by Australian businesses are hard to find because few businesses want to attract negative publicity. One Australian bank alone employs nearly thirty thousand people in India through a range of arrangements. Some estimates suggest that total direct and indirect employment by Australian companies in India now exceeds 300,000 people – which is around 3 per cent of the total Australian workforce.

The pandemic accelerated the trend towards outsourcing. When people started to work from home en masse, 'a lightbulb went on' says Johnny C. Taylor Jr, chief executive officer of the Society for Human Resource Management. The pandemic proved that remote work was quite effective, even for core business roles and leadership positions – and if people can be effective in these roles from home, then they can be effective from India. 'There was a time when I would have said "there's no way you can have these sorts of jobs be done remotely," and I don't say that anymore,' Taylor says. 'The pandemic proved the point for us.'[4]

The Indian business-process outsourcing industry continues to evolve, moving towards digital transformation and incorporating artificial intelligence, machine learning and other advanced technologies. As it grows, many Australian corporations will continue to outsource their work to India so they can focus on their core competencies and make critical decisions that will help the company grow.

12

DEMOCRACY

On a fateful summer night in 1975, as the Indian capital, New Delhi, slept under a warm blanket of sultry air, the wheels of a political upheaval were set in motion. It was a night that would alter the course of Indian democracy and instil fear in the hearts of millions. Prime Minister Indira Gandhi, the iron-willed daughter of Jawaharlal Nehru, had made an unprecedented decision – to suspend the Indian constitution and declare a state of emergency.

The city's streets, usually bustling with activity, were eerily silent, as if sensing the gravity of what was to unfold. In the corridors of power, a select few politicians and bureaucrats, loyal to Mrs Gandhi, were hastily summoned to her residence. It was there that they were informed of the impending declaration of the state of emergency. The order was given, and the machinery of the state began its relentless march towards an authoritarian regime. It was a time when a vast country of 600 million people was converted into a prison without walls.[1]

The clock struck midnight, and as 26 June dawned, the world's largest democracy was plunged into darkness. New Delhi awoke to the news that the city was under siege. Roadblocks had been set up, with armed police officers checking cars for signs of opposition leaders.[2] Civil liberties were suspended, opposition figures were arrested and the press was muzzled. The country that had once fought for freedom from colonial rule now found itself shackled by its own leader.

The Emergency sent shockwaves through the world, with many

fearing that the democratic foundations of India were crumbling. In Australia the news was greeted with alarm. *The Sydney Morning Herald* declared that it was a 'black day for ... third-world democracy, of which India was the champion and exemplar'.[3] John Howard, then an Opposition member of parliament, described it as 'a first-class tragedy for the parliamentary system throughout the world'.[4]

As the days turned into weeks, and the weeks stretched into months, the atmosphere of fear stifled dissent, and the state machinery was used to suppress opposition to Gandhi's rule.

The state of emergency finally ended after twenty-one months, but it cast a long shadow over Indian democracy and even over the concept of democracy in the new world. The emergency fed a global narrative that developing-country democracies were fragile. It played into a broader debate about whether democracy was even capable of producing the rapid economic growth that poorer countries so desperately needed.

Some intellectual critics had long claimed that democratic institutions create bureaucratic inefficiencies and policy paralysis, making it difficult to enact the necessary reforms for a strong economy. These critics argued that democratic politicians are forced to bend to popular demands at the expense of long-term national interests.[5] Other critics argued that democratic governments are too susceptible to populism[6] and unable to avoid the corrupting influence of powerful lobby groups who would direct national resources into 'unproductive profit-seeking activities'.[7] Using these arguments, critics asserted that more authoritarian governments have greater scope to impose economic reform and deliver nation-building change.

Through the course of the twentieth century, some of these criticisms appeared to play out. East Asian economies with weaker democratic institutions powered ahead. They were able to successfully execute outward-looking policies, which delivered rapid growth. Their strong central governments appeared to have the authority to direct national industries, stamp out corruption, resist business lobbying for protectionism and marshal the resources of the state to create the physical and human capital required to achieve global cost-competitiveness.

By contrast, emerging democracies seemed to struggle to make tough decisions due to political pressures. American political scientist Samuel P. Huntington argued in 1991 that economic development requires the ability to make hard choices, to allocate resources rationally and to implement policies effectively, and these are not qualities generally associated with democratic systems.[8]

India, the largest and most prominent democracy among the new post-war nations, became an emblem of the challenge for emerging democracies of delivering economic growth. As its economy faltered, and its growth remained sluggish, many economists concluded that its institutions were holding it back. In 1968, Gunnar Myrdal, an influential development economist, was sceptical about India's prospects, claiming its political system was a 'soft state', unable to deal with inefficiencies, delays and lack of decisiveness.[9]

For most of the twentieth century, up to the 1990s, India's experience seemed to be proving the critics of democracy right. The Indian system was plagued with political pressures, coalition politics and bureaucracy, slowing its decision-making. India's political system has been marked by a high degree of policy paralysis, as the ability to make decisions is often constrained by the need to build consensus and manage multiple constituencies.[10] Vested interests and pressure groups can obstruct reform. India's liberalisation agenda faced strong resistance from those who believed that a more open economy would lead to job losses, economic instability and greater income inequality.

The economic crisis of 1991 seemed the final proof that India's democracy was incompatible with a flourishing economy. India was facing severe economic problems, including high inflation, a large fiscal deficit and a balance of payments crisis. The government was heavily dependent on foreign loans and struggling to repay its debts.

But the crisis, rather than ruining India's democracy, galvanised it into action. By the late 1980s, there was a growing consensus among Indian policymakers, economists and intellectuals that the country's highly regulated economic system was unsustainable. The crisis provided the necessary impetus to push through changes.[11] India had no choice but to embark on a program of economic reform to meet the conditions set by the IMF and the World Bank for their support.[12]

Indeed, India's democracy produced the leadership required to implement the reforms. In 1991, the Indian people voted in a new government led by Prime Minister P.V. Narasimha Rao, along with finance minister Dr Manmohan Singh. The Rao–Singh team proved to be the driving force behind economic liberalisation, providing both the political will and the technical expertise required for the radical transformation of the Indian economy.[13]

The economic reforms in India during the 1990s fostered an environment that encouraged entrepreneurship, innovation and long-term stability. Over the years, India has managed to demonstrate that democracy and economic development can coexist.

Rather than letting democracy be a scapegoat for economic underperformance, India has shown that it can be a springboard for shared prosperity. After languishing with a low growth rate between 1960 and 2000, India is now growing rapidly. It sustained a per capita income growth rate of 4.6 per cent between 2000 and 2020 (see Figure 12.1), making it the second-fastest-growing major country in the world.[14]

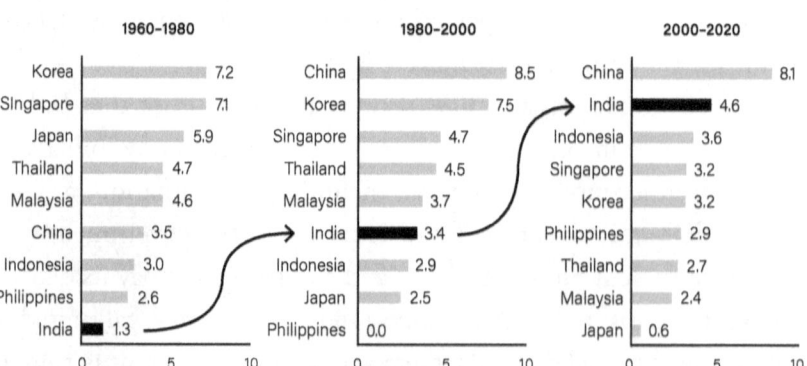

Figure 12.1 GDP per capita growth (% per annum) for select Asian economies

1960–1980		1980–2000		2000–2020	
Korea	7.2	China	8.5	China	8.1
Singapore	7.1	Korea	7.5	India	4.6
Japan	5.9	Singapore	4.7	Indonesia	3.6
Thailand	4.7	Thailand	4.5	Singapore	3.2
Malaysia	4.6	Malaysia	3.7	Korea	3.2
China	3.5	India	3.4	Philippines	2.9
Indonesia	3.0	Indonesia	2.9	Thailand	2.7
Philippines	2.6	Japan	2.5	Malaysia	2.4
India	1.3	Philippines	0.0	Japan	0.6

Source: World Bank data

With 1.4 billion people, India is the largest democracy in the world. It is also one of the strongest democracies in the world. India has a plurality of political parties, free elections and an independent judiciary. India's democracy is home to a multitude of media, including the largest circulation of newspapers in the world and hundreds of independent television stations. In a sign of a healthy democracy, these outlets present a wide variety of perspectives, many of which are critical of the government in office.

India is a laboratory among developing countries for testing how well democracy can lift a huge population out of poverty. Today, India has passed that test. It is richer than ever before, with rising global influence. It has shown that economic growth is possible in a gradual process of economic change within a democratic polity. India has provided the world with an alternative to authoritarian political settings and economic growth models. It has shown that a democracy can deliver an outward-looking economy that emphasises private sector and international trade. The strong performance of the Indian economy has answered questions in the twentieth century about the compatibility of democracy and development.

Since his election in 2014, Narendra Modi has played a significant role in shaping the country's democratic landscape. His tenure has seen enormous progress and development, but it has also been marked by controversy and criticism.

Modi's government has undertaken initiatives aimed at strengthening Indian democracy. The government has initiated several ambitious schemes targeting economic growth, poverty alleviation and improved sanitation and healthcare, such as Make In India, Swachh Bharat Abhiyan (a mission to improve sanitation) and Ayushman Bharat (a mission to deliver universal healthcare).

Critics have raised concerns about the treatment of political dissent in India in recent years, including the treatment of activists, academics and journalists, often under stringent laws like the 1967 *Unlawful Activities (Prevention) Act*.[15] The government's critics argue that this stifles freedom of speech and expression, essential aspects of a functioning democracy. According to the 2023 World Press Freedom Index, India ranks 161 out of 180 countries.

The impact of Modi's tenure on Indian democracy is a complex and highly debated topic. Critics argue that under Modi's government there has been an increase in religious polarisation. There are suggestions that the government's rhetoric and policies often favour the Hindu majority, which undermines the secular principles of Indian democracy. These critiques coexist with the fact that Modi remains a popular figure in Indian politics, as demonstrated by electoral outcomes. Overall, his policies have been well received, and Modi and his party won strong electoral mandates in 2014 and in a resounding re-election in 2019, which suggests significant public support for his leadership. There is also no question that India has substantially increased its economic and strategic power during the Modi administration.

The strength of India's democracy is important for the world, and for Australia. Democracy is a key factor that binds Australia and India together. The two countries share a commitment to democratic values, such as freedom of speech, the rule of law and respect for human rights. This shared commitment to democratic principles creates a strong foundation for cooperation and partnership. The shared values build long-term trust needed for cooperation on sensitive issues, including defence. As Australian foreign minister Penny Wong has said, 'India is a democracy and India is a country which shares so many of the values Australians look to. And India is a very important partner for Australia, particularly at this time.'[16]

And India's successful democracy is a beacon to the world. Former prime minister John Howard expressed Australia's admiration 'for the way in which the Indian people have embraced and held hold of democracy':

> It is a quite remarkable thing and there were so many cynics around in 1947 who said that the embrace of democracy in India would

not work. And at various stages democracy in that country has been challenged and it was temporarily suspended, but only for a relatively short period of time, and the natural democratic instincts of the Indian people came to the fore again. And it is the most astonishing achievement, [that] this huge nation, clearly the largest democracy in the world, has been so incredibly successful.[17]

As twin democracies in the Indian Ocean, Australia and India share a belief in the rules-based international order. Both countries have a strong interest in promoting economic growth and regional stability. As Prime Minister Narendra Modi has said: 'Australia and India share a commitment to a democratic, pluralistic and open society.'[18]

Australia and India are two exemplars of the power of democracy. As one of the world's multicultural success stories, Australia has shown that democracy can be consistent with pluralism. India, as a nation emerging from poverty to prosperity, has shown that democracy is consistent with economic growth.

13

DEFENCE AND SECURITY

On his visit to India in March 2023, Prime Minister Anthony Albanese boarded INS *Vikrant*, India's massive new indigenously built aircraft carrier. Ascending the gangway from the pier to the deck, he took in the sheer size of the vessel, which stretches across the area of three football fields. Albanese posed for photos with naval personnel and climbed into the cockpit of an Indian light fighter jet on the deck. He was the first foreign leader to set foot on the Indian navy's new jewel, an invitation that affirms New Delhi's growing defence ties with Canberra.

At its commissioning ceremony six months earlier, Prime Minister Narendra Modi declared, 'Today, INS *Vikrant* has filled the country with a new confidence and has created a new confidence in the country.' He called *Vikrant* 'a floating city' and declared it a symbol of 'India's efforts to become *Atmanirbhar* [self-sufficient] in the defence sector'.[1]

But for Modi, launching the largest ship ever built in the maritime history of India wasn't the only purpose of the day. To accentuate his nation's new maritime prowess, he added a symbolic flourish to the occasion. He announced that the Indian naval flag that flies above INS *Vikrant* and all other Indian naval ships would change. The old ensign, created in 1947, was framed by a St George's Cross – the red and white flag of India's former colonists. 'We've made history,' Modi said as he unveiled the new ensign, 'and discarded a sign of our subjugation.'[2]

Instead of the English cross, the new flag incorporates a blue octagonal shape inspired by the insignia of a seventeenth-century Hindu warrior king Shivaji I, who was instrumental in ending Mughal control over the Indian subcontinent and establishing the Maratha Empire. For Modi, the heraldic pennant of an ancient Indian empire fluttering above one of the most advanced warships in the world is an exquisite symbol of his vision of India's emergence as a modern nation.

Albanese was quick to use his presence on INS *Vikrant* to bolster the bilateral defence relationship. 'My visit,' he said, 'reflects my government's commitment to place India at the heart of Australia's approach to the Indo-Pacific and beyond.'[3] He announced from the carrier's deck that Australia will host Exercise Malabar for the first time.

The defence relationship that exists today between Australia and India would have been unimaginable a few decades ago. Indeed, when India purchased an aircraft carrier from the United Kingdom and leased a nuclear submarine from the Soviet Union in the 1980s as part of a naval build-up, Australia was alarmed. One member of the Australian parliament warned that India's naval expansion posed 'a very real direct threat to Australia and our trade routes'.[4] The Australian press echoed these concerns, with *The Australian* declaring, 'India's amazing build-up concerns us.'[5]

Three decades later, Australia's reaction to India's maritime capability is now almost entirely positive, thanks to an increasing convergence of interests in the maritime realm. Australia is no longer threatened by India; Australia wants to partner with India.

On his visit to India in 2022, the deputy prime minister and defence minister, Richard Marles, stated his overwhelming priority to 'ensure Australia has the capability necessary to defend itself in the toughest strategic environment we've encountered in over seventy years'. Marles recognised that Australia cannot develop this capability on its own, and will need to find partners to 'pool [our] resources and combine [our] strengths [to create] decisive competitive advantage'. Australia is building precisely those partnerships. 'When I look out at the world,' Marles said. 'India stands out.'[6]

Australia's security establishment has long formed the view that Australia must deepen its security engagement with India. Australia's region is 'too vast and complex for any country to succeed in protecting its interests alone', says Professor Rory Medcalf. 'There will be a premium on partnerships ... the Indo-Pacific is both a region and an idea: a metaphor for collective action, self-help combined with mutual help.'[7]

India's military power has grown rapidly in the last decade. India was the world's fourth-largest military spender in 2022, with its defence spending increasing by around 6 per cent annually. With over 1.4 million active personnel, it is the world's second-largest military force and has the world's largest volunteer army.

Self-sufficiency in defence has been one of the hallmarks of India's aspiration for the future. India used to be the biggest importer of arms, but now nearly three-quarters of defence production is domestic. In the last eight years, it has upped its defence exports by eight times. India now supplies arms and military technology to Italy, Saudi Arabia, France, Israel and Sri Lanka. India has also established a military base in the North Agaléga island of Mauritius, as well as bases in Bhutan, Madagascar, Tajikistan, Oman, Iran and Sri Lanka.

The Quadrilateral Security Dialogue, often referred to as the Quad, is an important strategic partnership between Australia, the United States, Japan and India. Established to promote regional security and cooperation, the Quad aims to maintain a free, open and inclusive Indo-Pacific region.

The idea for the Quad stemmed from the cooperation shown in the aftermath of the devastating 2004 Indian Ocean tsunami, where Australia, the United States, Japan and India were able to coordinate their emergency response. Some efforts were made in the following years to institutionalise the cooperation, although it was not intended initially as a military partnership.

The Quad was first tentatively proposed in 2006 when Indian prime minister Manmohan Singh visited Japan and noted in a joint statement with Prime Minister Shinzo Abe 'the usefulness of having dialogue among India, Japan and other like-minded countries in the Asia-Pacific region on themes of mutual interest'.[8]

After receiving support from the Bush administration in the United States, an exploratory meeting took place between the four countries in May 2007 on the margins of the ASEAN Regional Forum in Manila. The meeting, billed simply as an attempt to 'share some values and growing cooperation in the Asia-Pacific', attempted to be low-key, with no formal agenda and no decision about a subsequent meeting. Nonetheless, the new grouping generated enormous interest, curiosity and criticism. There were many calls for more clarity on the future of this 'four-cornered dialogue'. Observers questioned whether it would develop into a security arrangement, a ministerial forum, an alliance or an expansion of the existing Trilateral Strategic Dialogue between Australia, the United States and Japan. Some critics suggested it was an 'Asian NATO'.

Most of the participants in the meeting seemed to want it to continue. During his visit to India in 2007, Abe spoke of a 'broader Asia' that would also incorporate Australia and the United States. US presidential candidate John McCain upped the ante in late 2007 by announcing that he would 'institutionalise' the Quad if elected. Most significantly, the annual US–India Malabar exercise in 2007 was expanded to include Australia and Japan (and Singapore).

Exercise Malabar was the first tangible security activity of the Quad. It also proved to be the last, as the grouping was effectively disbanded for the next ten years. Pressure from China was the immediate catalyst to dissolve the grouping. Fearing the group was established to contain it, China officially asked each of the participants to withdraw from the group. Cracks in the Quad publicly emerged in late 2007, when the new Japanese prime minister, Yasuo Fukuda, indicated he intended to take a more benign attitude to China. In January 2008, on the eve of his first state visit to Beijing, Prime Minister Singh announced he would not be party to any initiative against China.

Australia also hesitated to advance the Quad. In July 2007, the Australian defence minister, Brendan Nelson, visited Beijing and 'reassured

China that so-called quadrilateral dialogue with India is not something that we are pursuing'.[9] Subsequently, in India, he reiterated that Australia 'doesn't want to do anything unnecessarily that upsets any other country'.[10] In late 2007, the newly elected Rudd government also formed the view that it would be wiser to invest further in a direct relationship with China before burdening that relationship with baggage from the many historical Sino–Japanese and Sino–Indian conflicts.[11] As Australia's former ambassador to China Geoff Raby later put it: 'Recognising that Australia is more dependent economically on China than any of the others, and by a big margin, it is curious why Australia would want to join a group which China sees as hostile to its interests.'[12]

The day after the 2022 election, just hours after they were sworn in, Prime Minister Albanese and Foreign Minister Wong were on a plane to Tokyo to attend the Quad leaders' meeting with Prime Minister Kishida, President Biden and Prime Minister Modi. The new government was clearly showing that its commitment to the Quad was strong. At the National Press Club in 2023, Wong recognised 'the power, weight and influence of Japan and India, which in their own right are contributing to strategic balance'.[13]

The restoration of the Quadrilateral Security Dialogue, 'Quad 2.0', began in 2017. The Japanese foreign minister, Taro Kano, confirmed in October that Japan would officially propose a revival. Both the Trump and Biden administrations saw the Quad as key to a pivot towards the Indo-Pacific region. The Quad leaders held their first formal summit in 2021, which produced a declaration of intent: 'We bring diverse perspectives and are united in a shared vision for the free and open Indo-Pacific. We strive for a region that is free, open, inclusive, healthy, anchored by democratic values, and unconstrained by coercion.'[14]

Beyond the Quad and other multilateral security engagements, Australia has been steadily deepening its direct defence ties with India. The 2017 Foreign Policy White Paper emphasised that 'India is in the front rank of Australia's international partnerships with congruent security interests'.[15]

India's interest in a defence relationship with Australia is also growing. The Indian Ocean is critical to India's economic security, with vital shipping lanes and significant natural resources. Australia, being an Indian Ocean rim country, can contribute to the maritime security of the region. Australia also has a role in supporting India's ambitious military modernisation, including by sharing defence technology, intelligence and expertise.

Australia's defence relationship took a step forward in 2023 when it hosted – and India took part in – the Malabar exercise. Malabar initially began as a joint naval exercise of the United States and India in 1992. Japan's inclusion became permanent in 2015, transforming it into a trilateral affair. In 2020, Australia joined, demonstrating the significance of the Quad as a platform for promoting a free, open and inclusive Indo-Pacific. By enhancing naval interoperability and military-to-military relationships, the exercise contributes to the promotion of a rules-based order, the safeguarding of freedom of navigation and the maintenance of peace and stability in the Indo-Pacific.

Malabar is complemented by a range of other cooperative exercises, including AUSINDEX, which has been conducted regularly since 2015 by the Royal Australian Navy and the Indian Navy, focusing on anti-submarine warfare, maritime patrol and surface warfare; Exercise Pitch Black, a multinational air combat exercise hosted by the Royal Australian Air Force; and Exercise Austra-Hind, which enhances cooperation on counterterrorism and counterinsurgency measures. These exercises have not only improved interoperability between the two nations but have also helped build trust and understanding. They reflect considerable alignment in strategic interests and prove that the ambivalence of the past is fading.

These exercises have been complemented by a range of forums for strategic dialogue and interaction between defence personnel. The most recent significant development came with inaugural 2+2 dialogue of foreign and defence ministers. There are only two nations in the world with which India has a 2+2 dialogue, an annual leaders' meeting and a trade agreement. Japan is one, Australia is the other.

Each year, Australia sends two officers to attend Indian military educational institutions: one officer attends India's Defence Services Staff College, while another attends its National Defence College. Sir Peter Cosgrove, former Australian chief of the defence force and former governor-general, is an alumni of the National Defence College exchange program, graduating in 1994. India also sends two officers to study in Australia annually, with one attending Australia's Command and Staff College and the other attending the Centre for Defence and Strategic Studies.

There remains much scope to increase defence ties, including longer-term reciprocal arrangements to access and coordinate capability. There is also great potential for additional defence industrial cooperation – to collaborate on artificial intelligence, cyber and space capabilities, quantum and other emerging technologies.

Australia and India also have further scope to work together on humanitarian and disaster relief. This would be a useful demonstration of India and Australia's combined value to the region. It would also be an opportunity for building greater operational experience between the two navies, and to engage other Indian Ocean nations.

Another useful area of cooperation between Australia and India would be to build upon shared interests in the Antarctic. The Antarctic Treaty System has governed affairs in Antarctica since 1961, but it is now struggling to cope with environmental threats and great power competition. India has three research stations in Antarctica, namely Bharati, Dakshin Gangotri and Maitri. Bharati Station, India's newest facility in the Antarctic, has created more scope for cooperation with Australia on oceanographic studies and ecosystem protection. Together, India and Australia could work to preserve Antarctica as a region devoted to peace and science, and reduce the potential for strategic competition.

Australia recognises India as a 'rising Indo-Pacific great power and an increasingly significant security partner for Australia, particularly in the maritime domain'.[16] Amid the dynamic geopolitical environment,

India and Australia have a shared vision for the Indo-Pacific region. Both countries are committed to contributing to a stable multipolar regional order based on the rule of law, which facilitates growing trade, expanded diplomatic engagement and continued peace.

PART III
FAMILIES

14

DIASPORA

For many twentieth-century immigrants and their children, it was a rite of passage: arriving in Australia, they adopted a new identity.

Real estate agent L.J. Hooker began life as Leslie John Tingyou but changed his last name to Hooker in 1925 because he thought that no one would buy real estate from a Chinese man and Hooker was his favourite position in rugby.[1] Businessman Richard Pratt was born in the free city of Danzig to Jewish parents who changed the family name from Przecicki to Pratt on arrival in Shepparton because the locals found it easier to pronounce.[2] Successful Greek Australian designer Alexandros Pertsinidis shortened his name to Alex Perry after his first mention in *Vogue* because he thought it would boost his career in the fashion industry.[3]

My brother, Kim Charlton, was adopted as an infant from Korea in the 1970s. He was born Tae Hong Kim, but our parents changed his name to Kim Tae Hong Charlton to give him their surname but retain his original names as a link to his ancestry.

Many Indian migrants modified their names when they came to Australia. Baljinder Singh became Bill Singh. 'When I was new here, Australians used to tell me that my name is too long for them,' Singh says. 'Some started calling me Bill instead – and gradually it became my name.'[4] Harmohan Singh Walia, a community leader who carried the torch in the 2000 Sydney Olympic Games representing the Indian community, is known to many of his friends as 'Harry'. He says many migrants to Australia had several motivations for changing their names, including to speed their assimilation and deter discrimination or just because they considered it better for the businesses they hoped to start in their new country.

As Australia's multicultural community matures, the pressure to Anglicise migrant names is waning. 'I just don't think it's important anymore to change your name,' says Sanjay Deshwal, a migration consultant. 'It's something we might have discussed twenty years ago, but not now.'[5] As the Indian community has grown and prospered, many members of the new generation feel more confident about their identity than some of their parents. Modern Australia provides more space for migrants to integrate without assimilation. First- and second-generation migrants are now free to create more authentic 'hyphenated identities'.

This reflects the blossoming of Australian multiculturalism. As migrant communities grow and flourish, they are increasingly able to cherish their own heritage while engaging in a fluid mixing of groups within a diverse Australian community. Journalist Rajni Luthra sees this as the emergence of a 'post-multicultural world' where identities are multilayered and young Australians truly believe they are all similar, regardless of geographical and faith boundaries. 'Look at the next generation of Indian Australian kids becoming adults here with their Aussie accents,' says Luthra. 'They resent being boxed into an ethnic silo that glosses over their multiple connections and multidimensional lives. They are unthinking Eurocentricism and rethinking integration.'[6]

The success of Australia's multiculturalism is an extraordinary national achievement. In many parts of the world, the blending of cultures and ethnic groups has been much less benign. Australia's relative harmony is a wonder and inspiration to many nations. But perhaps Australians celebrate the success of our pluralism so enthusiastically that we risk forgetting its hardships and occasionally brush aside the struggles that many migrants endure. We should remember that what we have in Australia is as rare as it is imperfect.

The success of Indian Australians is a powerful argument in favour of Australia's model of multiculturalism, but also a cautionary tale of its challenges. This section of the book describes the successful contribution of the Indian diaspora to Australia across many dimensions, including community, politics, faith, media and culture. It also looks at some of the challenges facing the Indian diaspora and what we must do to ensure that Indian Australians, as the latest and greatest wave of modern migration, are as successful as their predecessors.

One million strong

Australia is home to more than one million people with Indian heritage – nearly one in every twenty-five Australians. This broad Indian diaspora includes people born in India (673,354 people in the 2021 census), people with parents born in India (935,066 people recorded a father born in India and 917,541 people recorded a mother born in India), as well as those who claim Indian ancestry through grandparents or other relatives.[7] It comprises Australian citizens, permanent residents, international students and temporary workers.

As noted earlier, Indian-born Australians are now the second-largest group of first-generation migrants in Australia. They recently overtook Chinese-born Australians and New Zealand-born Australians and are just behind the number of Australians born in the United Kingdom.

Figure 14.1 Overseas-born Australians by country of birth in 2021

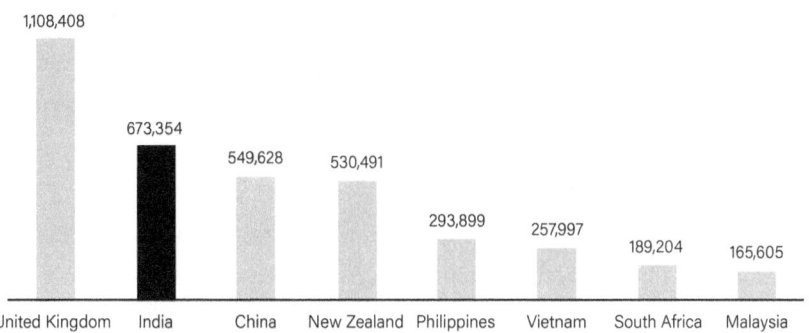

Source: ABS census 2021

The history of Indian migration to Australia goes back to the lascars and the camel drivers in the first decades of British settlement, and it grew in the mid-nineteenth century, when many Indians, including Hindus, Sikhs and Muslims, migrated to Australia to work on the goldfields. During the early 1900s, the White Australia policy curtailed immigration from non-European countries and the Indian community remained relatively small for several decades.

Following the relaxation of the White Australia policy in the late 1960s and its official abolition in 1973, there was a steady increase in Indian migration to Australia. Indian arrivals began to accelerate in the 1990s, when Australia shifted its immigration policy to prioritise skilled migration, focusing on attracting workers to fill labour market gaps. The points-based system introduced in 1999 favoured applicants with professional qualifications, work experience and English language proficiency, which made it easier for skilled Indian professionals to qualify for Australian visas.

On top of this, Australia's reputation as a provider of high-quality education attracted many Indian students. The Australian government promoted its education sector in India, and the number of Indian students enrolling in Australian universities and vocational institutions grew rapidly. This coincided with strong economic growth, higher disposable incomes and a rising middle class resulting from the Indian economic liberalisation of the 1990s. As a result, more Indians sought opportunities to live, work and study abroad, including in Australia.

Today, Indian Australians are the fastest growing of all the nation's largest ethnic groups. The number of people in Australia who were born in India has increased sevenfold in the last two decades. Nearly a quarter of the one million people who arrived in Australia from other parts of the world between 2016 and 2021 were from India.

On current growth rates, Indian-born Australians will soon become the largest migrant group. Indian-born Australians are growing ten times faster than the number of British-born Australians and five-times faster than the number of Chinese-born Australians. Between 2021 and 2016,

Australia added 217,966 Indian-born Australians compared with just 20,659 British-born Australians and 40,065 Chinese-born Australians.

Figure 14.2 Overseas-born Australians by country of birth between 2016 and 2021

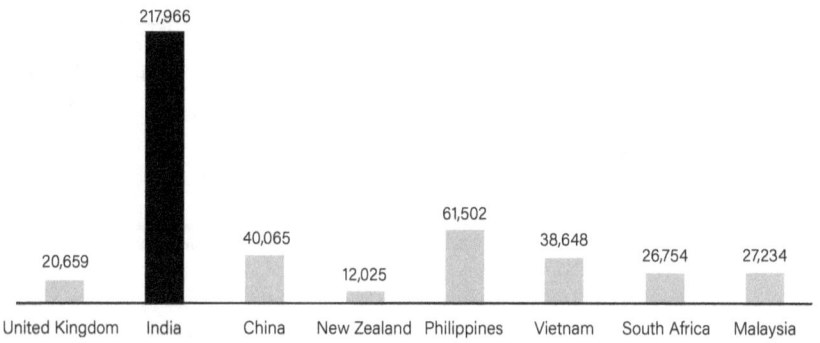

Source: ABS census 2021 and 2016

Australia's Indian population used to be largely concentrated in a few pockets in Sydney and Melbourne. But today the Indian diaspora is more spread out, with families building lives in the suburbs of every major city. The geographic distribution of the Indian diaspora broadly reflects Australian demographics, with nearly 70 per cent living in Victoria and New South Wales.[8]

The vast majority live in urban areas, with 93 per cent choosing to live in major cities of more than 100,000 people. Less than 1 per cent of Indian-born Australians live in rural areas. Australian residents with Indian ancestry reside in the highest concentrations in areas around Western Sydney, such as Parramatta and Blacktown, as well as in outer-suburban Melbourne, including south-western suburbs around Tarneit, south-eastern areas around Dandenong and northern suburbs around Glenroy.

The diversity of the nation's Indian population often gets overlooked. Most statistics consider Indian migrants as a single entity, but the reality is more complicated. One in ten people in Australia who list 'Indian' as their primary ancestry in the census also list a secondary ancestry. This includes Indian Australians who trace their roots to dozens of other countries, including Fiji, Sri Lanka, Malaysia, Singapore, Portugal, Nepal, South Africa, Iran, China and Japan.

This diversity is also reflected in the variety of languages spoken by Indian Australians. Nearly 27 per cent of Indian-born Australians speak Punjabi at home, 19 per cent speak Hindi, 8.8 per cent speak Malayalam, 8.7 per cent speak Gujarati and smaller numbers speak dozens of other languages.

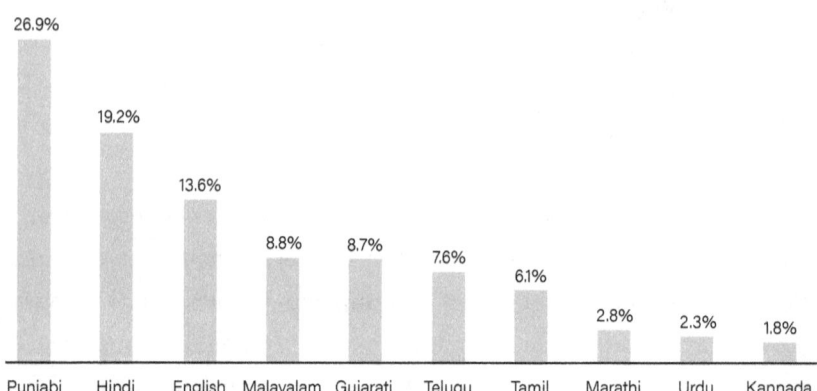

Figure 14.3 Languages spoken at home among Indian-born Australians

Source: ABS census 2021

By any measure, the Indian community has played an essential role in promoting cultural exchange and fostering strong ties between India and Australia through various cultural events, festivals and organisations. As this community continues to grow and integrate, the bonds between India and Australia are likely to strengthen further.

15

BUSINESS

'Indians, wherever we go, we work hard, have strong family values and contribute through sincere commitment to work ethics,' says Harmohan Singh Walia, author of the book *Challenges, Opportunities & Successes: 75 Inspirational Stories of Indo-Australians*. 'An Indian's proud moment is when they glowingly and proudly talk about their children of how well settled they are, job, career and finance wise.'[1]

Indian migrants to Australia are fabulously well qualified. Indian-born residents have much higher levels of educational attainment, with 64 per cent having a bachelor degree or higher, compared to 26 per cent of all Australian residents. That means Indian-born Australians are more than twice as likely to have a university degree. Almost 30 per cent of Indian-born residents aged over fifteen have a master's degree or higher.

The Indian diaspora is represented disproportionately in high-skill occupations, including in technology-enabled areas with skills shortages. Just under a half (49.3 per cent) of Indian-born workers in 2021 were working in either a managerial or a professional occupation. This compares with 38.4 per cent of Australian-born employed people. Indian-born Australians are six times more likely to be in an information communications technology (ICT) profession than the Australian average. The top occupations for Indian-born residents are ICT professionals, health professionals, business professionals and managers.

Figure 15.1 Percentages of Australians and Indian diaspora members in various professions

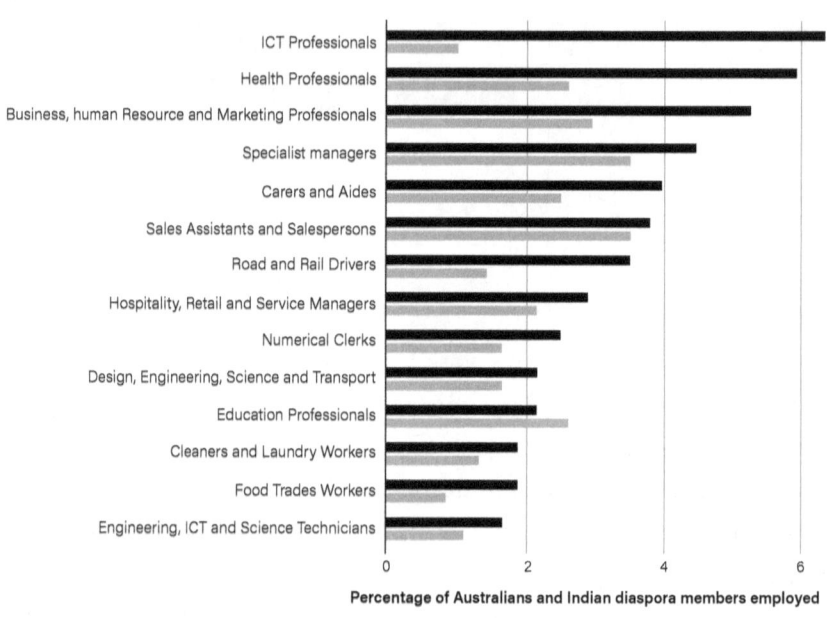

Source: ABS census 2016

'It is good for Australia to bring in more educated professionals who are tech-savvy and global citizens,' says Sheba Nandkeolyar, the first female chair of the Australia India Business Council. 'The professional migrants from India are highly aspirational, educated and they will grow the Australian economy through their entrepreneurial skills and professional qualifications. More professional migration, whether from India or elsewhere, can and will only benefit Australia.'[2]

Indian-born workers are among the highest income earners in Australia. Indian-born workers earned on average $82,321 per annum in 2021, compared with $77,657 per annum for Australian-born workers. Indian-born professionals earned on average $106,038 per annum, compared with an average of $97,609 per annum for Australian-born professionals.

Figure 15.2 Average income of migrants to Australia (median income per person)

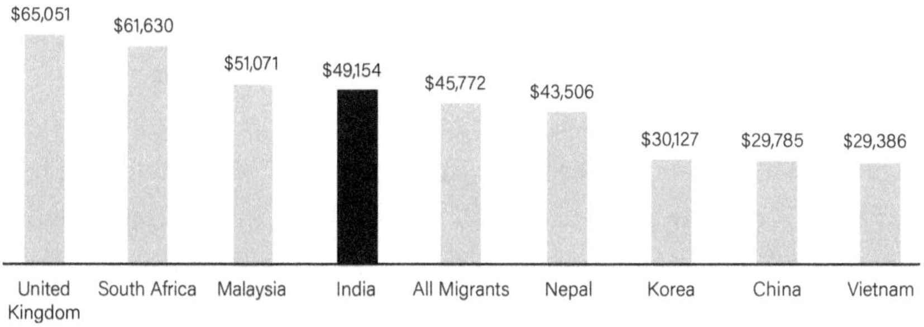

United Kingdom	South Africa	Malaysia	India	All Migrants	Nepal	Korea	China	Vietnam
$65,051	$61,630	$51,071	$49,154	$45,772	$43,506	$30,127	$29,785	$29,386

Source: ABS, Personal Income of Migrants, Australia, 2016–17

Australia could do more to attract skilled workers from India, says Lisa Singh, CEO of the Australia India Institute. 'We have skills gaps and if we are going to address those in both the short and long term, we have to look to India, to its tech talent and its young workforce, to help meet Australia's business and social needs,' says Singh. 'India has some of the best and brightest in the world, and we should be offering paths to permanent migration and more mobility options for people to move between the two countries.'[3]

Underemployment

When Mehak Sikka Bhatnagar migrated from India in 2018, she came with skills as an experienced dental surgeon. But arriving in Australia, she discovered she had to start at the bottom. 'I found that my overseas experience wasn't recognised anywhere. I needed local training on my CV and started work as a dental assistant in 2019.'[4]

It took her three years to pass the requirements of registering with the Dental Board of Australia. 'It's a huge financial drain to keep taking these exams, especially if you're unable to pass in the first attempt. A lot of people drop out because they can't afford it.'

Dr Sikka Bhatnagar's story is the flipside of India's migration story. While many migrants are finding high-skill jobs in the professions, medicine and technology, others end up in lower-skill roles working below their qualifications. Many Indian migrants find that their hard-earned degrees aren't always recognised by the Australian education system, putting them back to square one when looking for a job.

Indian-born people with a degree are much more likely to be working in low-skilled occupations than Australian-born people with degrees. For example, more than half (50.7 per cent) of Indian-born people working as labourers have a tertiary degree. By comparison, only 4.2 per cent of Australian-born people working as labourers have a degree. Similarly, 46.9 per cent of Indians working as machinery operators and drivers have a degree, compared to 3.4 per cent of Australian-born people working in the same field.

A study by the Australian National University's Professor Juliet Pietsch found that Indian migrants are more likely to be 'underemployed' in this way – that is, qualified for a professional occupation but actually working in a lower-skill job – than migrants from other countries, including China, South-East Asia, Southern Europe, Eastern Europe or Northern Europe. Tens of thousands of Indian immigrants struggle to gain professional work and pay in Australia even when they are qualified for it.[5]

New migrants trying to find jobs in Australia face a series of uphill battles: lack of qualifications recognition; undervalued foreign experience; and a greater risk of vulnerability and exploitation. Mohammad Al-Khafaji, the CEO of the Federation of Ethnic Communities' Councils of Australia, says, 'There is a culture in Australia where qualification doesn't really mean much ... In Australia, we have this obsession with "Australian experience".'[6] Al-Khafaji says this is a 'missed opportunity' for Australia, particularly in fields where there are skills shortages, such as engineering and health. 'If we continue on the path that we are on now, we will miss out on a huge percentage of very qualified, very innovative people that we should be welcoming,' he says. 'It's making some of our doctors or engineers end up driving taxis or Ubers.'[7]

Anthony Albanese announced during his visit to India in March 2023 the finalisation of the Australia–India Education Qualification Recognition Mechanism – the most comprehensive mutual recognition program between any two countries. The mechanism will go some way to recognising Indian qualifications in Australia. 'This agreement locks in the rules for mutual recognition to access education in both our countries, including the qualifications we provide online and offshore,' said the Minister for Education, Jason Clare.[8]

Improving the recognition of foreign qualifications is a win-win for Australia. It allows migrants to reach their full potential and gives businesses the skilled workers they need.

Business leadership
Tarun Gupta's father and mother both fled Pakistan to India as children when the subcontinent was partitioned into two independent states in 1947. Gupta's father became a police officer and the family moved through a series of towns and cities in Uttar Pradesh, India's most populous state. 'It was my father who actually encouraged me to apply to overseas universities,' Gupta says of the decision that brought him to Australia, and ultimately set him on a path to become the CEO of Stockland, one of Australia's largest property companies. 'I think he had a desire to study one day overseas. He was unable to do it. So maybe through his son, he was living the dream.'[9]

Gupta is one of many Indian Australians in senior leadership roles of top-listed companies, including Orica CEO Sanjeev Gandhi, Link CEO Vivek Bhatia, Pact CEO Sanjay Dayal and former Newcrest boss Sandeep Biswas. Their success mirrors the worldwide trend of major corporations being run by members of the global Indian diaspora, including Google's Sundar Pichai, the former PepsiCo CEO Indra Nooyi, Microsoft's Satya Nadella, former Mastercard chairman Ajay Banga (now head of the World Bank), former CEO of Citigroup Vikram Pandit, and more than fifty Fortune 500 companies currently run by CEOs of Indian descent.

'The common qualities I see across the group is they are all very hard-working, they are very grounded and they don't take things for granted. They know you have to put in 120 per cent and always be more prepared than the other person in the room,' says Vivek Bhatia. Bhatia sees a hunger for success among his fellow migrants in business leadership. 'You know that you have come here to prove a point. You know you have sacrificed, staying away from your family and friends, and if you have done that sacrifice then you might as well make the most of it,' he says, reflecting on his own experience. 'I didn't know anybody when I came to the country. I hadn't studied here. I didn't go to school or university here. I didn't know a single person. I had no fallback plans. Sometimes that's a good thing, right?'[10]

Indian business leadership extends from the big end of town to small businesses and startups. There are more than seventy thousand Indian-born business owners in Australia. These entrepreneurs are proving to be a source of national competitive advantage in export markets. Ashish Shah, who runs a trading business in Western Sydney supplying local grocers and supermarkets, explains that Australia's Indian diaspora has helped create many commercial opportunities. 'Many people in Australia want to buy Indian products, so trade has increased a lot in recent years,' he says.[11] His brother Parag Shah is building a manufacturing business in Pendle Hill that will supply groceries to Indian supermarkets and restaurants.

'Large Australian corporations have found it hard to invest in India, because they don't like risk and establishing a new presence in India seems very risky,' says Tim Thomas, the inaugural CEO of the Centre for Australia–India Relations. 'This is where small diaspora businesses can play an important role. They have a higher tolerance for risk and are better able to navigate India. Small businesses can show the way for large Australian companies.'[12]

The Indian diaspora also makes a strong contribution to business governance through their membership of company boards. There are an estimated 2840 directors and managers of Indian heritage out of a total of over 20,730 working in Australia. This corresponds to over 10 per cent of the total, while the diaspora represents approximately 3 per cent of the Australian population overall.[13]

Yet in larger companies, especially the biggest ASX-listed corporations, there is still a lack of diversity at board level. Over 8 per cent of Australia's population is born in Asia – a much higher percentage than in other Anglophone countries – yet only around 4 per cent of Australia's top two hundred publicly listed companies have board directors of Asian heritage.[14] The 2021 Board Diversity Index found that it would take eighteen years for ASX 300 boardrooms to reflect Australian cultural diversity.

The lack of diversity at board level means many companies don't have a deep understanding of Asian markets, including India. PwC Australia partner Andrew Parker said, 'I don't think we have the time to wait for [ethnic representation on boards] to happen and we can't take the chance ... because it might not and then we would've wasted a decade, so I do believe we need to take more positive action.'[15] Australia India Institute CEO Lisa Singh agrees that Australia's 'India literacy' is lacking. 'There's a lot of work to be done,' she says.[16]

Business groups

There are many organisations stepping into the void to build understanding and business links between Australia and India. The Australia India Business Council (AIBC) fosters trade and investment relations between the two nations. AIBC was established in 1986 by the governments of Australia and India. It now has chapters in six Australian state capitals as well as a presence in India. The council helps promote the bilateral business corridor, through policy and advocacy. 'India is the fastest growing major economy in the world,' says AIBC chair Jodi McKay. 'The relationship between Australia and India is not solely a government responsibility – business must be prepared to step up and it is AIBC's role to support and facilitate opportunities.'[17]

The India Australia Business and Community Alliance (IABCA) was established in 2014 by Sonia Gandhi, who came to Australia as an international student before forging a career in business and community leadership. IABCA builds awareness and understanding between the peoples and institutions of Australia and India. Its annual awards celebrate leaders who advance the India–Australia relationship and it has achieved international recognition for its role in cultural diplomacy and bilateral trade development.

Many other business-professional networks operate across the Indian diaspora in Australia. These groups facilitate professional networking but also complement the work of Australian industry and governments in supporting businesses seeking to engage the Indian market.

There is an extensive array of networks organised along cultural, geographic and community lines. Some, like the Little India Harris Park Business Association and Little India Australia, have been successfully promoting Indian cultural heritage, friendship and business opportunities for many years.

16

POLITICS

Lisa Singh, a senator from Tasmania, was the sole member of the Australian parliament with Indian heritage when she was elected in 2011.[1] In that same year, only one person with Indian heritage was serving across all the Australian state legislatures.[2] There was not a single mayor of Indian descent in any local government in the country. Despite being one of the largest immigrant groups in the country, Australians of Indian descent were barely represented in politics.

Twelve years later, Zaneta Mascarenhas, born in Kalgoorlie, Western Australia, to Indian immigrant parents of Goan descent who migrated from Kenya, was elected to represent the federal electorate of Swan. 'This is the most multicultural parliament we've had in history,' she said in her first speech. She acknowledged the diverse cohort of MPs around her, including four members of the forty-seventh parliament with South Asian heritage.[3] Standing on the floor of the House of Representatives in a stunning red sari, she declared: 'The public have spoken. They want to see a parliament that reflects their community.'[4]

In the NSW state parliament, the 2023 election was a high watermark for Australians of Indian descent. Charishma Kaliyanda, who migrated to Australia from India as a four-year-old, won the seat of Liverpool for Labor, and Gurmesh Singh, a fourth-generation migrant of Sikh Punjabi descent, retained his seat of Coffs Harbour for the Nationals. But what made the election special for Indian Australians was the diversity at the top of the winning ticket. The new deputy premier, Prue

Car, has Indian heritage through her father, who hails from Durgapur in West Bengal. The incoming treasurer, Daniel Mookhey, whose parents were Punjabi migrants, made history as the first minister to be sworn in on the Bhagavad Gita. 'The deputy premier and the treasurer both having Indian heritage in this government, is just such a sign of how as a parliament we are looking like the people we represent,' Mookhey said after the win. 'I don't think we deserve massive pats on the back for this as politicians, because frankly, we should have been achieving this already, but I do think we should mark the fact that progress has been made and there's more progress to be done.'[5]

Australians with Indian heritage have been steadily improving their representation in local government, albeit from a low base. Susai Benjamin was elected in 2012 to Blacktown City Council and he was joined on the same council by Moninder Singh in 2016. In the same year, Intaj Khan was elected to Wyndham City Council in Victorian local government elections.[6]

In 2021, three councillors with subcontinental heritage were elected to Strathfield Council: Sandy Reddy, Raj Datta and Sharangan Maheswaran. John Arkan was also elected to Coffs Harbour City Council, Sreeni Pillamarri was elected to Hornsby Shire Council and Usha Dommaraju was elected to Camden Council. In 2022, Barbara Ward, an Australian of Fijian Indian origin, was elected deputy mayor of Ku-ring-gai Council. The same year, Suman Saha, a Bangladesh-born Labor councillor with strong links across the Indian Australian community, became deputy mayor of Cumberland. 'I think it's a great honour and privilege that I came to this country as an international student and finished my studies and worked with the community,' Saha said.[7]

In 2023, Sameer Pandey became lord mayor of Parramatta, the first mayor from the Indian community. 'Indian Australians really want to see more Indian Australians elected to office, regardless of their party affiliation,' said migration consultant Sanjay Deshwal. 'My sense is that there is a lot of excitement among the Indian community to see Sameer stepping into this role.'[8]

While representation of Indian Australians has come a long way in the last few years, there is still more work to do to ensure that Indian Australians fully participate in our democratic structures. 'The strong perception among members of the Indian diaspora in Australia is that political parties are mainly concerned with ingratiating themselves with the community when it suits them, such as in the lead-up to elections, rather than genuinely representing the community's interests or proactively incorporating ethnic diversity into party structures,' says Surjeet Dogra Dhanji from the University of Melbourne.[9] Dr Dhanji points out that for a long time, many Indian Australians were put in unwinnable positions on party tickets. Her research on the 2019 federal election shows that of 1056 candidates standing for the lower house, twenty-one were Australians of Indian origin. Dave Sharma from the Liberal Party was the only one elected.

Political views
The Indian Australian community has a high level of political engagement. Strong English language skills and experience with Westminster democracy help Indian migrants quickly adapt to Australia's political system, according to Andrew Jakubowicz, an expert on ethnic communities at the University of Technology Sydney.[10] Indians generally are very politically conscious and politically aware. Ordinary people discussing politics at the corner chai shop or on the commute to work is commonplace in India. Many migrants bring that political interest to Australia. They might not have historical allegiances, but they have strong views. And they want to participate.

Australians with Indian heritage are not a homogenous voting block. Traditionally, many migrants tended to support Labor, partly because Labor seemed to be on the side of diversity and was naturally stronger in the outer suburbs where many migrants settled. Former federal Labor MP Laurie Ferguson says the Liberal Party was slow to recognise the political importance of multicultural communities. 'Barely five years ago, they really didn't care much about engaging ethnic groups.

They were not comfortable at the functions, if they turned up at all.' But Ferguson says that has changed recently. He feels there has been a decisive change among Liberal Party activists more recently to focus more on multicultural groups, especially the Indian community. 'The Indian community is possibly the single biggest battleground in ethnic politics, particularly in Sydney and Melbourne,' said Ferguson.[11]

The 'Indian vote' is important, says Pawan Luthra, who co-founded the Indian Link community media group in 1994, 'The Hindu community is a huge and growing community; it's one of the largest migrant groups in Australia. There are politicians at every Indian community event.' From all sides of politics, they attend cultural events, visit temples and shower the community with praise for its contribution to Australian society. Former prime minister Scott Morrison, for example, garnered attention for regularly posting Instagram selfies of himself cooking Indian curries and homemade 'ScoMosas'.

Figure 16.1 Indian Australian attitudes to Australian political parties

Respondents were asked the following question: 'Generally speaking, which political party, if any, do you identify with?'

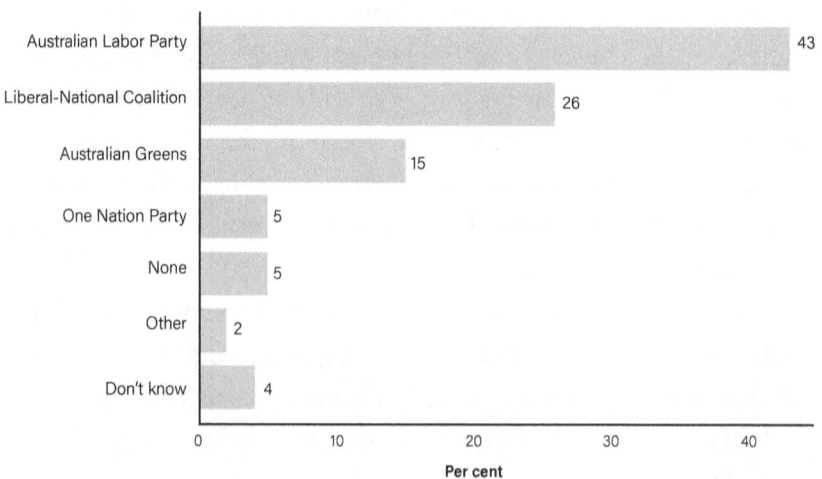

Note: There were 617 registered Australian voters surveyed.
Source: Carnegie Endowment for International Peace, 2022 survey of Indo-Australian attitudes

Concrete evidence of the voting patterns of Indian Australians is limited. One survey by the Carnegie Endowment for International Peace in 2022 found that 43 per cent of Indian Australians identified with Labor, 26 per cent of respondents identified with the Coalition and 15 per cent identified with the Greens, while 5 per cent selected One Nation.[12]

But while Labor has the support of the largest number of Indian Australian voters, the community's support is not monolithic. Many Indian Australians arrived in Australia recently, so they don't have a 'rusted-on' affiliation to either major party.

Cardiologist Yadu Singh, president of the Federation of Indian Associations of NSW, believes the Indian community is more conservative than the Carnegie polling suggests: 'Indians are not too much towards the left,' he says. He believes that many Indian Australians are small business owners – and any party that wants to attract them needs to appeal to their aspiration as well as their sense of social justice.[13] Pawan Luthra agrees that Indian Australians lean less to Labor than the data suggests. He believes many Indian migrants are natural swinging voters, switching their allegiance based on their perspective on which party is best at handling the issues.

The Carnegie survey of Indian Australians showed remarkably little difference in voting intentions based on religious identity. In the United Kingdom, Hindu voters have migrated away from the Labour Party over time and are more likely to vote for the Conservative Party, while Muslim and Sikh voters remain strong supporters of Labour. By contrast, Australians of Indian heritage show little evidence of political polarisation across religious groupings.

Indians in Australia are motivated by a range of issues. The top issues of concern for survey respondents were healthcare, the environment and the economy. Other important issues included housing, taxes, welfare, immigration and education.

The Carnegie survey found that members of the Indian diaspora in Australia care about bilateral relations with India. Indeed, three-quarters of people surveyed reported that a politician's position on India is either somewhat or very important for deciding who they will support in an election. However only 6 per cent of respondents listed Australia–India relations as their most important political issue.

Representative organisations

Over the past twenty-five years, a number of Indian organisations have come into existence across Australia to represent Indian Australians. Some of these are national bodies; others represent different regional or religious sections of the diaspora. These organisations have grown as the Indian Australian community itself has expanded. With the rapid influx of students and burgeoning growth of new Indian migrants, they seek to support the community and address the issues they face.

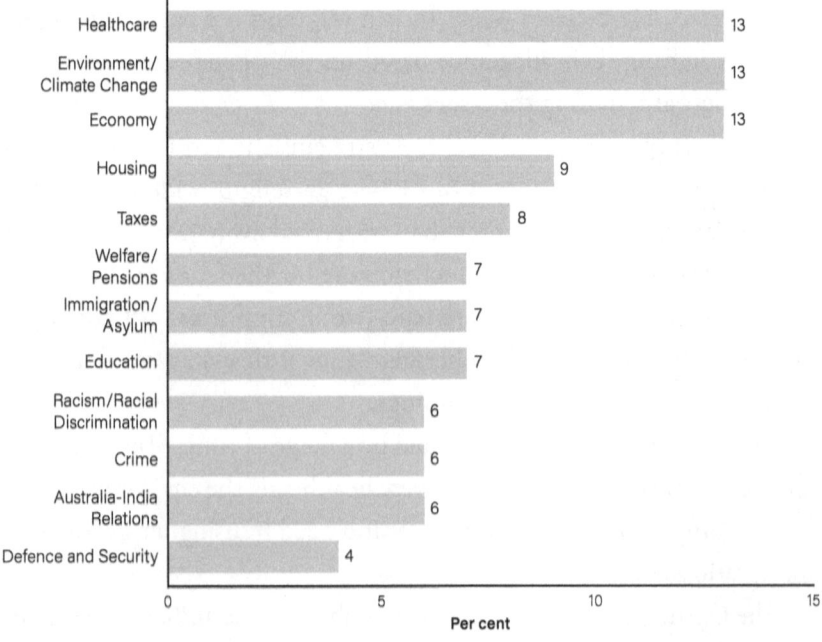

Figure 16.2 Top voter issues in Australia's 2022 election for Indian Australians

Note: There were 617 registered Australian voters surveyed.
Source: Carnegie Endowment for International Peace, 2022 survey of Indo-Australian Attitudes

The Australia India Society of Victoria, established in 1963, is one of the oldest Indian organisations in Australia. Its goal is to support new migrants and advance the needs of established Indian Australians. Through various activities, festivals and programs, it supports the diaspora and promotes participation in Australia's multicultural society.

The Indian Society of Western Australia was started in 1968 to support the growing Indian diaspora in the state. It inaugurated Western Australia's first Indian community centre in Perth in 2021, to create a cultural and social venue for the community. The centre is used for events, festivals and activities, including education programs and day care for the aged, as well as providing a dedicated space for locals with Indian heritage to come together and celebrate their culture and traditions.

The Federation of Indian Associations of Victoria was formed in 1989 to bring various regional, cultural and linguistic Indian groups together under the one umbrella organisation. Its main goals are to represent the cause of Indian Victorians and act as a lobby group for the Indian community in Victoria. By bringing together more than twenty-eight individual organisations into a unified body, it aims to strengthen the community and provide improved services to the Indian population in Victoria.

United Indian Associations was first established in 1994 to serve the Indian community in New South Wales. As an umbrella organisation, it has at different times included membership and links to many different organisations, including the Australian Punjabi Association, Gujarati Association of NSW, Sydney Kannada Sangha, Hindi Samaj, Sydney Malayalee Association, Marathi Association, Sydney Tamil Manram, Sydney Tamil Sangam and the Telugu Association of Australia.[14] It serves the Indian diaspora in Australia by engaging in social and community development.

The Federation of Indian Communities of Queensland was formed in 1997 to provide a common platform in representing and serving the Indian community in Queensland. Its membership includes nearly fifty Indian organisations, which represent people of Indian origin from mainland India, Fiji, South Africa, Malaysia and many other countries.

The Hindu Council of Australia is a peak body founded in 1998. It acts as a representative of the Australian Hindu community in dealing with the federal, state and local governments and reaches out to other Hindu organisations and institutions. The council's mission is to work for a strong, cohesive and active Hindu community in Australia. It aims to share and promote the Hindu faith while also creating links with other religious and cultural communities.

The Council of Indian Australians was inaugurated in 2011 to promote Indian cultural heritage, friendship and integration within multicultural Australia. The council is a secular and non-partisan organisation. It seeks to support the Indian Australian community with the challenges they face, including migration issues, settlement, employment and issues relating to foreign students.[15]

There are many more organisations across Australia that support different parts of the Indian diaspora. The vast majority of these are staffed by volunteers responding to the needs of their community.

Political influence in India

The diaspora is not only a political force in Australia; it also plays a role in politics in India. Australians with Indian heritage are part of the largest diaspora population in the world. There are nearly twenty million people of Indian origin living outside India across 146 countries.

The Indian diaspora makes up a large share of the population of many nations, including Singapore (where Indians make up 8 per cent of the population), Malaysia (7 per cent), Fiji (34 per cent), Trinidad and Tobago (35 per cent), Qatar (39 per cent), Canada (5.1 per cent), South Africa (2.4 per cent) and the United Kingdom (1.8 per cent). Australia's Indian diaspora makes up 4 per cent of the population.

The diaspora is now seen as integral to India's national development. It is a source of global soft power and a national asset with economic and strategic value. India no longer considers overseas migration of Indians a 'brain drain' but rather a 'brain circulation' that enhances India's global image and contributes back to India through homeward flows of remittances, business know-how and investment.

According to a recent report by the consulting firm McKinsey & Company, the twenty million Indians living abroad generate an annual income equal to 35 per cent of India's gross domestic product. Many send money home to family and friends. India receives more remittances from its diaspora than any other nation, with a total of US$100 billion flowing home in 2022.

The diaspora has been used by various Indian leaders over time to project India's soft power. Nehru engaged India's global diaspora to seek broad support for India's position as a non-aligned nation. Indira Gandhi used the diaspora to organise 'India Festivals' held in many nations to display and propagate India's cultural power. Rajiv Gandhi sought to leverage the diaspora to promote trade and investment.

More recently, Modi has stepped up India's engagement with its diaspora. His international visits have a strong focus on the diaspora. Before Modi, Indian embassies around the world would organise formal receptions with prominent Indians to coincide with prime ministerial visits. But Modi chooses instead to hold massive events, reaching out to larger numbers of people with Indian heritage through stadium events and parades where people line up on the streets to catch a glimpse of him, shake hands and take selfies with him.

Modi's political party, the BJP, has always had close ties with Indians abroad as part of its vision of a grand Indian civilisation. The former BJP prime minister Atal Bihari Vajpayee initiated an ambitious annual event called Pravasi Bharatiya Divas (Overseas Indian Day) in 2003, which is now celebrated around the world.

Modi's goal is to turn the Indian diaspora into an asset for India. 'You play a key role in shaping a positive image of India not just in America but also around the world,' Modi told a rapturous crowd of more than twenty-two thousand Indians in New York. BJP insiders call these events 'force-multipliers', with Modi's positive reception around the world building his image back home. During the 2019 elections, there were reports of members of the diaspora calling back home to explain to their family and friends the place of pride India enjoys in the eyes of the foreigners since the arrival of Modi as their leader in India.

These events have also added a new dimension to India's foreign policy. Modi wants to create politically assertive Indian communities abroad. The BJP has a goal to make members of the diaspora into supporters and cheerleaders for India's government with their local governments, media and communities.

In 2022, I met with Dr Vijay Chauthaiwale, who is in charge of the BJP's foreign affairs department, the Overseas Friends of BJP (OFBJP). In this role, he manages the BJP's outreach program overseas in cooperation with the prime minister, BJP party leaders and Foreign Minister Jaishankar. The OFBJP has chapters in more than forty nations. Chauthaiwale is constantly travelling and connecting between various units of the 'saffron *parivar* (family)', staying in touch with embassies, engaging with local Indian diaspora groups and preparing for Prime Minister Modi's visits, for which OFBJP coordinates various reception committees and events.

Chauthaiwale told me his goal is to project India's image as a growing power abroad and instil a sense of pride among the Indian community around the world.

17

EDUCATION

Sanjoli Banerjee is in her twenties but has the CV of someone much older. This young change-maker started her activism at age five, when she demonstrated with her parents in human-rights protests. At eight, she was recognised for her activism in women's empowerment by the chief minister of Haryana. Before she turned twenty, she had founded a free mobile school in rural India. At twenty-two, she was awarded the Diana Award, established in the memory of the Princess of Wales, for her work campaigning for gender equity and environmental degradation.

Banerjee graduated from school in 2016 with the highest mark in her state for Humanities. She was admitted to the prestigious Miranda House at Delhi University. But she had a desire to study abroad and decided to give it a shot. 'Modi had been elected to be the Prime Minister of India and the media was flooded with news of how he was working towards stronger foreign relations, which further grew my interest,' she explained. 'I wanted to explore India's place in the region and its relations with other countries.'[1]

After a lot of deliberation and research, Banerjee chose Australia. And just to be completely sure, she took a trip with her father to attend the open day at the Australian National University. 'I felt that the quality of education is better there ... ANU was ranked number 1 in Australia and was ranked sixth globally.'[2]

In the past two decades, more than one and a half million Indian students have studied in Australia. The number of Indian students studying in Australia has increased significantly over the years, growing by over 70 per cent since 2015. In 2023, Indian students became the largest group of international students in Australia, overtaking the Chinese. They are attracted to Australia's high-quality education system, with many universities here consistently ranking among the top hundred in the world. Catriona Jackson, Universities Australia chief executive, explains, 'We have a good product to offer, and [Indian students] know it.'[3]

The Albanese Labor government has implemented a range of student-friendly policies that have boosted applications from India. Migration agent Saurabh Smar said the federal government's 'efforts towards clearing the visa backlog accompanied by an improvement in grant rates for Indian student visa applicants has led to record growth in interest in Australian universities'.[4] Work rights during and after study are also an important drawcard for Indian students. In the aftermath of the pandemic, the government loosened restrictions on students' work hours and offered longer stays to former graduates. 'International students would be aware that Australia is facing a skills shortage and see the opportunity to not only study here but potentially stay on and work once they graduate,' Jackson said.[5]

Many Australian universities offer opportunities for students to participate in internships, student groups and other activities, further enhancing their international experience. When Banerjee was at ANU, she had the opportunity to be a member of the Australian parliament for a day, taking over the office of Senator Larissa Waters and even meeting then prime minister Scott Morrison. 'In India, you wouldn't get such an opportunity,' Banerjee reflected.[6]

Financial considerations are also an important factor for Indian students choosing to study in Australia. The average annual cost of education for Indian students in Australia is around $40,000. While this is expensive and can lead to significant financial pressures, it is more affordable than education in the United States or the United Kingdom.

Australia has mostly repaired the damage caused by the spate of violent attacks on Indian students in 2009. According to a survey conducted by the Indian High Commission in Australia, over 85 per cent of Indian students surveyed reported feeling welcome and safe in Australia. Australia is known for its high quality of life, friendly people and multicultural society. Indian students may find it relatively easier to adapt to life in Australia due to the presence of a large Indian diaspora and the acceptance of cultural diversity.

The fields of study that attract Indian international students to Australia are management and commerce, information technology, engineering, hospitality and health. According to the Department of Education, Skills and Employment, in 2020 Indian students accounted for 32.2 per cent of all international students enrolled in management and commerce courses in Australia, 30.6 per cent of all international students enrolled in information technology courses, and 24.5 per cent of all international students enrolled in engineering courses.

Figure 17.1 Top fields of study for international students from India in higher education and VET courses in 2020

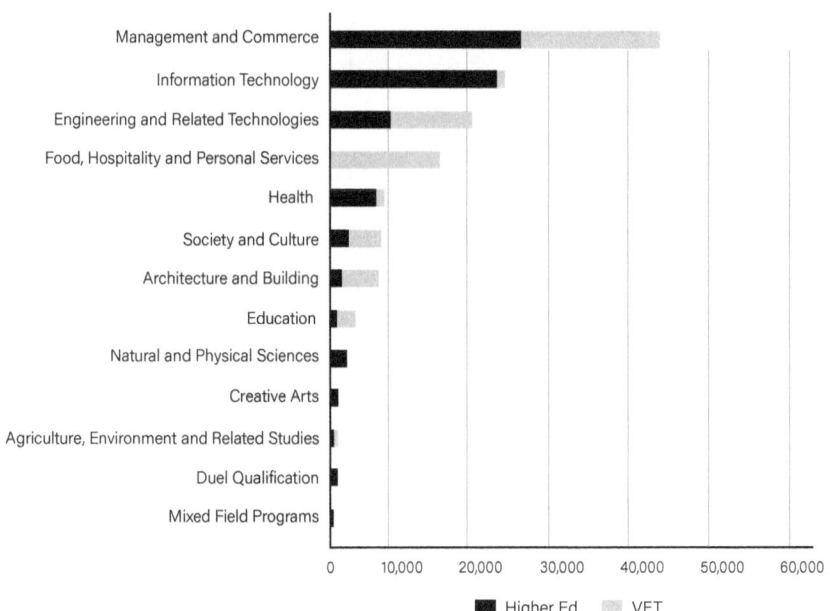

Source: PwC and the Department of Education, Skills and Employment

International students make a massive contribution to Australia. Total student spending on tuition fees, accommodation and living expenses was $37.6 billion in 2019, making it the fourth-largest export sector for Australia.[7] This spending supported approximately 250,000 full-time equivalent jobs in Australia, including direct employment and indirect employment in industries that provide goods and services to international students.[8] International students contribute to the Australian economy through income taxes, consumption taxes and other indirect taxes. In 2016, it was estimated that international students contributed $4.8 billion in taxes to the Australian government.[9]

International students who work part-time or after graduation also contribute to the Australian labour market. In some industries, such as healthcare and information technology, they help fill skill shortages, which boosts productivity and competitiveness.

Ketan Patel came to Australia as a student in 2001 and has since become a community leader and successful business owner. 'Actually, I never wanted to stay in Australia. I was just taking the opportunity to get an international education before I intended to apply to settle in the United States where my parents already lived in Chicago,' Patel says. In 2006, after completing his studies in information systems and working in property maintenance, he saw an opportunity to open an Indian grocery store in Harris Park. Today, his business, Radhe supermarkets, is one the fastest growing chains of Indian stores in Australia and branching out into restaurants. 'When I arrived in Australia, I liked it. And the weather is much better than Chicago, so I stayed!' Patel is an example of how Australia's education system can attract talent that contributes to the nation over the long term.[10]

More Indian students in Australia has led to more collaboration between Australian and Indian universities. For instance, in 2018 the Indian Institute of Technology Delhi and the University of Melbourne set up a joint research centre to 'facilitate high-quality research and training in the areas of nanoscience and nanotechnology, and promote the exchange of staff, students and ideas between the two institutions'.[11]

Deakin University is planning to establish an Indian campus. RMIT has launched a joint academy with the Birla Institute of Technology and Science, Pilani, to offer four engineering split-degree programs. This opens the door for students to split study time between Australia and India.

The Indian government has set a goal to double the percentage of students enrolled in higher education by 2035. 'That's nation-changing for India, and a genuine opportunity for Australian education providers to do more to collaborate with India,' says Education Minister Jason Clare.[12] Australia is among the countries that can help achieve that objective. India also wants to move its institutions up in the world rankings. Jyoti Arora, a researcher awarded an Australia India Research Students Fellowship, says that collaborative activities can help Indian universities lift their position in the global rankings. 'I'm keen to find out what strategies Australian universities use to both attain a high ranking and then keep it,' Arora says.

But Australia cannot take Indian students for granted, warns Gopalaswami Parthasarathy, former high commissioner of India to Australia. The rapid expansion of the middle class in India means parents can afford to send their children overseas to study, but they will only choose Australia if the quality of education remains high. 'People with garages posing as universities and colleges to lure Indian students gave a wrong impression of Australian education,' says Parthasarathy, but notes that these 'have now been closed down'. He wants Australia to continue to focus on the quality of education on offer for Indian students. 'It is clear that Australia will have to make a decision: does it want quality in quality institutions, or does it want numbers?'[13]

Indian students studying in Australia also face challenges. For many international students, finding affordable and suitable housing is difficult. According to the Indian High Commission in Australia, around 65 per cent of Indian students surveyed complained of this. Long commute times and hefty rental costs are common.

After completing her undergraduate studies at the ANU, Banerjee enrolled in a Master of Social Work degree at the University of

Wollongong. She lived at International House, student accommodation provided by the university, where she had a room to herself and shared a kitchen, dining room and bathroom. 'I consider myself lucky that I got student accommodation, as there are limited spots and it is quite expensive.'

Other challenges facing Indian students include financial pressures, exploitation by employers, discrimination and social isolation. According to a report by the Human Rights Commission, one in five international students in Australia has experienced discrimination or harassment, which can have a significant impact on their mental health and wellbeing.[14] According to a survey by the Council of International Students Australia, over 60 per cent of international students reported feeling lonely and isolated.[15] A report by the Fair Work Ombudsman showed that international students, including Indian students, are vulnerable to exploitation and underpayment by employers.[16] This can make it difficult for Indian students to earn a living and support themselves while studying in Australia.

Organisations such as the Indian Students' Association of Australia have been instrumental in providing assistance to Indian students, including advice on accommodation, part-time work and cultural events.[17] Additionally, several universities and educational institutions in Australia have established support services and resources to assist Indian students with their studies and social integration. Banerjee was elected to a representative role on campus to advocate for the welfare of international students in Australia. 'From my personal experience I felt homesick ... I want to make international students more close-knit, and a home away from home.'

Today, Banerjee manages campaigns as a full-time activist and director of an NGO in India. 'It was not an easy decision to study at a foreign university, being the first person to do so in the family.' Nonetheless, she reflects positively on her time in Australia, 'ANU transformed my life, from growing as a person to becoming a leader, with all the opportunities to work on myself and grow, I got to discover myself, life and the world, and for that I owe a lot to ANU.'

18

MEDIA

When Pawan Luthra began publishing the newspaper *Indian Link* in 1994, he would personally deliver bound stacks of each edition to Indian supermarkets and spice shops around the city in his own car. *Indian Link* was first published in Sydney but now reaches Melbourne, Adelaide, Brisbane, Canberra and Perth. Its goal has always been to 'help the Indian community assimilate into the Australian way of life', says Luthra, past winner of Multicultural Journalist of the Year. 'At the same time, *Indian Link* is aimed at helping Australians understand the Indian culture and beliefs.'

Before the internet, these newspapers were one of the few sources of information about events back in India and also played a crucial role connecting people across the local community. 'In the early days, we were a conduit back to India for migrant communities,' Luthra tells me. 'We catered to a hunger for information about India.' He remembers calling friends and family after the Indian national elections in 1996 to record the vote tallies, note down the number of seats each party would hold within the Lok Sabha, and pick up details of the short-lived new Vajpayee government, which lasted only thirteen days. His readers would rush to pick up the newspapers and read the latest dispatches from Delhi.

Indian newspapers, like many other ethnic media outlets, play an important role in providing information to migrant groups that mainstream media are largely unable to provide. In 1998, when the mainstream

Australian press was highly critical of India's nuclear tests, the Indian high commissioner in Canberra, Gopalaswami Parthasarathy, used *Indian Link* to channel a more nuanced message from the Indian government to the diaspora in Australia.

But the role of ethnic media has evolved over time. With the dawn of the internet, Luthra found that Indian Australians could tap into news about India more quickly and easily on the web. 'Once Google emerged in the late 1990s, the equation flipped,' Luthra recalls. People could access international news more easily, and local ethnic media focused more on the activities of the diaspora, including news of cultural and social activities and notices about forthcoming events.

The focus on local news matched the growth of the local diaspora. Indus Age, one of Australia's most successful multicultural media companies, launched by Minu and Rajesh Sharma, covers news, politics, culture, lifestyle and travel. It has built a loyal following among community leaders, businesspeople, students and families across the country, who rely on Indus Age as a necessary guide to community, religious, business and social activities. Its broad base is attractive to advertisers, especially among the maturing diaspora business sector, which has a growing appetite to increase its brand presence.

Alongside traditional print media is a burgeoning digital-media offering. Where once people would go to their local shops for the news, now they expect it in their inbox. Even older members of migrant communities are engaging in a broad range of online activities and collecting information more digitally than ever before. Along with his print newspaper, Pawan Luthra produces the *Indian Link E-Paper*, which is emailed directly to over twenty-five thousand subscribers each month. And he launched the first 24/7 Indian radio station in 2002.

A range of digital publishers have emerged within the Indian diaspora in recent years. Founded in 2021 in Melbourne, *The Australia Today* operates on the internet, Facebook, Instagram, TikTok and YouTube. It has grown rapidly, to offer Australian news, analysis and opinions in text and video formats. While the main focus of *The Australia Today* is the local diaspora, it also has a large following on the subcontinent. As the number of Indian migrants in Australia has grown, so has interest in Australia among their friends and family back in India. News that breaks in *The Australia Today* is regularly picked up by Indian newspapers and broadcast in Indian digital media.

The growth of social media over the last decade has changed the game again for multicultural publishers. 'Suddenly we were competing against "citizen journalists" who could report on festivals and events more quickly than we could,' says Luthra. One of the social-media giants is 'Indians in Sydney', a Facebook group created in 2007, which has grown to more than 116,000 members. The focus is on sharing information, discussing issues and making social connections. The group has more than a thousand posts per month, advertising events and discussing issues relevant to the diaspora. On top of public social media sites, thousands of disaggregated networks of WhatsApp groups disseminate information among friends and communities in an instant.

The growth of social media forced the established Indian newspapers to evolve their service to the needs of the community. Just providing local information to a local audience wasn't enough. 'We had to differentiate from social media by becoming a trusted source of news,' says Luthra. His biggest asset became his masthead, his reputation and the in-depth knowledge of his team.

On 9 June 2009, when the Indian population of Harris Park erupted in protest at the violence directed at Indian students, Luthra remembers a volatile situation. 'The media back in India were whipping up white-hot anger. They were reporting the attacks as evidence of endemic racism. On the other hand, the Australian media were reporting the attacks as a law-and-order issue and claiming the racial connections were coincidental.' Luthra felt a responsibility to come down in the middle. From within the Indian Australian community, he was well placed to temper the situation and provide objective facts. 'In a world full of so much social-media noise, we position ourselves as a voice of reason.'

The Indian and broader ethnic media played a crucial role in the COVID-19 pandemic. It was a tough time for all media outlets, with advertisement revenue drying up and the shops where the papers were normally distributed closed. But despite these challenges, ethnic media ensured multicultural communities stayed informed about the crisis and delivered vital health messages to diverse communities.

Ethnic media has made itself a valuable partner for governments. Governments often struggle to deliver information in many languages and cannot easily tailor their messages to capture the subtleties and nuances relevant to different communities. Multicultural media are therefore in a unique position to effectively communicate government initiatives at a grassroots level on many issues, from migration to health and education.

The role of multicultural media has never been so important. 'We as a community are racing forward and it is an exciting space to be in as we continue to be amazed and privileged to report on the achievements of Indian Australians – which are now wonderfully multifaceted,' says journalist Rajni Luthra. But she also acknowledges the role of the Indian media in the broader Australian cultural landscape. This role is changing from what she calls 'bridging' to 'bonding'.[1]

Bridging was about representation – that is, talking to the mainstream about the Indian Australian experience. It was about getting others to listen to a different perspective. The Indian media has successfully broken through as a political force. 'I think that politicians and officials did not see them as real newspapers for a long time, but that has changed now,' says Aisha Amjad, an adviser to state and federal politicians. 'Every important political candidate wants to give interviews and get coverage in the Indian media. Premiers, prime ministers – they all come wanting coverage in the fastest-growing migrant community.'[2]

'Bonding' is the other role of multicultural media. 'Bridging is between communities while bonding is within,' says Luthra. Bonding is about supporting the diaspora community as they navigate Australian society. In the short term, it means fostering engagement with local community and government institutions, and in the longer term catering to the need to belong, by participating in cultural, social, economic and political life.³

Ultimately, Luthra would like to see the term 'ethnic media' done away with. She warns against confining Indian voices to an ethnic silo. Instead, she applauds the trend of Indian commentators increasingly becoming part of the mainstream media. She points to Tarang Chawla, Neha Madhok, Charishma Kaliyanda, Pawan Luthra, Amar Singh and others who regularly appear in the mainstream media to give diverse perspectives on a broad range of topics, not just on ethnic issues. 'I am very hopeful that a post-multicultural media will reflect an ideal that reinforces the new integrative realities of Australia – one that captures our diversity.'

19

CULTURE

As the stage lights dimmed, the audience hushed reverently. The spotlight dropped on the ethereal figure of Sagarika Venkat, adorned in resplendent traditional attire. Her ensemble boasted vibrant shades of red, gold and green. The intricately woven patterns on her silk costume shimmered under the spotlight, creating an illusion of dancing flames.

The occasion was Venkat's *Arangetram*, which is a portmanteau of the Tamil words for 'stage' (*arangu*) and 'ascent' (*etram*) and loosely translates to a graduation ceremony for young performers. At just fourteen years of age, Venkat is one of Australia's most talented young performers of Bharatanatyam, a classical dance known for its sculptural poses, rhythmic footwork and intricate costumes.

The performance began with an invocation to the gods, as Venkat positioned herself in the traditional *samapada* stance. The rhythmic beats of the *mridangam*, a classical Indian percussion instrument, resonated through the theatre, melding with the melodious strains of the flute. The performer progressed through a series of intricate dance sequences. Her limbs moved fluidly, carving elaborate patterns in the air. Each *mudra*, or hand gesture, wove a vivid tapestry of stories, transporting the audience of several hundred people at the Riverside Theatre in Parramatta to the realms of ancient Indian mythology.

Venkat's mother, Manjula Viswanath, watched proudly from the side of the stage. A talented artist herself, she had painstakingly passed down the sacred art of Bharatanatyam to Sagarika, nurturing her into the accomplished dancer she is today. Viswanath is a skilled dancer, teacher and choreographer who is well known globally for her ability to combine tradition and innovation in performances across the world.

In recent years, Bharatanatyam has been experiencing a surge in popularity, emerging as a prominent art form within Australia's multicultural tapestry. The classical Indian dance form, with its rich history and tradition, has gained popularity not only among the Indian diaspora but also in the wider Australian community. Australians from various backgrounds have been drawn to the captivating rhythms, storytelling and expressive nature of Bharatanatyam.

The popularity of Bharatanatyam in Australia has been supported by a growing number of skilled teachers and dance schools, such as Manjula Viswanath's Rasika Dance Academy, the DK Alayam School of Music and Dance, and Chandralaya School of Dance in Melbourne, and the Lalithakalalaya School in Brisbane. These schools provide opportunities for students of all ages and backgrounds to learn and appreciate the beauty of Bharatanatyam, fostering a vibrant community of dancers and enthusiasts.

Festivals, community events and cultural showcases have increasingly incorporated Bharatanatyam performances, enabling the dance form to reach a broader audience and creating growing demand for performers.

Bharatanatyam is just one art form within the Indian community in Australia, whose strong cultural diversity reflects traditions from many parts of India and incorporates traditional and modern arts from various religious, linguistic and cultural groups. The vibrant and diverse cultures of India are maintained through a range of organisations, events and festivals throughout Australia – organisations such as the Tamil Arts and Cultural Association (TACA). Founded in 2011, TACA organises various cultural events, including Tamil music and dance performances, Tamil language classes and workshops. TACA plays a vital role in maintaining a strong connection to Tamil heritage for the Tamil community in Australia. Its leader, Anagan Babu, says the organisation aims to build a 'strong and cohesive Australian Tamil community that enriches, strengthens and contributes to multicultural Australia'.[1]

Indian culture in Australia has also evolved and adapted into modern art forms. While traditional high culture is kept alive, young people are developing a more pliable popular culture among second- and third-generation immigrants.

Indian films are growing in popularity in Australia. Bollywood films and Indian music have gained immense popularity, with many theatres screening Bollywood movies and hosting Indian film festivals. The Australian Indian Film Festival showcases Indian cinema in Australia each year, providing a platform for Indian filmmakers to share their work with Australian audiences. The festival has screened numerous critically acclaimed films, such as Leena Yadav's *Parched* (2015) and Garth Davis's *Lion* (2016), which is based on the true story of an Indian Australian man's search for his biological family.

Since migrating to Australia in 2001, Mitu Bhowmick Lange has contributed to every aspect of the local film industry. She started her Bollywood film career as a producer for the 2005 hit *Salaam Namaste*, starring Preity Zinta and Saif Ali Khan. Filmed in Victoria, it was the first Bollywood film to be shot completely overseas. '[*Salaam Namaste*] went on to create so much awareness for Melbourne in India. There was a hike in tourism to Victoria from India, with students coming to study here,' she says.[2] Following its success with local audiences, Bhowmick Lange established a company, Mind Blowing Films, which is the leading distributor of Bollywood and Indian cinema in Australia. She is also the director of the Indian Film Festival of Melbourne. Through her work, Bhowmick Lange has not only provided diaspora audiences with access to South Asian cinema, she has also built an ongoing relationship between the local and Indian film industries.

Indian Australian authors such as Roanna Gonsalves, Aravind Adiga and Suneeta Peres da Costa have made notable contributions to Australian literature. Gonsalves's collection of short stories, *The Permanent Resident*, explores the experiences of Indian immigrants in Australia.

Adiga, born in India and raised in Australia, won the Man Booker Prize for his 2008 novel *The White Tiger*, which explores the class struggle in modern India. Peres da Costa's 2018 novella *Saudade* delves into the life of a Goan family living in Angola during the country's struggle for independence. Literary festivals, such as the Sydney Writers' Festival and Melbourne Writers Festival, often feature Indian and Indian Australian writers, providing a platform for cultural exchange and dialogue.

The cultural influence of the Indian diaspora is growing via a new generation of social influencers and content creators. 'We are moving away from medicine, academics and IT (which is a platitude, just like cricket, curry and Commonwealth),' says Rajni Luthra. Instead, young Indian Australians are making waves in culture – and especially in new media – where their art bridges the gap between communities and makes our lived experience in Australia so much richer.

One of these young influencers is Priya Sharma, who has amassed 1.5 million followers and more than fifteen million views for her TikTok channel 'Hi My Name is Priya'. After quitting her job in the mining industry as an explosives engineer, Sharma started to produce short videos documenting her travels, daily adventures and love of Indian food. When she began to make videos full-time, she felt the pressure of *Log Kya Kahenge* ('what will people say') about her unconventional career choice, but Sharma believes it was only when she turned her back on the naysayers that she truly fulfilled her career aspirations. 'If you get caught up with what people will say, you are never going to move forward. I left those voices behind a long time ago,' Sharma says.[3] As a social media star, Sharma is part of a new generation contributing to a diverse media landscape in Australia.

Kirthana Selvaraj was a little surprised to find her self-portrait of a 'queer, brown, femme body' selected as a finalist for the 2021 Archibald portrait prize. 'It feels quite surreal, the Archibald has always been this institution that I felt would be impenetrable for someone like me,' she said. Her work was partly motivated by a frustration with traditional portraiture and conventions of the art world. In her portrait she is wearing a masculine suit that is reminiscent of the clothing that traditional white subjects in the Archibald would commonly wear to reflect their social position. 'I am wearing it subversively. Clothing doesn't have a gender.'[4] Selvaraj joins many other Australian artists with South Asian heritage, including Paean Sarkar and Ramesh Mario Nithiyendran, who explore their diverse identities through their work.

One element of Indian culture that has been thoroughly absorbed in Australia is yoga. Its origins can be traced to northern India over five thousand years ago. The word 'yoga' was first mentioned in the Vedas, ancient sacred texts written in Sanskrit. Yoga has seen a significant rise in popularity in Australia over the past few decades, becoming one of the most adopted elements of Indian culture in the country. Many Australian schools have incorporated yoga into their physical education curriculum, recognising its benefits for children's physical and mental health. Similarly, yoga classes are becoming a common feature of workplace wellness programs. Australians practise a wide range of yoga styles. Traditional forms such as hatha, ashtanga and Iyengar are popular, but Australians have also developed and adapted modern styles such as Vinyasa, power yoga, yin yoga and hot yoga. Yoga is an example of how Indian culture has been gradually absorbed by multiculturalism to a point where it has become common practice across many sections of modern Australia.[5]

Overall, both traditional and contemporary Indian art and customs have enriched Australia's multicultural fabric, with an increasing number of Indian films, musicians and writers gaining recognition and appreciation in the country. This cultural exchange fosters understanding and strengthens the bonds between the two nations.

20

FAITH

At the BAPS Swaminarayan mandirs across Australia, dedicated volunteers gathered during the COVID-19 pandemic to prepare fresh meals and care packages for needy communities in the Gold Coast, Adelaide, Brisbane, Sydney, Melbourne, Perth and other cities. Clad in protective masks and gloves, they worked diligently to chop ingredients, knead dough and stir simmering pots. Rows of stainless-steel tiffin boxes gleamed under the bright lights as they were laden with an assortment of dal, roti, rice, mango and chickpea pickle and vegetable curries. There was an unmistakable warmth in the kitchen, fuelled not only by the heat from the stovetops but also by the kindness and selflessness of the volunteers.

Outside the kitchen, other volunteers were busy assembling care packages containing essential supplies. Production lines of sadhus, volunteers and local politicians worked with precision to pack ration boxes with flour, dal, rice, oil, spices, tea, milk and toiletries. The rations were carefully packed into white boxes and sealed for delivery. Each box was emblazoned with a sticker which read 'In the joy of others lies our own'.

These words are the maxim of His Holiness Pramukh Swami Maharaj, the guru and leader of the Bochasanwasi Akshar Purushottam Swaminarayan Sanstha (BAPS), a major Hindu denomination. During his life, Pramukh Swami Maharaj built more than 1100 BAPS Hindu temples and inspired millions of devotees with his message of kindness and generosity.

BAPS has a significant presence in Australia, with temples in major cities including Sydney, Melbourne, Adelaide, Brisbane and Perth. These temples provide a place for devotees to engage in worship, spiritual education and community service. BAPS is known for its emphasis on traditional Hindu values, such as a vegetarian diet, abstaining from alcohol and drugs, and maintaining high moral standards.

One of the most notable BAPS temples in Australia is the BAPS Shri Swaminarayan Mandir in Melbourne. The temple, which was inaugurated in 2012, is a beautiful example of traditional Hindu architecture, featuring intricately carved stone and woodwork. It serves as a place of worship and a cultural centre for the local community.

The temple complex includes a *garbhagriha* (sanctum sanctorum), where the sacred *murtis* (idols) of Bhagwan Swaminarayan, Aksharbrahma Gunatitanand Swami, Shri Ghanshyam Maharaj and other deities are enshrined. Devotees visit the temple to offer prayers and participate in religious ceremonies. The complex also houses a cultural hall, where various events, educational programs and community gatherings take place.

Hinduism

Hinduism is the largest religion among the Indian diaspora in Australia. According to the 2021 Australian census, there were 684,002 Hindus in Australia, making up 2.7 per cent of the population. Hinduism is the fastest growing religion in Australia, mostly driven by high rates of immigration. Hinduism is also one of the most youthful religions in Australia, with 66 per cent of Hindus being under the age of thirty-four.

Hindus in Australia have built temples and community centres to practise their faith, and they celebrate various religious festivals. Diwali, also known as the Festival of Lights, is one of the festivals celebrated by Hindus (as well as Sikhs and Jains) in Australia. Most major Australian cities host large-scale public events for Diwali. In Sydney, the Opera House was illuminated in vibrant colours to mark the festival in 2022, while Melbourne's Federation Square was transformed into a bustling hub of music, dance and culinary delights.

Local councils get involved in Diwali as well, with many councils hosting community celebrations. Blacktown Council hosts an annual competition which encourages residents to decorate their homes with lights embracing the ancient festival. The contest has gained popularity – as well as mainstream attention – in the last five years. 'It's wonderful to see how the event has grown and the manner in which our residents have taken it on board,' Blacktown councillor Moninder Singh said.[1] Roneel Kumar, one of the winners of the competition, lit up his house with design light motifs featuring the om, lotus flower and oil lamp symbols. 'When we migrated to Australia eleven years ago, I started small with the lights, as my wife would miss the Diwali lights and celebrations we had back home,' Kumar said. 'Now it's amazing to see Diwali celebrations across Blacktown and Parramatta. We have lots of non-Hindus come to appreciate our lights and we have cars queuing with people wanting to take photos of our lights.'[2]

Holi, the festival of colours, has also gained popularity in Australia. This exuberant celebration of spring, love and the victory of good over evil is marked by the joyous throwing of coloured powders and water at one another. In recent years, Holi events have attracted thousands of participants from diverse backgrounds, highlighting the festival's broad appeal and inclusive nature. For example, the Holi celebrations take place across Melbourne, becoming annual events that draw people from all walks of life to partake in the festivities, while the Sydney Holi in the Parramatta's Prince Alfred Park draws thousands of people to enjoy colours, food, music and festivity. In addition to Diwali and Holi, other Hindu festivals such as Navratri, Ganesh Chaturthi and Janmashtami are also celebrated by the Hindu community in Australia.

Hindu beliefs are diverse, and Hinduism can be thought of as a family of religions rather than a single religion. For example, the Hinduism practised by the large Tamil community in Australia contains elements of ancient Dravidian traditions. Lord Murugan, the patron god of the Tamil people, gives its name to several Tamil temples in Sydney, Melbourne, Canberra and Perth. Each temple has its own distinctive festivals and traditions. At Sydney's Murugan temple, the Thiruvizha festival is held in the month of Panguni of the Tamil calendar and attracts thousands of devotees to watch the chariot be pulled through the crowd. Rishi Rishikesan, a young community leader participating in the festival explained: 'Australian Tamils keep up the same culture in Australia as back home, with the festivals and clothing. It keeps our community strong.'

Jainism
Jainism, which shares elements of Hinduism, is a small but growing religious group among Australia's Indian diaspora. Jainism teaches that the path to enlightenment is through nonviolence and reducing harm to living things (including both animals and plants). Jains are strict vegetarians – in fact they avoid eating root vegetables because removing the root would kill the plant. Some Jains even avoid brushing their teeth too vigorously, to prevent harm to microorganisms present in their mouths. Like Hindus, Jains believe in reincarnation and that the cycle of birth, death and rebirth is determined by one's karma.

The Sydney Jain community is currently building a new temple at Girraween. The project began around 2014; it has taken many years to purchase and prepare the site. The process is painstaking because the temple, consistent with the principle of nonviolence, uses no nails or iron. Instead, the structure is built from thousands of pieces of solid marble and held together with fibreglass rods. When complete, the temple will service the growing Jain community around Western Sydney. Ashish Shah, owner of an import business, says the 'Jain community is very religious. Today I have a small idol in my house that I pray to. When the temple is built it means we can pray properly, we can observe the daily rituals in the traditional way, and we can come together as a community.'[3]

The Melbourne Jain community place of worship was founded in 2008, when Nitin Doshi, president of Melbourne Shwetambar Jain

Sangh, built a small temple in his backyard. 'We converted our four-car garage, where we used to play table tennis,' said his daughter Nimita. The makeshift temple is a beautiful space replete with stunning marble carvings and perfumed with aromatic incense. Ten years later, the Melbourne Jain community began construction of a large new temple in Moorabbin. The temple is made of white Makrana marble from India, very similar to the kind used to build many iconic monuments in India, including the Taj Mahal. Nitin Doshi said, 'Seventy families, or maybe even less, contributed to the tune of about $2.5 million ... in about two and a half hours. It was the faith of every family in our God, in our system, in our rituals, in our religion and in our guru that helped them make a decision to contribute an enormous amount of money.'[4]

Islam

Islam is the second-largest religion among the Indian diaspora in Australia. Early Muslim migrants (known as 'Ghans') entered outback Australia as camel drivers in the late 1800s from colonial India. Indian Muslims began migrating in larger numbers in the 1970s and 1980s, primarily from the states of Uttar Pradesh, West Bengal and Bihar. Islam has grown to 813,392 people in Australia by 2021, which is 3.2 per cent of the Australian population – but this number includes people from many nations outside India. Indian Muslims in Australia participate in religious activities at local mosques and celebrate Islamic holidays such as Eid al-Fitr and Eid al-Adha.

Many South Asian Muslims in Australia migrated from Pakistan and Bangladesh. There are many mosques across Australia where South Asian Muslims can perform their prayers and engage with their community. Some mosques may offer sermons (*Khutbah*) in Urdu, the national language of Pakistan, as well as in English to accommodate the diverse linguistic backgrounds of their congregation. These Australians worship by performing the five daily prayers (*Salah*), fasting during the month of Ramadan, giving charity (*Zakat*) and, if financially and physically able, undertaking the pilgrimage to Mecca.

The Ahmadiyya Muslim Community is a minority Islamic sect that originated in India. The Ahmadiyya have faced violent persecution for centuries. Followers are defined by their belief in the Prophet Mirza Ghulam Ahmad. But the religion has been rejected by the greater Islamic community around the world as heresy against the Prophet Mohammed.

Ahmadi Muslims began migrating to Australia in the late 1980s. They have established a strong community presence and are able to freely practise their faith. 'We are aware of how lucky we are to be free here,' said the president of the Ahmadiyya Muslim Youth Australia organisation, Waqas Ahmed.[5]

There are an estimated four thousand Ahmadi Muslims in Australia, most of whom are immigrants from Pakistan, but some are from India, Bangladesh, Ghana and Sierra Leone. There are at least four Ahmadiyya mosques across Australia, including the Baitul Huda Mosque in Marsden Park, Sydney, the Baitul Masroor Mosque in Logan City, Brisbane, the Bait Us Salam Mosque in Melbourne and the Mahmood Mosque in Adelaide. Thousands of members of the Ahmadi Muslim community in Australia attend their annual conference, known as Jalsa Salana.

Sikhism

The first Sikh to arrive in Australia was believed to be an Indian hawker known as Hawker Singh, who arrived in 1890. The significant influx of Sikhs occurred after the Commonwealth of Australia was established in 1901. Many Sikhs arrived in Australia as part of the British Indian Army and were deployed to fight in World War I and World War II. Some of them decided to stay after the wars and settle. Others came to Australia to seek economic opportunity.

Sikhs formed close-knit communities and established their own *gurdwaras* (places of worship) in the major cities of Australia. They also established social and cultural organisations, such as the Khalsa Diwan Society and the Australian Sikh Association. These organisations played a crucial role in preserving Sikh culture and traditions in Australia.

Today, the Sikh community is thriving, diverse and active in all aspects of Australian society. Sikhs are engaged in a wide range of professions, including business, medicine, law, engineering and education. They have made significant economic contributions and established their own businesses and enterprises.

Many Australian Sikhs practise traditional customs which may include the 'Five K's' (five articles of faith): *Kesh* (uncut hair), *Kara* (a steel bracelet), *Kachera* (cotton undergarments), *Kirpan* (a ceremonial sword) and *Kangha* (a wooden comb). Adherence to these articles helps some Sikh Australians to maintain their distinct identity and symbolise their commitment to their faith.

Sikhs worship in gurdwaras found in many cities and towns across Australia, with some of the more prominent ones being the Gurudwara Sahib in Sydney, the Sri Guru Singh Sabha in Craigieburn, Melbourne, and the Guru Nanak Sikh Temple in Woolgoolga, New South Wales. Gurdwaras are the hub of community events, language classes and cultural programs, helping Sikhs maintain their identity and traditions while integrating into Australian society.

The most significant religious festival for Sikhs is Vaisakhi, observed in the second week of April, marking the Sikh New Year and the harvest season.[6] The Sikh community in Melbourne and Sydney often celebrate Vaisakhi with religious processions that involve singing hymns and reciting prayers, accompanied by music. The procession usually starts from a gurdwara and moves through the local streets, allowing the wider community to participate. People often distribute free food and drinks to the public along the route. Participants adorned in colourful traditional Punjabi outfits recite religious slogans and passages from the holy scriptures (Sri Guru Granth Sahib).

During the Vaisakhi celebrations, gurdwaras host various cultural performances, such as Bhangra and Giddha, traditional Punjabi folk dances. These performances showcase the rich cultural heritage of the Sikh community and add a festive atmosphere to the celebrations. They also serve *langar*, a free community meal which is open to all, regardless of faith or background, and symbolises equality, humility and the spirit of selfless service.

The Sikh community in Australia operates a strong youth program, Sikh Youth Australia (SYA). Satwant Singh Calais co-founded SYA in 1999 to foster model Australian citizens and leaders in their chosen professions and the community. Calais arrived in Australia in the 1970s, when the White Australia policy was operating and there were very few South Asians (let alone Sikhs). As a young man, Calais had to establish his identity among the mainstream 'Aussies' at a time when the concept of multiculturalism in Australia was still emerging. Calais is the president of SYA and uses the organisation to empower Sikh youth to understand and enjoy their identity and contribute to the broader Australian community. SYA seeks to provide opportunities for Sikh youth to network and expand their social horizons by meeting other Sikhs. Sikh entrepreneurs, community leaders and mentors volunteer their time to inspire and engage the Sikh youth to realise their potential.

The Sikh community in Australia is involved in promoting interfaith dialogue and understanding. The Australian Sikh Association has organised numerous events and programs to promote greater understanding and cooperation between different faiths and cultures. The Sikh community is active in charitable and humanitarian work. It has established several organisations that provide assistance to those in need, including the homeless, the elderly and the disadvantaged. The Australian Sikh Association has also been involved in disaster relief efforts, providing aid to those affected by natural disasters such as bushfires and floods.

Amar Singh is the president and founder of charity organisation Turbans 4 Australia. In 2023, Singh was awarded the Australian of the Year Local Hero award for supporting the community during floods, bushfires, drought and the pandemic. He founded the charity after experiencing racial discrimination and insults because of his Sikh turban and beard. 'It saddened me that my turban, my spiritual crown, the most sacred object on my body, had become an object of fear. My experiences of discrimination were far from the accepting multicultural Australian society I had known and loved since I arrived here as a fifteen-year-old. I wanted Australians to see Sikhs as people they could trust and turn to in times of need.' Singh responded by showing people they didn't need to be afraid and began helping struggling Australians. 'I thought: what better way to teach others about my community and my faith than through charity work?'[7] Every week, Turbans 4 Australia package and distribute up to 450 food-and-grocery hampers to people experiencing food insecurity in Western Sydney. It has delivered supplies to farmers experiencing drought and food to flood victims in Lismore and bushfire-impacted people on the South Coast.

The Sikh community has established itself as an integral part of Australian society. Today, Sikhs are involved in all aspects of Australian life and are making significant contributions to the social, cultural and economic fabric of the country.

Christianity
Christianity is the third-largest religion in India, with about thirty million Christians making up more than 2 per cent of the population.

St Thomas the Apostle is said to have sailed to the Malabar region in present-day Kerala in 52 CE and introduced Christianity to India.

The St Thomas Christian community was strengthened in the medieval period by waves of Christian migrants from the Middle East. In the fourth century, the Knanaya colonies were established in South Kerala. Christian missionaries Mar Sabor and Mar Proth arrived in the ninth century and built a church at Kollam with the blessing of Kerala's then emperor.

Despite their numerical minority, Christians have played a significant role in India's social and cultural spheres, contributing to such fields as education, healthcare, social services and politics.

The Christian community is also a major cultural force in India, particularly in states such as Goa and Kerala, where their influence is evident in architecture, music, dance and festivals.

This rich blend of religious history, cultural practices and social services underscores the fact that even a relatively small demographic in India can have a profound impact on the history and culture of different regions.

21

HEALTH AND COMMUNITY SERVICES

When his father reached the age of ninety-two, Harish Velji faced a difficult dilemma. After multiple strokes, his father, Harry, had lost mobility and needed constant care. Harish's instinct was to look after his father at home, but his mother, then eighty-seven, was not in a position to look after Harry's needs and required some care herself. The hospital recommended that Harish put his father in a home where he could receive the care he needed. But Harry's needs were deeper than medical care and living assistance. In his last years of life, he valued his ritual of having masala tea a few times a day. He loved his traditional Indian vegetarian meal. And while not being very religious, Harry still needed to celebrate religious and cultural festivals. Although Harry spoke English, some of his visiting friends would not and might need to talk with staff in an Indian language.

Harish's dilemma is typical of the challenges faced by many migrant families, who live with the tension between integration and tradition. It is easy to understand why someone – especially in their later years – might want to live with people who speak the same language, eat the same comfort food and practise the same religion.

Sri Om Care is one of the organisations trying to offer culturally sensitive care options for Australians from diverse backgrounds. Understanding the challenges that migrants often face, such as language barriers, cultural differences and limited social-support networks,

Sri Om Care provides aged-care facilities and services for the South Asian community in Sydney. Established in 2004, it offers a range of services designed to help seniors maintain their independence, stay connected with their cultural roots and engage with others in a supportive environment.

Sri Om Care also offers tailored support services for individuals with disabilities, helping them lead fulfilling lives and participate fully in their communities. These services include personal care, skill development, social and recreational activities, and assistance with daily-living tasks.

Around Australia there are hundreds of organisations emerging to meet the demand for culturally sensitive care options required by growing multicultural communities – across child care, disability care and aged care.

The Tamil Seniors Association organises regular social gatherings and cultural events, such as music and dance performances, storytelling sessions and traditional celebrations.

The Strathfield Community Centre in Homebush is buzzing every Thursday, as members of the association gather to share stories, play bridge and scrabble, discuss current events or do classes in knitting, patchwork and handicrafts. It established a housing cooperative in 1998. This accommodation enables Tamil seniors to live with others from similar backgrounds and retain a sense of familiarity and belonging.

The Pink Sari Project is focused on boosting the number of women in Indian and Sri Lankan communities in New South Wales being screened for breast cancer. Since launching in September 2014, the grassroots movement has been raising awareness about breast cancer and encouraging breast screening for women in these communities. Through community events and social-media campaigns, the project is making a difference to women across the state.

The Toongabbie Legal Centre (TLC) is a community-based legal centre providing free legal advice, referral services and information to those who cannot afford to pay private lawyers or do not know where to go when they encounter a legal problem. The TLC was founded by the solicitor Susai Benjamin, who saw there was a need within the local community for help navigating the legal system. The centre is staffed by nearly forty volunteers and includes a team of solicitors, migration agents, law students and social workers.

Harinder Kaur and her husband, Maninder Singh, founded the Harman Foundation in 2013. Inspired by the devastating loss of their eldest son, Harman Preet Singh, in a car accident, the foundation initially set out to provide grief counselling. But the service quickly expanded to include support for those experiencing domestic and family violence, mental-health challenges and bullying. The foundation has also started a shelter called Her House to support and empower women who seek refuge from violent living conditions. During COVID-19 the foundation distributed thousands of food hampers.

As we mature as a multicultural nation, Australia needs a more capacious and sensitive sense of individual and community health. A landmark study by the Australian Institute of Health and Welfare (AIHW) using 2021 census data shows stark differences in health outcomes across multicultural communities.[1] The study analysed the prevalence of several chronic health conditions, including asthma, cancer, mental health, lung conditions, dementia, heart disease, stroke, diabetes and kidney disease.

The data shows that Australians born in India generally have good health outcomes, with just 20 per cent reporting a chronic condition in the 2021 census. This was lower than Australians born in Iraq (29 per cent), Lebanon (26 per cent), Greece (25 per cent), Italy (23 per cent) and Malaysia (21 per cent). The data showed that people born in Australia, England and New Zealand had the highest prevalence (more than 30 per cent) of at least one long-term health condition, with a higher than average prevalence of arthritis, asthma, cancer, lung conditions and mental health conditions.

Figure 20.1 Percentage of population, by country of birth, with one or more chronic health conditions

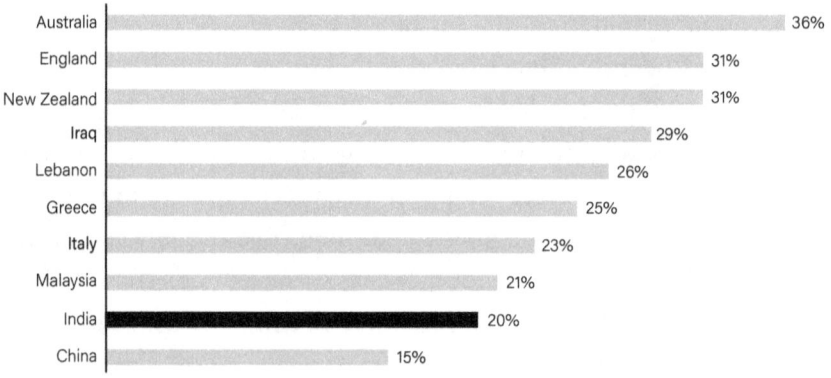

Country	%
Australia	36%
England	31%
New Zealand	31%
Iraq	29%
Lebanon	26%
Greece	25%
Italy	23%
Malaysia	21%
India	20%
China	15%

Note: The data is age-adjusted.
Source: AIHW

The positive health outcomes in the Indian community may be caused by the circumstances in which they come to Australia or their ability to access healthcare when they arrive. 'Many people arrive in Australia through our skilled migration scheme where there's strict eligibility criteria and often people are highly educated,' the AIHW concluded. Strong English proficiency and education among some members of the Indian diaspora may cause fewer language and awareness barriers to accessing Australian healthcare relative to other migrant groups. Also, many Indian communities have relatively healthy lifestyles due to religious beliefs and cultural practices that lead to reduced alcohol and meat consumption.

Health data needs to be interpreted carefully, especially when it relates to culturally and linguistically diverse groups. Some conditions are under-reported in many communities due to cultural contexts. In communities where anxiety and mental issues are considered taboo, they may be under-reported due to social stigma. Language barriers can also cause under-reporting in survey responses.

Despite the overall strong results, there are areas where Indian-born Australians have poor health outcomes. People born in India are more than twice as likely to have diabetes as people born in Australia. The survey results are backed by clinical evidence on diabetes in Western Sydney. Glen Maberly, professor of public health at the University of Sydney, says that tests for diabetes in Blacktown and Mount Druitt emergency departments show that South Asian people have a 60 per cent higher diabetes rate than people born in Australia. 'People of Indian origin face a higher risk of diabetes due to genetic and socio-economic factors,' says Maberly. They have a lower threshold for developing diabetes at an earlier age, which may be related to the way their bodies store fat and their reduced ability to produce insulin. They also encounter stress, discrimination and lifestyle changes when they move to a new country, which can aggravate their diabetes risk and complications.

Maberly has been building relationships with trusted local businesses and community leaders in communities at risk of diabetes. 'Health alone can't fix the diabetes problem, so we are working closely with community leaders who can raise awareness of the disease and promote healthy living options at a grassroots level,' Maberly says.[2] Culturally sensitive public health initiatives can help reduce stigma and discrimination associated with certain health conditions or behaviours.

The Lions Club of Sydney Indians is one of the community organisations enlisted in the fight against diabetes. 'Diabetes is an epidemic in our community and we need as many organisations as possible to collaborate and spread the diabetes awareness message to our people who may be at risk,' club president Padmanabhan Karamil said.[3]

Healthy Living Toongabbie is a group of health-conscious business and community leaders in Western Sydney mobilising residents to fight against diabetes. This not-for-profit group organises events including shopping centre visits and forums to raise awareness of diabetes and promote healthy lifestyles in their community. One of the group's leaders, Dr Sithamparapillai Thava Seelan, was honoured with an OAM for championing holistic healthcare in Western Sydney.

Engaging communities and incorporating their cultural values, beliefs and practices in public-health interventions strengthens the community's sense of ownership and involvement, ultimately improving the effectiveness and sustainability of these interventions. 'Place-based mobilisation is an exciting concept that aims to drive disease prevention by local influencers who have the ears of their community and the passion to help them beat type 2 diabetes,' Maberly says. 'We are encouraged by the depth of commitment from local leaders who take the threat of diabetes, and all the related health issues and complications, so seriously that they have become advocates for awareness and champions of prevention.'

Cultural sensitivity in public health is essential for fostering trust, reducing health disparities and designing effective interventions that meet the unique needs of diverse populations. As understanding of the needs of Australia's Indian diaspora grows, it will lead to improved outcomes and greater equity in healthcare access and delivery.

PART IV

PARTNERS

22

INVESTMENT

Australia's pivot to India is an opportunity to strengthen our nation by adding another chapter to our multicultural story and forging an alliance with the emerging superpower in our region. If we are successful, it will help deliver harmony at home and security in the world.

This opportunity has only recently drifted within reach. Despite many similarities of geography and history, the distance between Australia and India seemed unbridgeable for many decades. This book has argued that our colonial experiences left us with fundamentally incongruent outlooks on the world. Economically, Australia became a trading nation, while India focused on self-reliance. Strategically, India's preference for non-alignment was diametrically opposed to Australia's enthusiasm for alliances. These orthogonal approaches prevented us from creating a relationship of substance in the second half of the twentieth century. They created a lacuna at the core of our relationship that no amount of diplomatic effort could fill.

As the Indian proverb reads, 'Nobody is born friend or born enemy, only circumstances bind you.' Changing circumstances in the 1990s – including the fall of the USSR, India's economic reforms and the changing pattern of Australia's migration – allowed that lacuna to be slowly filled. Over the next two decades, these events allowed Australia and India to drift together. As the Cold War ended, India began to look east. As our regional security environment began to change, Australia began to look west. As India's economy leapt ahead, our bilateral trade grew. As Indian migrants and students arrived in Australia, our people-to-people links flourished. As our interests gradually came into alignment, our relationship came into focus.

By the time Prime Minister Albanese and Prime Minister Modi embraced in front of a packed stadium in Sydney in 2023, the friendship between Australia and India was undeniably warm. Modi is the first Indian prime minister to visit Australia twice. Albanese is the first Australian prime minister to visit India twice in one year. The elevation of the Quadrilateral Security Dialogue has cemented our strategic relationship. The signing of the Australia-India Economic Cooperation and Trade Agreement links our two economies. The annual summits between leaders, foreign and defence ministers are testament to our political relationship.

This diplomatic intensity reflects the substantial role that each country hopes the other will play in its future. But neither nation is entirely clear about exactly what part it is willing to play, or what it expects of the other. Australia hopes that India will help promote regional security and allow us to participate in its extraordinary economic growth. India hopes Australia will substantially and symbolically support its recognition as a first-rank global power. Whether or not we are able to fulfil each other's aspirations depends on how our relationship develops in the future. As with any friendship, its real strength is only tested in challenging times.

Australia should not mistake expressions of friendship for an alliance that implies any formal or exclusive obligation. Nearly two thousand years ago, a Tamil poet wrote, '*Yaadhum Oore, Yaavarum Kelir*', which means, 'To us, all towns are one, all men our kin'. This theme runs through Indian grand strategy, going back to the ancient Sanskrit treatise on statecraft, the *Arthashastra*, which exhorts rulers to work together with all parties rather than singling them out. This refusal to pick a side is the common thread that links Nehru's post-independence stance of non-alignment with Modi's modern dictum of multi-alignment.

India's statecraft, in all its guises, has always sought to keep options open. Yes, India is a part of the Western Quad, but it's also in the Beijing-led Shanghai Cooperation Organisation. It routinely attends trilateral meetings with both China and Russia. It participates in the BRICS forums, comprising Brazil, Russia, India, China and South Africa. Subrahmanyam Jaishankar, India's external affairs minister, makes clear in his book on the subject that the core objective of his foreign policy is to 'give India maximum options in its relations with the outside world'.[1]

Australia's pivot to India should aspire to build a distinctive relationship that goes beyond transactional engagement and circumstantial alignment. It requires us to take a warm friendship produced by favourable circumstances and turn it into a genuine partnership. The essence of that partnership is to deepen the relationship with mutual investment in common endeavours across every sphere of our interactions.

This will require us to significantly lift our investment: Australia currently invests less than $20 billion in India. That is less that we invest in Papua New Guinea, less than a third of what we invest in Singapore and just a twentieth of what we invest in the United States.[2] Correspondingly, India's investment in Australia isn't much better.

When one country invests in another, it gives each a stake in the other's future. When Australian businesses and superannuation funds invest in India, it means that young Australians know their prosperity is tied to India's success. And it means Indian people see Australia as a supporter of their development and a participant in their growth. Mutual investment is the essential binding agent that cements a true partnership.

Right now, the door is open, because India needs massive foreign investment to build the roads, railways, ports, factories and homes that will support its rapid economic growth. India's economy is in a phase of remarkable acceleration. It took India's economy sixty years to reach US$1 trillion by gross domestic product. It then took eight years for Indian GDP to reach US$2 trillion. Then only another six years to pass US$3 trillion. On current projections it will take just four years to reach

US$4 trillion and a further three years to reach US$5 trillion. Around that point, India will have overtaken Japan and Germany to become the world's third-largest economy and the Indian economy will account for one-fifth of the entire world's GDP growth. If economic and demographic trends continue on this trajectory, India might reach the end of the twenty-first century as a global power with unrivalled scale.

India is seeking to attract foreign capital to fuel its rapid economic growth. A suite of investment-friendly policies has enticed hundreds of billions of dollars of investment from companies in the United States, Japan, China and Europe. Apple recently announced plans that could see it produce up to 20 per cent of its iPhone handsets in India. Taiwanese technology giant Foxconn is looking to build a US$20-billion semiconductor plant in India with a domestic partner. The stock of inward and outward direct and portfolio investment has grown from a little over 1 per cent of GDP in 1990 to more than 30 per cent,[3] and Stanford economist and Nobel laureate Michael Spence declared that 'India is the outstanding performer now', noting that the country 'remains the most preferred investment destination'.[4]

But investment from Australia is still slow. Only a few Australian companies – Wesfarmers, Telstra, Macquarie, ANZ, BHP and a small number of others – have made significant direct investments in India. Despite Australia having the fourth-largest pension system in the world, our funds have very modest allocations to India. By dragging our feet on investment, Australia is passing up the opportunity of a lifetime.

Beyond the business sector, Australia should also be making investments in every sphere of our relationship. We should be investing more through our universities in the Indian education sector. We are investing through our defence complex in joint capability sharing with India. We should be investing in regional initiatives and multilateral forums in maritime technology, global health, space, artificial intelligence and many other areas. This is what will switch our interactions from transactional to mutual and elevate our relationship from friendship to partnership.

There is a simple reason for Australia's low level of investment in India today. What retards Australian investment is what retards *all* types of investment: risk. Australian superannuation funds fear that Indian markets are too risky and they won't get the returns they need; Australian businesses fear operational and regulatory risks in their Indian subsidiaries; Australian universities fear that cultural, financial and institutional risks will prevent them attracting the students they would need to create a viable foreign offshoot.

The best way to reduce and manage risk is to increase mutual understanding, build relationships and breed familiarity. Former high commissioner Peter Varghese sees an urgent need 'for both sides really to have a much deeper and much more contemporary understanding of the economic opportunities between the two countries'. Varghese believes that the Australian business community, in particular, needs to have 'a more up-to-date understanding of what's happening in India'.[5]

Deepening Australia's appreciation of India starts with the recognition that it is one of the most diverse countries on earth. It defies reductions and stereotypes. It encompasses a kaleidoscope of languages, traditions and religions. India's first prime minister described his country's rich cultural fusion as 'some ancient palimpsest on which layer upon layer of thought and reverie had been inscribed'.[6]

Australians also understand that our own nation's true genius lies in our synthesis. We often refer to ourselves as the world's most successful multicultural society and celebrate the flourishing of successive waves of migrants over the past seventy-five years. But India has been a multicultural nation since the Aryans arrived in the Indus Valley more than three thousand years ago. Memories have always been long in India, and the Hindu concept of time, attuned as it is to eternity, folds the ancient into the modern. Over the centuries, India has absorbed a succession of regimes and new ways of thinking, changing each time but always keeping its essential character.

Perhaps this long history of diversity is one of the reasons that Indian migrants have so readily settled into modern Australia. The

Indian Australian diaspora now numbers more than one million. India is Australia's biggest source of skilled migrants and our second-biggest source of international students. Members of the Indian diaspora are active across all aspects of Australian life: business, medicine, arts, academia, politics, civil society and sport. This diaspora is young, energetic, ambitious, dynamic and influential.

As Australia's ties with India continue to mature, members of the diaspora will contribute their expertise and energy to the relationship. They have become an essential guide to help us understand and navigate the complexity of India. They have the connections, language skills and relationships to build our national awareness of India's intricate politics and markets. And they can help to influence the perception of Australia within them. As Varghese has said, they 'can go into the nooks and crannies of a relationship where governments cannot. They can shape perceptions in a way governments cannot. And they create personal links, in business, the arts, education, and civil society which can help anchor the relationship.'[7] In doing so, the diaspora is a vital part of Australia's pivot to India.

NOTES

Preface
1. Capability enhancement is defined as the forecast absolute increase in military expenditure above existing levels at estimated defence sector purchasing power parity, constant 2022 prices (2023–30): 'Lowy Institute Asia Power Index', Lowy Institute website, 2023, https://power.lowyinstitute.org/data/future-resources/defence-resources-2030/military-capability-enhancement-2030.
2. Penny Wong, 'Interview with Pawan Luthra, *Indian Link*, 24 May 2023.

1. Little India, Big India
1. The West Bengal house was the home of another navy surgeon, Dr Wilson. See *Watercolour of Homes at Maidapur in West Bengal*, by an unknown artist working in the Murshidabad style, Hyde Collection, British Library, c. 1790–1800. Inscribed on the back, in ink and pencil, are the following words: 'South East or back view of Mr. Oldfield's House at Moidapore and Doctor Wilson's Bungalow near it.'
2. In 1789, James Ruse, a former convict, produced the first successful wheat harvest in New South Wales. John Harris purchased land from Ruse in 1793.
3. Nehru had previously changed the name of the street to Rajpath, a Hindi translation of the street's former colonial name, Kings Way.
4. This observation was made by the Dutch explorer Jan Carstensz while en route through the Torres Strait. However, the descriptor 'Indian' was used widely in those days to refer to a range of very diverse populations outside Europe and didn't necessarily imply any genealogical relationship with South Asians.
5. Thomas Henry Huxley, 'On the Geographical Distribution of the Chief Modifications of Mankind', *Journal of the Ethnological Society of London*, vol. 2, no. 4, 1870.

6   Irina Pugach et al., 'Genome Wide Data Substantiate Holocene Gene Flow from India to Australia', *Proceedings of the National Academy of Sciences*, vol. 110, no. 5, 29 January 2013.
7   M. Rasmussen et al., 'An Aboriginal Australian Genome Reveals Separate Human Dispersals into Asia', *Science*, vol. 334, no. 6052, 22 September 2011, pp. 94–8.
8   Note that other researchers suggest that tools were present in archaeological deposits near Sydney dating back to about eight thousand years ago and in northern Queensland to around fifteen thousand years ago.
9   Anna MacDonald, 'Research Shows Ancient Indian Migration to Australia', *PM*, ABC Radio, 15 January 2013.
10 Governor John Hunter, Letter to the Duke of Portland, 25 September 1798, in F.M. Bladen (ed.), *Historical Records of NSW, Vol. III: Hunter, 1796–1799*, Sydney: Charles Potter, Government Printer, 1895, p. 492.
11 Patrick Suckling, 'Australia and India – Bound Together by Times of War', Australian High Commission in New Delhi, 9 September 2014.
12 Peter Stanley, *Die in Battle, Do Not Despair: The Indians on Gallipoli*, Warwick: Helion & Co., 1915.

2. False Dawns and First Dates

1   Jawaharlal Nehru, 'A Tryst with Destiny', Speech to the Indian Constituent Assembly, 14 August 1947.
2   'First Independence Day Celebration at Canberra', Indian High Commission to Australia, 2011, www.hcicanberra.gov.in/docs/1528097690flag-history.pdf. The Indian tricolour was officially hoisted at India House, the high commissioner's residence by Sir Raghunath Paranjpye at 0730 hrs IST (1200 hrs local time at Canberra) on 15 August 1947, in the presence of the then Australian Minister for External Affairs, Dr Herbert V. Evatt, and over three hundred guests. The national flag of independent India was first unfurled at a midnight ceremony held in New Delhi's Constitution Hall on the night of 14–15 August 1947. But it was not unfurled outdoors until 8.30 the next morning.
3   As early as 1893, Alfred Deakin, who would go on to become prime minister of Australia, declared that 'the future relations of India and Australia possess immeasurable potencies. Their geographical proximity cannot but exercise a very real and reciprocal influence upon the forces of national life in each.' See Senate, 'Australia-India Relations: Trade and Security', Report of the Senate Standing Committee on Foreign Affairs, Defence and Trade, Canberra: Australian Government Publishing Service, 1990.
4   Eric Meadows, 'Australia's Relations with India: Some of the History', Australian Policy and History, 12 November 2017, https://aph.org.

au/2017/11/australias-relations-with-india-some-of-the-history. The then British secretary of state for India and Burma, Leo Amery, asked all dominions to establish such a relationship as part of an effort to foster diplomatic relations between them, but Australia was the first to do so.
5   Herbert Vere Evatt cited in Kevin Rudd, 'From Fitful Engagement to Strategic Partnership', Address to the Indian Council of World Affairs, 12 November 2009.
6   Ian Hall, 'Australia's Fitful Engagements of India', in Ian Hall (ed.), *The Engagement of India: Strategies and Responses*, Washington, D.C.: Georgetown University Press, 2014.
7   Gough Whitlam, 'Speech, New Delhi', *Australian Foreign Affairs Record*, no. 44, June 1973, pp. 393–94.
8   M.J. Cook, Letter to Patrick Shaw, 18 April 1974, NAA: A1838, 169/10/1 PART 2.
9   Senate, 'Australia-India Relations'.
10 Mark Pierce, 'India at 75: Opportunities for Australia', India Australia Institute, University of Melbourne, 17 March 2022, https://aii.unimelb.edu.au/india-at-75-opportunities-for-australia.
11 'Trade and Investment at a Glance 2021', DFAT, Canberra, 2021.
12 'Statistics on Who Invests in Australia', DFAT, Canberra, 2021.
13 See for example: Meg Gurry, Ian Hall, Eric Meadows, Michael Wesley, Surjeet Dogra Dhanji, Aarti Betigeri, Harsh V. Pant, David Lowe, Auriol Weigold, Lisa Singh, Jodi McKay, Rory Medcalf and David Brewster.

3. Listless Leadership

1   Meg Gurry, *India: Australia's Neglected Neighbour? 1947–1996*, Griffith: Centre for the Study of Australia-Asia Relations, 1996.
2   'Annual Political Report for 1951' (National Archives of India, vol. 3, no. 31, R&I/52), cited in David Lowe and Eric Meadows, *Rising Power and Changing People: The Australian High Commission in India Canberra*, Canberra: ANU Press, 2022.
3   Evatt had met Nehru in London in 1938 at Stafford Cripps's home along with British leaders Bevan Attlee and Herbert Morrison. Iven Mackay to H.V. Evatt, Dispatch from Delhi, DFAT Archive, 10/98, 1946.
4   H.V. Evatt to Ben Chifley, 24 October 1948, cited in Pamela Andre (ed.), *Documents on Australian Foreign Policy, 1937–49, Vol. 14, Australia and the Postwar World: The Commonwealth, Asia and the Pacic 1948–49*, Canberra: Department of Foreign Affairs and Trade, 1998, p. 147.
5   N.B. Khare to Iven Mackay, cited in Lowe and Meadows (eds), *Rising Power and Changing People*.
6   H.V. Evatt in 1848, cited in Rudd, 'From Fitful Engagement to Strategic Partnership'.

7   Christopher Waters, 'War, Decolonisation and Postwar Security', in David Goldsworthy (ed.), *Facing North: A Century of Australian Engagement with Asia, Volume 1: 1901 to the 1970s*, Carlton South: Melbourne University Press, 2012, p. 108.
8   Nehru, 'A Tryst With Destiny'.
9   David Fettling, 'When Chifley Met Nehru', *Inside Story*, 18 April 2018.
10 Gregory Pemberton, 'An Imperial Imagination: Explaining the Post-1945 Foreign Policy of Robert Gordon Menzies', in Frank Cain (ed.), *Menzies in War and Peace*, Sydney: Allen & Unwin, 1997, p. 159.
11 Walter Crocker cited in Pemberton, 'An Imperial Imagination'.
12 Meg Gurry, *Australia and India: Mapping the Journey 1944–2014*, Carlton: Melbourne University Publishing, 2015.
13 Gurry, *Australia and India*.
14 Robert Menzies, 'Speech to 18th Parliament – 1st Session', House of Representatives, 19 March 1947.
15 Jawaharlal Nehru's speech is cited in W.R. Crocker, *Nehru: A Contemporary's Estimate*, London: Allen & Unwin, 1966.
16 David Walker, *Stranded Nation: White Australia in an Asian Region*, Crawley: UWA Publishing, 2019.
17 Peter Heydon, Letter, 5 July 1958, cited in Meg Gurry, 'Leadership and Bilateral Relations: Menzies and Nehru, Australia and India, 1949–1964', *Pacific Affairs*, vol. 65, no. 4, 1993, p. 510–26.
18 N. Mansergh (ed.), *Documents and Speeches on Commonwealth Affairs 1952–1962*, London: Oxford University Press, 1963, pp. 389–91.
19 Robert Menzies, 'Statement in Parliament', *Hansard*, 11 April 1961.
20 Sunanda Datta-Ray, 'Where Good Anglo-Indians Go to Die', *The Sydney Morning Herald*, 28 November 1983, p. 9.
21 AAP, 'Nehru's Views on White Australia', *The Advertiser*, 25 February 1949, p. 3.
22 'General Cariappa Deplores White Australia Policy', *The Canberra Times*, 22 June 1954, p. 1.
23 *Calcutta Statesman*, 24 June 1954, p. 4.
24 Iven Mackay to H.V. Evatt, 'Dispatch 52/46', 22 December 1946, in W.J. Hudson and Wendy Way (eds), *Documents on Australian Foreign Policy, Vol. 10: July–December 1946*, Canberra: Department of Foreign Affairs and Trade, 1993, p. 534.
25 Vikas Pathak, 'Nehru Had Oz Worries', *Hindustan Times*, New Delhi, 6 January 2010.
26 Cited in Chris Waters, 'Diplomacy in Easy Chairs: Casey, Pearson, and Australian–Canadian Relations, 1951–7', in Margaret MacMillan and Francine McKenzie (eds), *Parties Long Estranged: Canada and Australia in the Twentieth Century*, Vancouver: University of British Colombia Press, 2003, p. 220.

27 Walter Crocker quoted in Judith Brett, *Robert Menzies' Forgotten People*, Carlton: Melbourne University Press, 2007.
28 Gurry, 'Leadership and Bilateral Relations'.
29 Frank Bongiorno, 'The Price of Nostalgia: Menzies, the "Liberal Tradition" and Australian Foreign Policy', *Australian Journal of Politics and History*, vol. 51, no. 3, 2005, p. 410.
30 Gough Whitlam quoted in Gurry, *Australia and India*.
31 Gough Whitlam, 'International Affairs', Parliamentary Debates, House of Representatives, 24 May 1973, 2643> Cited in Lowe and Meadows, *Rising Power and Changing People*.
32 Lowe and Meadows, *Rising Power and Changing People*.
33 Gough Whitlam, Speech, New Delhi, *Australian Foreign Affairs Record*, vol. 44, June 1973.
34 Address by Australian High Commissioner, Mr Bruce Grant, to the Press Club of India, 20 December 1973, NAA: A1838, 169/10/1 PART 26.
35 Shaw to the Department of Foreign Affairs, 10 June 1973, NAA: A1838, 169/10/11/2/5 PART 3, cited in Lowe and Meadows, *Rising Power and Changing People*.
36 Curtis quoted in Gurry, *Australia and India*, p. 119.
37 Graham Feakes, Letter to Raymond Greet, 18 December 1984, cited in Gurry, *Australia and India* .
38 Malcolm Fraser, 'Prime Minister's Statement for Indian Television', 14 December 1978, NAA: A1838, 169/10/11/2/7 PART 6.
39 Peter Henderson to Gordon Upton, 17 November 1983, cited in Lowe and Meadows, *Rising Power and Changing People*.
40 Bob Hawke, *The Hawke Memoirs*, Melbourne: William Heinemann Australia, 1994, p. 324.
41 Bill Hayden, 'Australian Government's Views on the Indian Ocean', *Australian Foreign Affairs Record*, vol. 55, no. 6, 20 June 1984, pp. 576–84. By the end of 1984, Hayden was urging Bob Hawke to endorse a new India strategy. Relations with India, Hayden wrote, had 'been allowed to drift in recent years ... and Australian foreign policy has develop[ed] without a full appreciation of India's present and potential importance ... [There would be considerable] material economic benefits from a closer relationship.'
42 Gareth Evans, 'Address to the South Asian Association for Regional Cooperation', Monash University, Melbourne, 26 October 1990.
43 Before he became prime minister, Bob Hawke had told a rude joke at Indira Gandhi's expense in a public forum in front of seven hundred people. The anecdote is shared in Barrie Cassidy, 'Politicians and Fruit Cakes: A Tawdry Tale', *The Drum*, 19 October 2012.
44 Rajiv Gandhi, 'Comments at State Dinner at Old Parliament House', October 1986.

45 Hamish McDonald, 'A Testing Time for India – and Australia', *The Sydney Morning Herald*, 3 September 2011.
46 *Australian Financial Review*, 25 October and 1 November 1985, NAA: A1831 169/10/1 Pt. 5.4
47 Graham Feakes, interviewed by Michael Wilson, 18 October – 24 November 1993, Australian Diplomacy Oral History Project, National Library of Australia.
48 Bob Hawke, Statement in House of Representatives, 17 October 1986, *Australian Foreign Affairs Record*, vol. 57, no. 10, 1986, pp. 954–56.
49 Rajiv Gandhi, Speech, in *Rajiv Gandhi: Selected Speeches and Writings*, New Dehli: Publications Division, Ministry of Information and Broadcasting, Government of India, 1986.
50 Department of Foreign Affairs, Cabinet Submission, October 1996.
51 Alexander Downer, Press Release, 12 May 1998.
52 Hamish McDonald, 'Bush Counters China Through New Best Friend', *The Sydney Morning Herald*, 4 March 2006.
53 A number of domestic commentators also criticised Australia's handling of the tests. Professor Ian Copland argued: 'Mr Howard's gratuitous outpourings, on our behalf, of "disgust" and "outrage" … were … actually counter-productive, since we have lost whatever little influence we had there.' Senate Foreign Affairs, Australia's response to nuclear tests in South Asia, Defence and Trade Committee, Canberra, 1999–2002.
54 John Howard, Press Conference, New Delhi, 11 July 2000.
55 'PM's India Visit to Have Trade Focus', *The Sydney Morning Herald*, 2 March 2006.
56 John Howard, Address to Australia India Business Council Lunch, Sydney, 1 September 2006.
57 Gurry, *Australia and India*.
58 Robert Laurie, interviewed by Michael Wilson, 7 August 2007, cited in Gurry, *Australia and India*.
59 Stephen Smith, Address to the Indian Council of World Affairs, New Delhi, September 2008.
60 'Australian PM Kevin Rudd to Visit India', *Hindustan Times*, 7 August 2009.
61 Greg Sheridan, 'Strengthen Team India', *The Australian*, 21 May 2009.
62 Michael Clarke, 'The Fraser Government's "Uranium Decision" and the Foundations of Australian Non-Proliferation Policy: A Reappraisal', *Australian Journal of Politics and History*, vol. 58, no. 2, 4 June 2012, pp. 221–25.
63 Gareth Evans, 'Nothing Gained by Treating India as an Outlaw', *The Age*, 15 December 2011.

64 John Howard had signalled his intention to lift the ban on uranium sales to India in the last months of his government in August 2007, but it was not supported by the Labor party. Gillard managed to change the ALP national platform in 2011 – no small feat given that 65 per cent of Labor voters were opposed to lifting the ban. See Lowy Institute Poll, 2012.

65 While uranium was the centrepiece of Gillard's visit, she also came with an intent to appeal to the Indian people. Reinforcing sporting links, she visited a cricket clinic run by the Magic Bus Organisation, which mentors 250,000 children from impoverished areas. At the event, she announced that the Order of Australia (rarely granted to a foreigner) would be awarded to Indian cricket legend Sachin Tendulkar. The announcement created considerable media attention and public goodwill, with Tendulkar himself expressing gratitude and a hope that his award would cement the bond between India and Australia. Tendulkar was the first foreign cricketer to receive the honour since Brian Lara in 2009. Two West Indian cricketing greats, Clive Lloyd and Garfield Sobers, have also received the award.

66 Frédéric Grare, *India Turns East: International Engagement and US-China Rivalry*, London: Hurst, 2017.

67 During his tenure, Tony Abbott continued the trend of his predecessors by focusing on both economic and strategic cooperation. The signing of the civil nuclear agreement in 2014, building on the work of Julia Gillard, was a significant achievement for the Abbott government, as it removed a major obstacle to closer cooperation between Australia and India in the energy sector. The Abbott government worked to boost bilateral trade and investment, including efforts to further negotiations on the Comprehensive Economic Cooperation Agreement.

68 Phillip Coorey, 'Time to Take India Relationship to a New Level: Malcolm Turnbull', *Australian Financial Review*, 10 April 2017.

69 The report set out ambitious goals, including to lift India into Australia's top three export markets, to make India the third largest destination in Asia for Australian outward investment, and to bring India into the inner circle of Australia's strategic partnerships, with people-to-people ties as close as any in Asia. The report also identified ten sectors where Indian demand and Australian supply can work together, including four 'lead sectors' in education, resources, agribusiness and tourism, as well as six more sectors where there are complementarities between the two economies: infrastructure, health, financial services, sport, science and innovation.

70 The government agreed on an implementation plan for Varghese's recommendations, including a Memorandum of Understanding between Austrade and Invest India to promote bilateral investment flows; the establishment of an Australia-India Food Partnership, opening up new opportunities for our agri-tech and services companies; Australia-India Strategic Research Fund grants to help researchers solve challenges shared by both nations; and the expansion of the Australia-India Mining Partnership at the Indian School of Mines.
71 At this summit, they made progress particularly in the areas of economic cooperation and energy. Modi and Morrison unveiled a new vision statement on maritime cooperation, finalised a logistics support agreement to facilitate future humanitarian and disaster relief efforts and joint exercise, and elevated the relationship to a 'Comprehensive Strategic Partnership'.
72 Sarah McPhee, '"Blood on Your Hands": PM Labels Slater's India Ban Comments "Absurd"', *The Sydney Morning Herald*, 4 May 2021.
73 Amy Gunia, 'After Australia Banned Its Citizens in India From Coming Home, Many Ask: Who Is Really Australian?', *Time*, 19 May 2021.
74 '"Historic" Trade Agreement With India Signed After Decade of Negotiations', ABC, 2 April 2022.
75 Meg Gurry, 'Neither Threat Nor Promise: An Australian View of Australian–Indian Relations Since 1947', *South Asia*, vol. 13, no. 1, 1990, pp. 85–101.

4. Setbacks and Squalls
1 Matthew Wade, 'Big News: The Indian Media and Student Attacks in Australia', *Cosmopolitan Civil Societies Journal*, vol. 7, no. 3, 2015.
2 'Another Indian Student Attacked in Australia', The Times of India, 28 May 2009.
3 Comments by Indian prime minister Manmohan Singh, 9 June 2009, cited in 'PM "Appalled" at Attacks on Indian students in Australia', *Hindustan Times*, 9 June 2009.
4 Kevin Rudd, Interview with Neil Mitchell, Radio 3AW, 10 June 2009.
5 Andrew Trounson, 'Indian Attacks Opportunistic – Study', *The Australian*, 12 August 2011.
6 Peter Spolc and Murray Lee, 'Indian Students in Australia: Victims of Crime, Racism or the Media?', ISANA Conference Proceedings, 2009.
7 Ashok Mali, Christopher Kremmer, Gopalaswami Parthasarathy, John McCarthy, Maxine McKew and Sanjaya Baru, *Beyond the Lost Decade: Report of the Australia India Institute Perceptions Taskforce*, Melbourne: Australia-India Institute, 2012.

8   Vinod Mehta, quoted in Matthew Wade, 'Big News: The Indian Media and Student Attacks in Australia', *Cosmopolitan Civil Societies Journal*, vol. 7, no. 3, 2015.
9   Nalin Mehta, quoted in Wade, 'Big News'.
10 Wade, 'Big News'.
11 Syed Firdaus Ashraf, 'Bollywood Says NO to Australia', Rediff.com, 5 June 2009.
12 Dan Harrison, 'Indian Student Visa Applications Fall by Half', *The Sydney Morning Herald*, 7 January 2010.
13 *Crook: It's Good to Be Bad* is a 2010 Indian film directed by Mohit Suri and produced by Mukesh Bhatt. It was released on 8 October 2010.
14 John Clarke, 'Report of the Inquiry Into the Case of Dr Mohamed Haneef', Attorney-General's Department, Canberra, 2008.
15 'Racism a Factor in My Arrest: Haneef', *The Sydney Morning Herald*, 21 January 2008.
16 Sharda Ugra, 'The Rivalry is Ruined', *India Today*, 21 January 2008.
17 Gurry, *Australia and India*.
18 Rekha Chowdhary, *Jammu and Kashmir: 1990 and Beyond: Competitive Politics in the Shadow of Separatism*, New Dehli: SAGE Publishing India, 2019.
19 Shekhar Gupta, 'Militant Movement Holds Kashmir in a State of Violent Siege, Separatism Gets New Legitimacy', *India Today*, 31 January 1990.
20 On the evening of 21 January, a large group of protesters reached Srinagar's wooden Gawkadal Bridge. Security forces fired on the crowd, leading to the death of at least fifty people. The casualties sparked mass unrest across Kashmir, which was covertly sponsored by Pakistan. During months of increasing tension, India built up a force of two hundred thousand regular and paramilitary troops in Kashmir. Five brigades of its most sophisticated attack unit, the Indian Army Strike Corps, were deployed 50 miles from the Pakistani border. Pakistan, which was by far the weaker side militarily (having lost three wars against India since 1947), stationed its main armoured tank brigades along the Indian border.
21 In May 1990, then US-President George H.W. Bush dispatched an envoy to Pakistan in response to intelligence that the Pakistani military was poised to pre-empt a confrontation with India (that it would likely lose) by using a covert nuclear weapon. Uday Bhaskar, 'The Forgotten India–Pakistan Nuclear Crisis: 25 Years Later', *The Diplomat*, 2015.
22 Gurry, *Australia and India*.
23 The Mirage had been Australia's main strike fighter from 1965 to 1988 before it was replaced by the F/A-18 Hornet. Due to their age, the Mirages were challenging to sell, and the Department of Defence dropped the price from $100 million to $36 million to secure a sale to Pakistan.

24 Ministry of External Affairs, 'Statement on Australia's Decision to Ship Mirage 111 Aircraft to Pakistan', Press Release, New Delhi, 19 October 1990, cited in Gurry, *Australia and India*.
25 Foreign Minister Gareth Evans tried to mollify the Indian government by suggesting that Australia wouldn't go ahead with the sale in the event that they might be used by Pakistan in a conflict with India. He said in August 1990 that 'if hostilities should seem more imminent than they do at the moment [between] Pakistan and India – then Australia would review the terms of the contract'. The situation became farcical when heavy artillery fire was exchanged along the Kashmir border. The Australian government was under pressure to suspend the arms deal, but instead Evans narrowed the definition of what it would take to review the contract. The term 'hostilities', he told parliament, 'was intended to refer to full-scale war between the two countries rather than simply the exchange of fire'. See Gareth Evans, 'Minister for Foreign Affairs and Trade Remarks at a Press Conference in Islamabad', 5 August 1990. See also Parliament of Australia, Senate, *Hansard*, 18 September 1990.
26 *The Sydney Morning Herald*, 15 May 1998, p. 8.
27 Indian Government Statement on Nuclear Tests, 11 May 199.8
28 Pawan Luthra, 'Forging a Future', *Indian Link*, August 2012.
29 Gareth Evans and Bruce Grant, *Australia's Foreign Relations: In the World of the 1990s*, Carlton: Melbourne University Press, 1995.

5. Divergent Economies

1 William Dalrymple, *The Anarchy: The Relentless Rise of the East India Company*, London: Bloomsbury Press, 2019.
2 Raihana Sayeeda Kamal, 'Jagat Seth of Bengal: Banker of the World', *The Business Standard*, 4 February, 2020.
3 The Mahajanapadas were sixteen kingdoms or oligarchic republics that existed in ancient northern India from the sixth to fourth centuries BCE.
4 Vera Anstey, *The Economic Development of India*, London: Longmans, Green & Co., 1929.
5 Nehru writes that one of the English flagships during the Napoleonic wars had been built by an Indian firm in India: Jawaharlal Nehru, *The Discovery of India*, Delhi: Oxford University Press, 1947.
6 Dalrymple, *The Anarchy*.
7 Dalrymple, *The Anarchy*.
8 *Riyaz-us-Salatin*, published in Bengal 1788, is the first British-era historical book on the Muslim rule in Bengal.
9 P.J. Marshall, *East Indian Fortunes: The British in Bengal in the Eighteenth Century*, Oxford: Oxford University Press, 1976.

10 Christopher de Bellaigue, 'The Pillage of India', *The New York Review of Books*, 11 June 2020.
11 Shashi Tharoor, *Inglorious Empire: What the British Did to India*, Brunswick: Scribe Publications, 2017.
12 Anonymous publication of 1767 cited in Dalrymple, *The Anarchy*.
13 Jack Greene, *Evaluating Empire and Confronting Colonialism in Eighteenth-Century Britain*, New York: Cambridge University Press, 2013.
14 The famine in Bengal ultimately affected company revenues, forcing the executives to ask for a massive government bailout in 1772. Edmund Burke wrote an official report the following year.
15 In 1776, Adam Smith published his famous tract 'The Wealth of Nations', which became a framework for modern economics. The book contains an oblique reference to the East India Company and draws the general conclusion that 'the government of an exclusive company of merchants is, perhaps, the worst of all governments for any country whatever'.
16 Peter Lloyd, 'The First 100 Years of Tariffs in Australia: The Colonies', *Australian Economic History Review*, vol. 57, no. 3, 2017, pp. 316–44.
17 Noel Butlin, *Investment in Australian Economic Development, 1861–1900*, Cambridge, Cambridge University Press, 1964.
18 For further information on India's industrial growth during the colonial period, see for example: D.R. Gadgil, *The Industrial Evolution of India in Recent Times, 1860–1939*, 5th edn, Oxford: Oxford University Press, 1971; P.A. Wadia and K.T. Merchant, *Our Economic Problem*, Bombay: Vora, 1957; D.H. Buchanan, *The Development of Capitalistic Enterprise in India*, New York: Macmillan, 1934.
19 Junie Tong, *Finance and Society in 21st Century China: Chinese Culture Versus Western Markets*, Florida: CRC Press, 2011.
20 Radhakamal Mukerjee, *The Economic History of India: 1600–1800*, London: Longmans, Green and Company, 1939.
21 Nehru, *The Discovery of India*.
22 Nehru, *The Discovery of India*.
23 Ha-Joon Chang, *Kicking Away the Ladder: Development Strategy in Historical Perspective*, London: Anthem Press, 2002.
24 Renato Aguilar, 'Latin American Structuralism and Exogenous Factors', *Social Science Information*, vol. 25, no. 1, March 1986, pp. 227–90.
25 Samir Amin, *Unequal Development: An Essay on the Social Formations of Peripheral Capitalism*, New York: Monthly Review Press, 1976.
26 Jawaharlal Nehru, *Glimpses of World History*, New Delhi: Penguin Books, 1934.
27 Jawaharlal Nehru, *Soviet Russia: Some Random Sketches and Impressions*, Allahabad: Law Journal Press, 1928.

28 G. Feldman, 'On The Theory of Growth Rates of National Income', in N. Spulber (ed.), *Foundations of Soviet Strategy for Economic Growth: Selected Soviet Essays, 1924–1930*, Bloomington: Indiana University Press, 1964.
29 Independent India's first major policy document, the Industrial Policy Resolution of 1948, outlined a 'national consensus' on India's economic policies. This national consensus called for a state-led mixed economy and focused on self-reliance.
30 Rahul Mukherji, 'The State, Economic Growth, and Development in India', *India Review*, vol. 8, no. 1, 2009, pp. 81–106.
31 Kasturi Rangan, 'India Demands "Know-How" and 60% Share of Coca-Cola Operation', *The New York Times*, 9 August 1977.
32 Amanda Ciafone, *Counter-Cola: A Multinational History of the Global Corporation*, Oakland: University of California Press, 2019.
33 Sam Dolnick, 'Waning Days of an Indian Soda Pop', *The New York Times*, 23 February 2009.
34 Salman Rushdie cited in 'Postcard', *Saraba*, no. 2, 23 April 2009, p. 32.
35 Note that the government's approach varied by sector. It was particularly hostile to foreign companies in 'low tech' consumer goods industries and substantially more tolerant of foreign companies in 'high tech', advanced industries.
36 Prithwiraj Choudhury and Tarun Khanna, 'Charting Dynamic Trajectories: Multinational Enterprises in India', *Business History Review*, vol. 88, Spring 2014, pp. 1–38.
37 Harpreet Dusanjh and A.S. Sidhu, 'Policy Framework for Multinational Corporations in India: A Historical Perspective', *Indian Journal of Economics and Business*, 2010, pp. 527–9.
38 Nehru and his daughter Indira Gandhi both believed that economic independence was an important complement to political independence. Together they sought to use the public sector to rapidly industrialise the economy. 'The public sector was conceived as the base of Indian industry,' Indira Gandhi said in 1967. 'It also ensured India's freedom. To the extent India depended on imports, its independence was compromised.'
39 Edward Gargan, 'A Revolution Transforms India: Socialism's Out, Free Market In', *The New York Times*, 29 March 1992.
40 Sarah Sargent, 'India, Once Bitten, Twice Shy', *Australian Financial Review*, 18 May 1990.

6. Strategic Misalignment
1 Samir Puri, *The Shadows of Empire: How Imperial History Shapes Our World*, London: Pegasus, 2021.

2   Allan Gyngell, *Fear of Abandonment: Australia in the World Since 1942*, Carlton: La Trobe University Press, 2021.
3   Jawaharlal Nehru, Speech at Asian Relations Conference, 1947.
4   The Asian Relations Conference established India as a leader of the newly independent nations in the post-colonial world and set down the principles of non-alignment that would guide India's contemporary foreign policy stances. India advocated for communist China's recognition at the UN. And it avoided taking sides in the Cold War, refusing to censure the Soviet Union over its interventions in Eastern Europe and Czechoslovakia.
5   Robert Menzies, Extract from Australian House of Representatives, Commonwealth Parliamentary Debates, vol. HR6, 1955.
6   Robert Menzies, *The Measure of the Years*, Melbourne: Cassell, 1970, p. 44.
7   Nehru was openly hostile to the SEATO pact. Its whole approach, he said, was 'wrong and dangerous … and may antagonise a great part of Asia'.
8   If Nehru considered Menzies a 'stooge' of the United States, Menzies saw Nehru as, at best, naive to the communist threat and, at worst, prejudicial to the efforts of democracies to keep communism at bay. India's initial sympathy with China raised Australian fears about being surrounded by militant nationalist Asian states that leant towards socialism.
9   Gurry, *Australia and India*.
10 Nehru agreed to a Chinese proposal in 1952 of converting India's Mission in Lhasa (Tibet) to a Consulate General. This Mission was the outcome of the India-Tibet treaty, commonly known as Simla Agreement of 1914. The Chinese had never accepted this agreement. But as Tibet was an autonomous region, so China didn't have any reason to object to this agreement. See Arun Anand, 'How Nehru's Love for China Sealed Tibet's Fate and Compromised India's Interest', *News18*, 17 December 2022.
11 Paul McGarr, *The Cold War in South Asia: Britain, the United States and the Indian Subcontinent, 1945–1965*, Cambridge: Cambridge University Press, 2013, pp. 330–1.
12 Angadipuram Appadorai (ed.), *Select Documents on India's Foreign Policy and Relations 1947–1972*, vol. 1, New Delhi, Oxford University Press, 1982, p. 62.
13 Rajan Menon, 'India and Russia', in David Malone, C. Raja Mohan and Srinath Raghavan (eds), *The Oxford Handbook of Indian Foreign Policy*, New York: Oxford University Press, 2015, pp. 509–21.
14 Sydney Schanberg, 'Pact Said to Bury India's Nonalignment', *The New York Times*, 14 August 1971.

15 First Assistant Secretary Malcolm Booker, Letter to Minister, n.d., NAA: A1838, 169/10/1/1 part 1, cited in Gurry, *Australia and India*.
16 Senate, 'Australia-India Relations: Trade and Security', Senate Standing Committee on Foreign Affairs, Defence and Trade, 1990, p. 70.
17 Chandrashekhar Dasgupta, *India and the Bangladesh Liberation War*, New Delhi, Juggernaut, 2021.
18 Comments made by High Commissioner Peter Curtis, expressing his hope that Prime Minister Malcolm Fraser would recognise the primacy of India. Curtis was High Commissioner to India from 1976 until 1980. Cited in Gurry, *Australia and India*.
19 Senate, 'Australia-India Relations: Trade and Security', Senate Standing Committee on Foreign Affairs, Defence and Trade, 1990.
20 Jim Walsh, 'Surprise Down Under: The Secret History of Australia's Nuclear Ambitions', *The Nonproliferation Review*, Fall 1997.
21 Praveen Davar, 'Rajiv Gandhi's Outstanding Defence Policy Turned India Into Master of the Region', *National Herald*, 22 May 2020.
22 India's growing regional assertiveness was demonstrated in its intervention in the Maldives. In 1988, a political crisis erupted in the Maldives when a group of Maldivian rebels, backed by foreign mercenaries, attempted a coup d'etat to overthrow the government of President Maumoon Abdul Gayoom. The Maldivian government appealed to India for help, citing concerns for the safety of its citizens and the territorial integrity of the country. India, under the leadership of Prime Minister Rajiv Gandhi, launched a military intervention, codenamed Operation Cactus, to restore the democratically elected government and thwart the coup attempt. The Indian Air Force airlifted a contingent of troops to the Maldives, which swiftly secured the capital city of Malé and other key installations. The intervention was effective and the Maldives government was able to retain power. However, India's actions also drew criticism from some quarters, which had concerns about the potential implications for regional stability and questions about the legality and legitimacy of foreign military intervention in the internal affairs of a sovereign nation.
23 Barbara Crossette, 'Military Moves; India Is All Over, and South Asia Resents It', *The New York Times*, 27 November 1988.
24 Gurry, *Australia and India*.
25 Krishna Menon, Speech at the United Nations, 6 September 1954.
26 Shaw to DFA, 19 February 1973, 30 January 1973, NAA: A1838, 169/10/11/2/5 part 1, cited in Gurry, *Australia and India*.
27 Gareth Evans, Speech to ASEAN PMC, Brunei, 2 August 1995, *Insight*, vol. 4, no. 14, 22 August 1995, cited in Gurry, *Australia and India*.

28 For India's foreign policy establishment, regional stability is a key policy objective because it provides the best conditions for economic growth. India's major challenge remains domestic poverty reduction. The example of the Bharatiya Janata Party's 2004 'India Shining' campaign is still relevant. In the national elections, the ruling BJP campaigned on the emergence of India as a great power, all but oblivious to the daily struggles of the population. The BJP's routing at that election served as a lesson for Indian leaders in prematurely celebrating their country's foreign policy clout.
29 Seema Sirohi, 'Testing Times Ahead for India's New Foreign Minister S. Jaishankar', *IndiaTimes* 12 June 2019.
30 See '"Issue-Based Alignments" May Be the Focus of Jaishankar's Foreign Policies', *Hindustan Times*, New Delhi, 2 June 2019.
31 In November 2022, Indian Foreign Minister S. Jaishankar travelled to Moscow, where he stood alongside his Russian counterpart Sergey Lavrov and called their countries' relationship 'steady and time-tested'.
32 Lauren Frayer, 'A Year Into the Ukraine War, the World's Biggest Democracy Still Won't Condemn Russia', *Morning Edition*, NPR, 20 February 2023.
33 See 'Issue-Based Alignments' , *Hindustan Times*.

7. Pivot: Three C's and Four D's
1 John Button, *Flying the Kite*, Sydney: Random House, 1994, p. 149.
2 Gurry, *Australia and India*.
3 Barry O'Farrell, 'Australia-India Institute Oration', Australia India Institute, New Delhi, 4 April 2022.

8. Cricket
1 Dicky Rutnagur, 'The Australians in India, 2000–01', *ESPN Cricinfo*, 2002.
2 Rajasthan Royals, 'Shane Watson: Why I Love India!', YouTube, 29 April 2011, www.youtube.com/watch?v=SL48D1NpkCc.
3 Robin Chipperfield, 'Alana King Didn't See Cricketers Like Her Growing Up. Now She's an Australian Icon', *SBS News*, 8 July 2022.

9. Cuisine
1 Rajni Luthra, 'Five Indian Restaurants in This Year's Chef Hat Awards', *Indian Link*, 18 February 2022.

10. Commonwealth
1 Jawaharlal Nehru, Speech at the Lahore session of the Indian National Congress, 1940.

11. Commerce

1. Edward Gargan, 'Scandal Taints India's Move to Economic Liberalization', *The New York Times*, 6 July 1993, Section D, p. 1.
2. John Burns, 'India Economic Reforms Yield a Measure of Hope', *The New York Times*, 15 January 1995.
3. Pankaj Mishra, 'Narendra Modi and the New Face of India', *The Guardian*, 16 May 2014.
4. Konrad Putzier, 'Next Wave of Remote Working Is About Outsourcing Jobs Overseas', *The Wall Street Journal*, 11 April 2023.

12. Democracy

1. Kuldip Nayar, *The Judgment: Inside Story of the Emergency in India*, New Delhi: Vikas Publishing House, 1977.
2. Ramachandra Guha, *India After Gandhi*, New Delhi: Pan Macmillan, 2007.
3. *The Sydney Morning Herald*, 27 June 1975, p. 6, cited in Gurry, *Australia and India*.
4. John Howard, House of Representatives, Debates, 9 September 1975.
5. Samuel P. Huntington, *The Political Order in Changing Societies*, New Haven: Yale University Press, 1968.
6. Anne Krueger, 'The Political Economy of the Rent-Sseeking Society', *American Economic Review*, vol. 64, 1974, pp. 291–303.
7. Jagdish Bhagwati, 'Democracy and Development: New Thinking on an Old Question', *Indian Economic Review*, 1995, vol. 30, 1995, pp. 1–18.
8. Samuel P. Huntington, *The Third Wave: Democratization in the Late Twentieth Century*, Norman: University of Oklahoma Press, 1991.
9. G. Myrdal, *Asian Drama: An Inquiry into the Poverty of Nations*, New York: Pantheon Books, 1968.
10. P.B. Mehta, 'India's Governance Challenge', Carnegie Endowment for International Peace, 2011, carnegieendowment.org/2011/03/30/india-s-governance-challenge-pub-43207.
11. R. Rajan and Arvind Subramanian, 'India's Pattern of Development: What Happened, What Follows?', *Journal of Monetary Economics*, vol. 53, 2006, pp. 981–1019.
12. Rajan and Subramanian, 'India's Pattern of Development'.
13. Rob Jenkins, *Democratic Politics and Economic Reform in India*, London: Cambridge University Press, 2000.
14. 'World Development Indicators', World Bank, 2021, https://wdi.worldbank.org.
15. 'India 2022', Amnesty International, 2023, www.amnesty.org/en/location/asia-and-the-pacific/south-asia/india/report-india.
16. Penny Wong, Interview with James Valentine, ABC Radio Sydney, 24 May 2023.

17 John Howard, Address to Australia India Business Council, Sydney, 1 June 2006.
18 Narendra Modi, 'Joint Statement on the Visit of Prime Minister of India to Australia', Prime Minister's Office of India, 18 November 2014.

13. Defence and Security

1   'INS Vikrant: Inside India's Newly Commissioned Aircraft Carrier', *BBC News*, 2 September 2022.
2   Manu Pubby, 'PM Modi Unveils New Navy Ensign, Says "Slavery Traces" Removed', *India Times*, 3 September 2022.
3   Anthony Albanese, Remarks on INS *Vikrant*, 9 March 2023.
4   Ken Aldred, Speech in Parliament, *Commonwealth Parliamentary Debates*, House of Representatives, vol. 159, no. 23, February 1988, pp. 526–7.
5   *The Australian*, 10 February 1989, cited in Gurry, *Australia and India*.
6   Richard Marles, Speech at the National Defence College, New Delhi, 22 June 2022.
7   Cited in Marles, Speech at the National Defence College.
8   Tanvi Madan, 'The Rise, Fall and Rebirth of the "Quad"', *War on the Rocks*, 16 November 2017.
9   Madan, 'The Rise, Fall and Rebirth'.
10 Madan, 'The Rise, Fall and Rebirth'.
11 Kevin Rudd, 'The Convenient Rewriting of the History of the "Quad"', *Nikkei Asia*, 26 March 2019.
12 Phillip Coorey, 'Australia Backs Restoration of "Anti-China" Security Grouping', *Australian Financial Review*, 7 November 2017.
13 Penny Wong, 'Australian Interests in a Regional Balance of Power', National Press Club Address, 17 April 2023.
14 Quad Leaders' Joint Statement, 'The Spirit of the Quad', 12 March 2021.
15 Australian Government, Foreign Policy White Paper, Canberra, 2017.
16 'Press Statements Following India-Australia 2+2 Ministerial Meeting', Ministry of External Affairs, Government of India, 11 September 2021.

14. Diaspora

1   Andrew Taylor, 'Real Estate Noss Janusz Hooker and the Weight of a Famous Name', *The Sydney Morning Herald*, 16 September 2018.
2   Matthew Schulz, 'Life and Times of Richard Pratt', *Herald Sun*, 2 May 2009.
3   Catherine Keenan, 'Smart Alex', *Sunday Life*, 14 September 2009.
4   Vivek Asri, 'When Baljinder Becomes "Bill" and Ankur, "Jayden": Why Do Indians Change Their Names in Australia?', *SBS Hindi*, 24 October 2017.
5   Author interview with Sanjay Deshwal, May 2023.
6   Rajni Luthra, Speech to Indian Consulate, Sydney, 2023.
7   Australian Bureau of Statistics, Australian Census 2021, Canberra.

8   Of all Indian-born Australians, 38 per cent live in Victoria, 31 per cent in New South Wales, 11 per cent in Queensland, 9 per cent in Western Australia, 7 per cent in South Australia, 3 per cent in the Australian Capital Territory and 1 per cent in Tasmania and the Northern Territory.

15. Business

1   Harmohan Singh Walia, 'Challenges, Opportunities & Successes: 75 Inspirational Stories of Indo-Australians', self published, 2022.
2   Gus McCubbing, 'India Is Top Source of Migrants', *Australian Financial Review*, 28 June 2022.
3   Emma Connors, 'Why Australia Needs India More Than Ever', *Australian Financial Review*, 8 March 2023.
4   Rhea Nath, '"About Time": New Taskforce to Re-evaluate Indian Qualifications in Australia', *Indian Link*, 23 March 2022.
5   Juliet Pietsch, 'Diverse Outcomes: Social Citizenship and the Inclusion of Skilled Migrants in Australia', *Social Inclusion*, vol. 5, no. 1, 2017, pp. 32–44.
6   Farz Edraki, '"Doctors and Engineers End Up Driving Taxis": The Uphill Battle Facing Migrants to Australia', *This Working Life*, ABC Radio National, 31 October 2019.
7   Edraki, '"Doctors and Engineers"'.
8   Jason Clare, 'Students and Education Providers to Benefit From New Agreement Struck by India and Australia', Media Release, Department of Education, 3 March 2023.
9   Michael Bleby, 'New Stockland CEO's Plan to House Australia', *Australian Financial Review*, 16 July 2021.
10 Patrick Durkin, '"I Kept All My Rejection Letters": Rise of the Australian-Indian CEOs', *Australian Financial Review*, 22 October 2021.
11 Author interview with Asish Shah.
12 Tim Thomas, Centre for Australia-India Relations Roundtable Discussion, 3 May 2023.
13 Department of Foreign Affairs and Trade, 'Australia's Indian Diaspora: A National Asset – Mapping the Community's Reach into the Australia-India Economic Relationship', Canberra: DFAT, 2022.
14 Fazal Rizvi, Kam Louie and Julia Evans, 'Australia's Diaspora Advantage: Realising the Potential for Building Transnational Business Networks With Asia', Melbourne: Australian Council of Learned Academies, 2016.
15 Jennifer Duke, '"Enormous Talent Pool": Push for More Asian Australians in Leadership Roles', *The Sydney Morning Herald*, 3 July 2020.
16 Matt Wade, 'It Will Soon Be the World's Most Populous Nation, So It's Time We Got to Know India Better', *The Sydney Morning Herald*, 19 April 2023.

17 Jodi McKay, 'From the National Chair', AIBC Press Release, n.d., https://aibc.org.au/from-the-national-chair.

16. Politics

1 Lisa Singh was a senator from 2011 to 2019. Dave Sharma was a member of the House of Representatives from 2019 to 2022. While Senator Lisa Singh is often cited as 'the first person of Indian origin elected to the Australian Parliament' and Dave Sharma MP is noted as 'the first Indian-origin politician to be elected to the House of Representatives', there are several other federal politicians with Ango-Indian links. According to 'country of birth' data collected in the Parliamentary Handbook, there have been four federal parliamentarians born in India: Senator Christabel Chamarette, John Eldridge MP, Chris Hurford MP and Senator Malcolm Roberts. Based on Register of Senators' Qualifications and Register of Members' Qualifications data (collected since 2017), there have been three federal parliamentarians with parents and/or grandparents born in India: Andrew Leigh MP, Zaneta Mascarenhas MP and Tim Wilson MP.
2 Trevor Khan, a Nationals member of the Legislative Council served from 2007 to 2022. Anne Warner previously served in the Queensland Legislative Assembly from 1983 to 1995 and was a government minister under Wayne Goss from 1989 to 1995.
3 Michelle Ananda-Raja was born in London to Tamil parents who had fled from Sri Lanka; Zaneta Mascarenhas has Goan heritage; Cassandra Fernando is the first ever Sri Lankan-born member of the Australian Parliament; Senator Mehreen Faruqi has Pakistani heritage.
4 Zaneta Mascarenhas, First Speech to Parliament, July 2022.
5 Khushaal Vyas, 'NSW Treasurer Daniel Mookhey: We Now Look Like the People We Represent', *Indian Link*, 4 April 2023.
6 S.D. Dhanji, 'Australians of Indian Origin in Politics: Interrogating the "Representation Gap" in Australia', Working Paper, Faculty of Arts, University of Melbourne, September 2020 .
7 Joanne Vella, 'Cumberland Council Elects Suman Saha as Deputy Mayor', *The Daily Telegraph*, 29 September 2022.
8 Author interview with Sanjay Deshwal, 2023.
9 Dhanji, 'Australians of Indian Origin in Politics'.
10 Matthew Knott, '"We've Got the Numbers": Why Politicians Are Wooing Indian Australians', *The Sydney Morning Herald*, 15 April 2022.
11 Tanveer Ahmed, 'How Conservatives Can Win the Ethnic Vote', *Quadrant*, 1 April 2013.
12 Caroline Duckworth, Devesh Kapur and Milan Vaishnav, 'Indo-Australian Voters and the 2022 General Election', Washington, D.C.: Carnegie Endowment for International Peace, 18 May 2022.

13 Knott, 'We've Got the Numbers'.
14 'About UIA', United Indian Association, accessed April 2023, www.uia.org.au/about.html.
15 These issues are specified by the Council of Indian Australians, the Hindu Council and other organisations.

17. Education
1 'Meet Sanjoli Banerjee', ANU, 28 September 2021, https://bellschool.anu.edu.au/news-events/stories/8189/meet-sanjoli-banerjee.
2 Agrima Srivastava, 'Life in a Foreign University', *The Indian Express*, 16 March 2023.
3 Julie Hare, 'India Drives Record Rebound in Foreign Students', *Australian Financial Review*, 5 January 2023.
4 Avneet Arora, 'India Emerges as the Largest Group Applying for Student Visas to Australia', *SBS Online*, 19 January 2023.
5 Arora, 'India Emerges'.
6 'Meet Sanjoli Banerjee', ANU.
7 Australian Bureau of Statistics, 'International Trade: Supplementary Information, Calendar Year, 2019', ABS, 27 August 2020.
8 Deloitte Access Economics, 'The Value of International Education to Australia', Canberra: Australian Government Department of Education and Training, 2018.
9 Deloitte Access Economics, 'The Economic Impact of Improving Schooling Quality', Canberra: Australian Government Department of Education and Training, 2016.
10 Author interview with Ketan Patel, 27 April 2023.
11 'India–Australia Research Centre for Nanoscience and Nanotechnology,' Indian Institute of Technology Delhi, accessed 3 April 2023, https://ird.iitd.ac.in/newinitiatives/IARC.html.
12 Jason Clare, 'Australia–India Visit to Boost Australian Higher Education Sector', Media Release, 28 February 2023.
13 Pawan Luthra, 'Forging a Future', *Indian Link*, August 2012.
14 Australian Human Rights Commission, 'Supporting International Students in Australia', September 2021, https://humanrights.gov.au/our-work/education/supporting-international-students-australia.
15 'CISA National Report 2019', Council of International Students Australia, October 2019, www.cisa.edu.au/wp-content/uploads/2019/10/CISA-National-Report-2019.pdf.
16 Fair Work Ombudsman, 'Exploitation of International Students in Australia', Australian Government.
17 'Indian Student Association of Australia,' ISAA, accessed 4 April 2023, www.isaa.org.au.

18. Media
1. Author interview with Rajni Luthra.
2. Author interview with Aisha Amjad.
3. Author interview with Rajni Luthra.

19. Culture
1. Author interview with Anagan Babu.
2. Vyshnavee Wijekumar, 'The Melbourne Woman Who Helped Indian Cinema Conquer Australia', *The Age*, 1 February 2023.
3. Suhayla Sharif, 'Priya Sharma: The South Asian Aussie Spicing Up Social Media', *Indian Link*, 28 April 2023.
4. Bageshri Savyasachi, 'Kirthana Selvaraj in Her "Green Suit" at the Archibald', *Indian Link*, 1 June 2021.
5. There is also widespread criticism of the West's cultural appropriation of yoga.

20. Religion
1. Rajni Luthra, 'Blacktown's Diwali Lights Contest: Joint Winners', *Indian Link*, 29 October 2022.
2. Blacktown Council, 'Blacktown City Council's Diwali Lights Competition Dazzles Locals', *Council*, 15 December 2022.
3. Author interview with Ashish Shah.
4. Siobhan Hegarty, 'Meet the Jains of Melbourne, Who Are Doing No Harm', *The Spirit of Things*, ABC Radio National, 22 September 2018.
5. Camille Bianchi, 'Ahmadiyya Muslim Minority Find Religious Freedom in Australia', *SBS News*, 27 December 2015.
6. It also commemorates the formation of Khalsa panth of warriors under Guru Gobind Singh, the tenth Sikh Guru, in 1699.
7. Turbans for Australia, accessed 2023, www.t4a.org.au.

21. Health and Community Services
1. 'Chronic Health Conditions Among Culturally and Linguistically Diverse Australians', Australian Institute of Health and Welfare, 2021.
2. Author interview with Glen Maberly, 3 May 2023.
3. 'Indian Community Rallies to Beat Diabetes Together', *The Pulse*, 28 May 2019.

22. Investment
1. S. Jaishankar, *The India Way: Strategies for an Uncertain World*, New Delhi: HarperCollins India, 2020.

2   '5352.0 International Investment Position, Australia: Supplementary Statistics, 2019', Australian Bureau of Statistics, 7 May 2020.
3   Peter Varghese, 'India Economic Strategy: A Report to the Australian Government by Mr Peter N Varghese AO', Canberra: Department of Foreign Affairs and Trade, 2018.
4   Arvind Subramanian and Josh Felman, 'Why India Can't Replace China', *Foreign Affairs*, 9 December 2022.
5   Vivek Asri, 'India Economic Strategy to 2035: Is India Aligned With Australia?', *SBS Hindi*, 7 August 2018.
6   Jawaharlal Nehru, *The Discovery of India*, New Delhi: Penguin Random House, 1946.
7   Varghese, 'India Economic Strategy'.

RECOMMENDED READING

Amin, Samir, *Unequal Development: An Essay on the Social Formations of Peripheral Capitalism*, New York: Monthly Review Press, 1976.

Andre, Pamela (ed.), *Documents on Australian Foreign Policy, 1937–49, Vol. 14, Australia and the Postwar World: The Commonwealth, Asia and the Pacic 1948–49*, Canberra: Department of Foreign Affairs and Trade, 1998.

Anstey, Vera, *The Economic Development of India*, London: Longmans, Green & Co., 1929.

Appadorai, Angadipuram (ed.), *Select Documents on India's Foreign Policy and Relations 1947–1972*, vol. 1, New Delhi, Oxford University Press, 1982.

Bladen, F.M. (ed.), *Historical Records of NSW, Vol. III: Hunter, 1796–1799*, Sydney: Charles Potter, Government Printer, 1895, p. 492.

Buchanan, D.H., *The Development of Capitalistic Enterprise in India*, New York: Macmillan, 1934.

Butlin, Noel, *Investment in Australian Economic Development, 1861–1900*, Cambridge, Cambridge University Press, 1964.

Button, John, *Flying the Kite*, Sydney: Random House, 1994.

Cain, Frank (ed.), *Menzies in War and Peace*, Sydney: Allen & Unwin, 1997.

Chang, HaJoon, *Kicking Away the Ladder: Development Strategy in Historical Perspective*, London: Anthem Press, 2002.

Chowdhary, Rekha, *Jammu and Kashmir: 1990 and Beyond: Competitive Politics in the Shadow of Separatism*, New Dehli: SAGE Publishing India, 2019.

Ciafone, Amanda, *CounterCola: A Multinational History of the Global Corporation*, Oakland: University of California Press, 2019.

Crocker, W.R., *Nehru: A Contemporary's Estimate*, London: Allen & Unwin, 1966.

Dalrymple, William, *The Anarchy: The Relentless Rise of the East India Company*, London: Bloomsbury Press, 2019.

Dasgupta, Chandrashekhar, *India and the Bangladesh Liberation War*, New Delhi, Juggernaut, 2021.

Gadgil, D.R., *The Industrial Evolution of India in Recent Times, 1860–1939*, 5th edn, Oxford: Oxford University Press, 1971.

Goldsworthy, David (ed.), *Facing North: A Century of Australian Engagement with Asia, Volume 1: 1901 to the 1970s*, Carlton South: Melbourne University Press, 2012.

Grare, Frédéric, *India Turns East: International Engagement and US-China Rivalry*, London: Hurst, 2017.

Greene, Jack, *Evaluating Empire and Confronting Colonialism in Eighteenth-Century Britain*, New York: Cambridge University Press, 2013.

Guha, Ramachandra, *India After Gandhi*, New Delhi: Pan Macmillan, 2007.

Gurry, Meg, *Australia and India: Mapping the Journey 1944–2014*, Carlton: Melbourne University Publishing, 2015.

Gurry, Meg, *India: Australia's Neglected Neighbour? 1947–1996*, Griffith: Centre for the Study of Australia–Asia Relations, 1996.

Hall, Ian (ed.), *The Engagement of India: Strategies and Responses*, Washington, D.C.: Georgetown University Press, 2014.

Hawke, Bob, *The Hawke Memoirs*, Melbourne: William Heinemann Australia, 1994.

Hudson, W.J., and Wendy Way (eds), *Documents on Australian Foreign Policy, Vol. 10: July–December 1946*, Canberra: Department of Foreign Affairs and Trade, 1993.

Huntington, Samuel P., *The Third Wave: Democratization in the Late Twentieth Century*, Norman: University of Oklahoma Press, 1991.

Huntington, Samuel P., *The Political Order in Changing Societies*, New Haven: Yale University Press, 1968.

Jaishankar, S., *The India Way: Strategies for an Uncertain World*, New Delhi: HarperCollins India, 2020.

Jenkins, Rob, *Democratic Politics and Economic Reform in India*, London: Cambridge University Press, 2000.
Lowe, David, and Eric Meadows, *Rising Power and Changing People: The Australian High Commission in India Canberra*, Canberra: ANU Press, 2022.
MacMillan, Margaret, and Francine McKenzie (eds), *Parties Long Estranged: Canada and Australia in the Twentieth Century*, Vancouver: University of British Colombia Press, 2003.
Mansergh. N. (ed.), *Documents and Speeches on Commonwealth Affairs 1952–1962*, London: Oxford University Press, 1963.
Marshall, P.J., *East Indian Fortunes: The British in Bengal in the Eighteenth Century*, Oxford: Oxford University Press, 1976.
McGarr, Paul, *The Cold War in South Asia: Britain, the United States and the Indian Subcontinent, 1945–1965*, Cambridge: Cambridge University Press, 2013.
Menon, Rajan, 'India and Russia', in David Malone, C. Raja Mohan and Srinath Raghavan (eds), *The Oxford Handbook of Indian Foreign Policy*, New York: Oxford University Press, 2015.
Menzies, Robert, *The Measure of the Years*, Melbourne: Cassell, 1970.
Mukerjee, Radhakamal, *The Economic History of India: 1600–1800*, London: Longmans, Green and Company, 1939.
Myrdal, G., *Asian Drama: An Inquiry into the Poverty of Nations*, New York: Pantheon Books, 1968.
Nayar, Kuldip, *The Judgment: Inside Story of the Emergency in India*, New Delhi: Vikas Publishing House, 1977.
Nehru, Jawaharlal, *The Discovery of India*, New Delhi: Penguin Random House, 1946.
Nehru, Jawaharlal, *Glimpses of World History*, New Delhi, Penguin Books, 1934.
Nehru, Jawaharlal, *Soviet Russia: Some Random Sketches and Impressions*, Allahabad: Law Journal Press, 1928.
Puri, Samir, *The Shadows of Empire: How Imperial History Shapes Our World*, London: Pegasus, 2021.

Spulber, N. (ed.), *Foundations of Soviet Strategy for Economic Growth: Selected Soviet Essays, 1924–1930*, Bloomington: Indiana University Press, 1964.

Stanley, Peter, *Die in Battle, Do Not Despair: The Indians on Gallipoli*, Warwick: Helion & Co., 1915.

Tharoor, Shashi, *Inglorious Empire: What the British Did to India*, Brunswick: Scribe Publications, 2017.

Tong, Junie, *Finance and Society in 21st Century China: Chinese Culture Versus Western Markets*, Florida: CRC Press, 2011.

Wadia, P.A., and K.T. Merchant, *Our Economic Problem*, Bombay: Vora, 1957.

Walker, David, *Stranded Nation: White Australia in an Asian Region*, Crawley: UWA Publishing, 2019.

INDEX

Abbott, Tony 36, 38
Abe, Shinzo 130–1
Aboriginal Australians 6–8, 80
Adiga, Aravind 176–7
Africa 24, 28, 53, 63, 82, 184 *see also* South Africa
aged care 159, 186, 189–90
Ahmadiyya Muslim Community 184
Ahmadiyya Muslim Youth Australia 184
Ahmed, Kafeel 43
Ahmed, Waqas 184
airline industry 71
aitihasik kshan 5
Aksharbrahma Gunatitanand Swami 180
Al-Khafaji, Mohammad 148
Albanese, Anthony 16–17
  and cricket 106
  and defence 128–9
  and education 149, 164
  and the Quad 132
  visits to India by 39, 106, 149, 198
alcohol 8, 180, 192
Ali Khan, Saif 176
Allen, Darrell 41
ALP (Australian Labor Party) 23, 27, 30, 153–7, 164 *see also* Albanese, Anthony; Whitlam, Gough
Ambassador (car) 48–50, 70
Amjad, Aisha 172
Andrews, Kevin 43
Anglocentricism 24, 33, 83, 105
Anglo–Dutch Wars 55
Anglosphere 33, 151
Antarctica 134
anti-colonialism 4–5, 24, 63–5
ANU 33, 148, 163–4, 167–8

ANZ bank 118, 200
ANZAM 83
ANZUS treaty 83
apartheid 16, 25, 31 *see also* South Africa
APEC 34, 91, 113, 117
Apple 200
archaeology 7
Archibald prize 177–8
architecture 1–2, 4, 50, 52, 180, 182–3, 187
Argentina 63
Arkan, John 154
arms industry 86, 94, 130 *see also* nuclear weapons
Arora, Jyoti 167
Arthashastra 198
ASEAN (Association of Southeast Asian Nations) 34, 91–2, 118, 131
Asia-Pacific Economic Cooperation forum (APEC) 34, 91, 113, 117
Asian and Pacific Council (ASPAC) 84, 91
Asian Relations Conference (1947) 23, 82, 84
'Asian Tiger' economies 50, 79
ASPAC (Asian and Pacific Council) 84, 91
assimilation 140, 169
Atmanirbhar Bharat (self-reliant India) 37, 115, 128
Atta (restaurant) 110
Aurangzeb, Emperor 52
AUSINDEX 133
Australia Day 3
'Australia in the Asian Century' (white paper) 34–5
Australia India Business Council (AIBC) 31, 146, 151
Australia India Institute 147, 151
Australia India Research Students Fellowship 167

Australia India Society of Victoria 159
The Australia Today 170–1
Australia–India Economic Cooperation and Trade Agreement 38–9, 198
Australia–India Education Qualification Recognition Mechanism 149
Australian Greens (political party) 156–7
Australian Indian Film Festival 176
Australian Indian Sports, Educational and Cultural Society 105
Australian Labor Party *see* ALP
Australian Medical Association 38
Australian National University 33, 148, 163–4, 167–8
Australian Punjabi Association 159
Australian Sikh Association 184, 186
autarky 63, 71
automotive industry 48–9, 50, 62, 65, 70, 79
Ayushman Bharat 125

Babu, Anagan 175–6
Bait Us Salam Mosque (Melbourne) 184
Baitul Huda Mosque (Marsden Park, Sydney) 184
Baitul Masroor Mosque (Logan City, Brisbane) 184
Bandung Conference (1955) 24–5
Banerjee, Sanjoli 163–4, 167–8
Banga, Ajay 149
Bangladesh 92 *see also* Bengal
  Australians originating in 108, 154, 183, 184
  independence of 87–8
Bangladesh Liberation War (1971) 87
banking 51, 71, 116, 119
bankruptcy 68, 71, 99, 115
BAPS (Bochasanwasi Akshar Purushottam Swaminarayan Sanstha) 179–80
BAPS Shri Swaminarayan Mandir 180
BAPS Swaminarayan mandirs 179
Basu, Kaushik 116
Beazley, Kim 90
Bengal 1–2, 154 *see also* Bangladesh
  early trade with 8, 55
  emigration from 183
  famine in (1770–71) 56–7
  independence of 87
  wealth of 50–3, 60
Benjamin, Susai 154, 191
Bezos, Jeff 51

Bhagwan Swaminarayan 180
Bharatanatyam 174–5
Bharatiya Janata Party (BJP) 11, 36, 161–2
Bhatia, Vivek 149, 150
Bhowmick Lange, Mitu 176
BHP 200
Biden, Joe 132
Birla Institute of Technology and Science, Pilani 167
Biswas, Sandeep 149
BJP (Bharatiya Janata Party) 11, 36, 161–2
Blacktown 143, 154, 181, 193
Bochasanwasi Akshar Purushottam Swaminarayan Sanstha (BAPS) 179–80
Bollywood 3, 42, 176
Bongiorno, Frank 27
Bose, Netaji Subhas Chandra 4
Brazil 63, 73, 199
BRICS forum 199
British Commonwealth *see* Commonwealth, British
British Empire 4, 8, 53–61, 80–1, 107, 111
bureaucracy 20, 67–8, 70, 71, 75, 122–3
Burke, Edmund 57
Bush, George W. 131
business groups 151–2
business leadership 149–51
Button, John 99, 101

Calais, Satwant Singh 186
call centres 118, 119
Caltex 70
Cambodia 92
Camden Council 154
camel drivers 142, 183
Campa Cola 68–9
Canada 17, 35, 93, 160
Car, Prue 153–4
Cariappa, K.M. 26
CECA (Comprehensive Economic Cooperation Agreement) 34, 37, 38, 118
Central Food Technological Research Institute 69
Centre for Australia–India Relations 150
Centre for Defence and Strategic Studies (Australia) 134
Chandralaya School of Dance 175
charitable works 183, 186–7
charkha (spinning wheel) 64
Charles II, King 55

Charlton, Kim 139
Chauthaiwale, Vijay 162
Chawla, Tarang 173
Chifley, Ben 16, 23–4, 111
child care 190
China
   and APEC 91
   and Australia 17–19, 35, 76–8, 91, 132
   civil war in 84
   cuisine of 107–8
   diaspora of 3, 100, 107, 139, 141–4
   diplomatic recognition of 28, 85, 90–1
   economic development of 61–3, 67, 71–4, 79, 93
   and education 148, 164
   Indian trade with 53, 200
   India's relations with 86, 91, 93, 107, 199
   India's war with (1962) 84–5, 87
   manufacturing industry of 62, 72
   and nuclear weapons 46, 88
   Open Door Policy of (1978) 67
   and Pakistan 46, 85, 91
   population of 10
   and the Quad 131–2, 199
   and Russia 94
   tariffs in 66
   and USSR 84
Christianity 187–8
cinema 3, 42, 176
Citigroup 149
Clare, Jason 149, 167
Clive, Robert 52–3, 54
Coca-Cola 68–70, 114
Coffs Harbour 53, 154
Cold War
   end of 33, 92, 94, 99–100, 197
   and Non-Aligned Movement 25, 81–2, 84
Coles supermarkets 118
Colombo Plan 112
colonialism/colonisation 26–7 *see also* British Empire; East India Company; post-colonialism
   of Australia 80
   and cuisine 108
   of India 50, 53–61, 80–1
   symbols of 4–6
   and trade 63, 76
Command and Staff College (Australia) 134

Commonwealth, British 24–6, 80, 101 *see also* 'three C's'
   creation of 111
   criticism of 112–13
   and defence 83, 112
Commonwealth Heads of Government Meeting (CHOGM) 113
Commonwealth Scholarship and Fellowship Plan (CSFP) 112
Commonwealth Strategic Reserve 83
communism 25, 71, 83, 90
community services 180, 191
company directors 150–1
Comprehensive Economic Cooperation Agreement (CECA) 34, 37, 38, 118
Conservative Party (UK) 157
consumerism 49, 114, 116–17
corruption 71, 73, 75, 122
Cosgrove, Peter 134
Council of Indian Australians 160
Council of International Students Australia 168
Countering Violent Extremism (CVE) Unit 112
COVID-19 pandemic 38, 44, 119–20, 164, 172, 179, 186, 191
cricket 27, 33, 38, 44, 101, 102–6 *see also* 'three C's'
Cripps, Stafford 23
Crocker, Walter 24, 27
cuisine 101, 107–10, 177, 179, 181 *see also* food; 'three C's'
cultural diversity 10, 110, 140, 143–4, 165, 173, 175, 201 *see also* multiculturalism
   lack of 151
   in politics 153–5
Cumberland Council 154
currency of India (rupee) 70
curry *see* cuisine; 'three C's'
Curtis, Peter 29
cybersecurity 37, 113, 134

dance 3, 174–5, 181, 185, 187, 190
Dandenong 143
Darling Ranges (in WA) 6
Dasgupta, Rana 117
Datta, Raj 154
Datta-Ray, Sunanda 25
Davis, Garth 176
Dayal, Sanjay 149
Deakin University 167

decolonisation 23–4, 28, 82 *see also* post-colonialism
defence and national security 10, 31–2, 34, 37–8, 45, 118, 128 *see also* arms industry; 'Four D's'; military strength and expenditure; nuclear weapons; Quadrilateral Security Dialogue (the Quad)
    and China 84, 131–2
    cooperation between India and Australia for 129, 132–4
    and Indian self-sufficiency 128–30
    and Pakistan 85–6
    and treaties 83–4, 86, 90, 131
    during WWII 8, 23
Defence Services Staff College (India) 134
deindustrialisation of India 58–61
Delhi Streets (restaurant) 110
Delhi Sultanate 52
democracy *see also* 'Four D's'
    in Australia 80, 155
    and economic development 11, 65, 76, 79, 122–4
    in India 81, 125–7
    revocation of (1975) 121–2
    threats to 121–2
    traditions and values of 8, 10, 79, 101, 126
Deng Xiaoping 67, 71
deregulation 99, 115–16
Desai, Santosh 69
Deshwal, Sanjay 140, 154
Dhanji, Surjeet Dogra 155
diabetes 193–4
diaspora, Chinese *see* China: diaspora of
diaspora, Indian ix–x, 101 *see also* 'Four D's'; migration
    and cricket 104–5
    cultural influence of 177, 202
    diversity of 143, 201–2
    education of 145, 192
    history of 142, 183–4
    location of 143, 160
    and Narendra Modi 37, 161–2
    occupations of 145–6, 150
    and politics 160–2
    power and potential of 6, 9–10, 149, 160–1, 202
    and remittances 161
    size of x, 2–3, 10, 36, 141–3, 151, 160, 202

dingo (Australian wild dog) 7
diplomacy ix, 8–9, 15–17, 29, 32, 34, 46, 91–3, 117 *see also* Quadrilateral Security Dialogue (the Quad)
disability services 190
disaster relief 134, 186, 187
Diwali 3, 180–1
DK Alayam School of Music and Dance 175
domestic violence 191
Dommaraju, Usha 154
Dosa Hut (restaurant) 109
Doshi, Nimita 183
Doshi, Nitin 182–3
dosti (friendship) 10, 101 *see also* 'Four D's'
Double Seven (soft drink) 69
Downer, Alexander 31, 46
Dragon House (restaurant) 108
Dravid, Rahul 102, 103
Dravidian traditions 181–2

East Asia Summit 34, 113, 118
East Asian hemisphere 92
East India Company 54–8
economy of Australia 10, 59–60, 75–9
    benefits of Indian diaspora to 146, 151, 166, 198
    and China 132
    history of 8, 21, 50, 63, 197
    and outsourcing 118
economy of China 71–2, 132
economy of India 58 *see also* manufacturing industry; tariffs; trade
    in the 1700s–1800s 53–5
    centralisation of 65, 73
    in the future 199–200
    growth of x, 5, 32–4, 72–4, 124, 151, 199–200
    at Independence (1947) 61, 70, 73
    and investment 74
    as inward-looking 9, 21, 37, 48–50, 61–8, 71–3
    liberalisation of 49, 114–15, 123–4
    in medieval times 50–2
    in Mughal period 52–3
    plundering of 50, 53–60
    reform of in 1990s ix, 9, 33, 49, 70, 99, 114–18, 123–4
    and self-reliance 61–8, 71
    size of 5, 200
education *see also* students

of Australians in India 112, 117, 134,
    163–8
  cost of 164
  of Indians in Australia 36, 112, 134, 142
  investment in 200, 201
  partnerships for 112, 149, 166–7
  quality of 167
  recognition of qualifications 147–9,
    167, 192
  standards of in India 61, 100, 145–7
Eid al-Adha 183
Eid al-Fitr 183
emergency, state of (India, 1975–77) 121–2
England *see also* Commonwealth, British
  manufacturing in 60
  Navy of 53
  population of 53
  trade with 54–9
  wealth of 51, 59
entrepreneurship 66, 72, 116, 124, 146, 150,
    157, 186
Eurocentricism 24, 27, 140
Europe 24–5, 32, 52–4, 93, 200
Evans, Gareth 31, 47, 92
Evatt, Herbert Vere 'Doc' 16, 23
Experiment Farm 2
exports
  from Australia 9, 21, 50, 63, 76, 79, 117,
    150 (*See also* education: of Indians
    in Australia)
  from Britain 56, 58–9
  from China 62, 72
  from East Asia 9, 50, 61–2, 79
  from India 50, 60–1, 65–6, 72–4, 115, 130

Fabian Society 64
famine, in Bengal (1770–71) 56–7
Feakes, Graham 29, 30, 45
federation of Australia (1901) 80, 184
Federation of Ethnic Communities' Councils
    of Australia 148
Federation of Indian Associations of NSW 157
Federation of Indian Associations of Victoria
    159
Federation of Indian Communities of
    Queensland 159
Fenwick, Captain 51
Ferguson, Laurie 155–6
Fernandes, George 69
Fiji 108, 144, 154, 160

First Fleet 8, 80
First War of Independence 57
Fischer, Tim 31, 46
'Five K's' (Sikh customs) 185
Five Power Defence Arrangements 84
five-year plans (for India's economic
    development) 65
flag of India 15, 64, 128
food 181, 185 *see also* cuisine; 'three C's'
  lack of 8, 187, 191
  trade in 76
foreign currency exchange 70, 74, 115–16
foreign direct investment (FDI) 115
Fortune 500 companies 149
fossil fuels 71, 89, 94, 115
'Four D's' 10, 101
Foxconn 200
France 27, 55, 65, 90, 130
Fraser, Malcolm 29, 35, 91
free-trade agreements 34, 37–9, 92, 133, 198
freedom of the press 125–6
Fukuda, Yasuo 131

G20 11, 37, 113
Gallipoli 8
Gandhi, Indira
  and state of emergency (1975) 121
  and diaspora 161
  and foreign investment 68
  and foreign policy 30, 85–7
  and nationalisation 71
  and privatisation of banks 71
Gandhi, Mahatma 64, 82, 114
Gandhi, Rajiv 30–1, 36, 115
  and diaspora 161
  and military defence 89
Gandhi, Sanjeev 149
Gandhi, Sonia 152
Ganesh Chaturthi 181
Gaur, Aman 105
GDP (gross domestic product) 32, 58, 67,
    72–4, 116, 124, 199–200
genetic links between Indians and Australians 6
geology 6
geopolitics 9, 21, 81–2, 87, 93–5, 134 *see also*
    Cold War; colonialism/colonisation
George V, King 4
George VI, King 112
Germany 5, 74, 117, 200
Ghana 63, 184

'Ghans' 183
ghulami ki mansikta 5
Gilchrist, Adam 104
Gillard, Julia 34–5
Gini index (of income inequality) 73
Girraween 182
Glenroy 143
'Golden Bird' (medieval India) 50–3
Gond people 7
Gondwana region of India 7
Gondwanaland 6–7
Gonsalves, Roanna 176
Google 149
Grant, Bruce 28
gross fixed capital formation 74
Gujarati Association of NSW 159
Gully Ravine 8
Gupta, Tarun 149
gurdwaras (Sikh places of worship) 184, 185
Gurkha Bluff 8
Gurry, Meg 27, 32, 45
Guru Nanak Sikh Temple (Woolgoolga, NSW) 185
Gurudwara Sahib (Sydney) 185
Gyngell, Allan 22

Hall, Ian 16
Haneef, Mohamed 43–4
Hansen, John 44
Harman Foundation 191
Harris, John 1–2, 6
Harris Park (in Western Sydney) 2–3, 166, 171
Hasluck, Paul ix, 16
Hawke, Bob 30–1, 46, 91
Hayden, Bill 30
Hayden, Matthew 102
healthcare 125, 157–8, 166, 187, 190–4
Healthy Living Toongabbie 193
Henderson, Peter 29
Heydon, Peter 25
'Hindi Chini Bhai Bhai' (India and China are brothers) 84–5
Hindi Samaj 159
Hindu Council of Australia 159
'Hindu rate of growth' 72
Hinduism 4, 45, 126, 128, 156, 157, 160, 179–82, 201
Hindustan Motors 49
Holi 181
Holt, Harold 86
homelessness 186
Hong Kong 61, 63
Hooker, L.J. 139
Hornsby Shire Council 154
House of Jagat Seth 50–2
housing 157, 167, 190
Howard, John 31–3, 46, 122, 126–7
human rights 28, 112–13, 126, 163, 168 *see also* apartheid; race and racial attitudes
humanitarian efforts 134, 186
Huntington, Samuel P. 123
Hutchison Telecommunications 118
Huxley, Thomas Henry 6

IABCA (India Australia Business and Community Alliance) 152
IBM 70
Imam, Bulu 7
imperialism 4, 24, 48, 54–9, 69, 81–2, 90, 111 *see also* British Empire
import substitution 62–3, 66, 75, 79 *see also* exports
income levels
  in Australia 146–7
  in India 61, 72–4, 116, 123–4, 142
  of international diaspora 161
independence of Australia 80
independence of India 15–16, 23–7
  centenary of 6
  and the economy 57, 61–8
  and foreign policy 81–2, 111, 198
  struggle for 80–1
  symbols of 4, 15
India Australia Business and Community Alliance (IABCA) 152
'An India Economic Strategy to 2035: Navigating from Potential to Delivery' (report, 2018) 37
India Festivals 161
India Gate (in New Delhi) 3–4, 6
India–CLMV (Cambodia, Laos, Myanmar and Vietnam) Business Conclave 92
India–Myanmar–Thailand Trilateral Highway 92
Indian Film Festival of Melbourne 176
Indian Independence Day (15 August) 64
Indian Institute of Technology Delhi 166
Indian Link (newspaper and media group) 156, 169–70
Indian National Congress 111

Indian Ocean Rim Association (IORA) 113, 118
Indian Premier League (IPL) 38, 101, 104–5
Indian Republic Day (26 January) 3
Indian Society of Western Australia 159
Indian Students' Association of Australia 168
'Indians in Sydney' (Facebook group) 171
Indians' opinions of Australia 84, 99
Indigenous Australians 6–8, 80
Indo–China War 87
Indonesia 24, 35, 91
Indo–Pakistani War 85, 87
Indo–Soviet Treaty of Peace, Friendship and Cooperation 86
Indukuri, Praveen 109
Indus Age 170
Industrial Policy Statement (1948) 70
industrialisation 61–4
inequality 64, 73, 116, 123
information technology industry 116, 119, 145
innovation 49, 51, 71, 75, 124, 148, 175
INS *Vikrant* (aircraft carrier) 128–9
insurance industry 71
International Monetary Fund (IMF) 124
investment
    in Australia 20, 78
    and economic growth 73–4, 197–202
    in India 20, 114–15, 150, 199–202
inward-looking economy *see under* economy of India
IPL (Indian Premier League) 38, 101, 104–5
Ish (restaurant) 110
Islam 45, 142, 183–4

Jackson, Catriona 164
Jagat Seth family 50–2
Jahangir, Emperor 54–5
Jainism 180, 182–3
Jaishankar, Subrahmanyam 93, 94, 162, 199
Jakubowicz, Andrew 155
Jalsa Salana 184
Janata Party 69
Janmashtami 181
Japan
    and ASPAC 91
    Australia's trade with 19, 28, 76–7
    and defence 38, 91, 93, 130–3
    economy of 5, 61–3, 72–3, 200
    Indian trade with 53, 79, 92, 117
    investment by 200
    investment in 64, 74

Kaladan Multi-Modal Transit Transport Project 92
Kaliyanda, Charishma 153, 173
Kano, Taro 132
Karamil, Padmanabhan 193
karma 182
Karpurapu, Anil Kumar 109
Kashmir 45, 85, 87
Kaur, Harinder 191
Kerala 187
Khalsa Diwan Society 184
Khan, Intaj 154
Khawaja, Usman 105
Khorshid, Omar 38
Khutbah 183
King, Alana 105
King, Philip Gidley 59
Kishida, Fumio 132
Kohli, Virat 103
Korea *see* South Korea
Korean War 83, 84
Krishna, S.M. 34
Kumar, Roneel 181
Kumar, Shravan 40
Kuring-gai Council 154

Labour Party (UK) 157
Lakshmi, Padma 108
Lalithakalalaya School 175
langar 185–6
languages
    barriers caused by 189, 192
    diversity of 144, 177, 183, 201
    proficiency in English 142, 155, 202
    teaching of 35, 175, 185
Laos 92
Laurie, Robert 33
Laxman, V.V.S. 102, 103
Lee, Brett 104
legal assistance 190–1
Let's Chaat Food (restaurant) 110
Li, Francis 108
Liberal Party of Australia 155–7
Liberal–National Coalition 156–7
'Licence Raj' 115
life expectancy 61
Life Insurance Corporation of India 71
Lions Club of Sydney Indians 193
literacy 61, 65 *see also* education
literature 176–7

'Little India' (in Western Sydney) 1–3, 6, 107
Little India Australia 152
Little India Harris Park Business
 Association 152
local government representation 153–4
Log Kya Kahenge ('what will people say') 177
London Declaration (1949) 111–12
'Look East' policy 92
Lord Murugan 181–2
Lowy Institute 17–19
Luthra, Pawan 156, 157, 169–71, 173
Luthra, Rajni 140, 172–3, 177
Lutyens, Edwin 4, 6

Maberly, Glen 193–4
Mackay, Iven 26
Macquarie Group 118, 200
Madhok, Neha 173
Mahajanapadas 52
Maharaj, His Holiness Pramukh Swami 179
Maheswaran, Sharangan 154
Mahindra & Mahindra 49
Mahmood Mosque (Adelaide) 184
Make In India 125
Malabar military exercise 38, 129, 131, 133
Malaya 8, 83, 84
Malaysia 72, 79, 84, 144, 160, 191
Maldives 89
Mani, Shekar 109
Manjit's Wharf (restaurant) 110
manufacturing industry 21, 200
 in Australia 118, 150
 in Britain 59–60
 in East Asia 50, 79
 in India 37, 48–9, 52–3, 60–70, 116
Marar, Ara Sharma 38
Maratha Empire 129
Marathi Association 159
Marles, Richard 129
Maruti Suzuki 49
Marxism 63–4
Mary, Queen 52
Mascarenhas, Zaneta 153
Mastercard 149
McCain, John 131
McCarthy, John 41, 43
McGrath, Glenn 102, 103
McInnes, Neil 26
McKay, Jodi 151
Medcalf, Rory 130

media 125, 169–71
Mehta, Nalin 41
Mehta, Vinod 41
Melbourne Shwetambar Jain Sangh 182–3
Melbourne Writers Festival 177
members of parliament 153–5, 164
mental health 192
Menzies, Robert 24–7, 83, 86
mercantilism 58–60
Mexico 63
Microsoft 149
middle class 32, 42, 88, 99–100, 116, 142, 167
migration *see also* diaspora; White Australia
 policy
 to Australia from China 107, 139, 142
 to Australia from India 100, 139–44,
  183–4
 from China to India 107
 policy 26, 100, 142
 from Punjab 108–9, 185
military exercises 38, 129, 131, 133
military strength and expenditure x, 5, 85,
 88–90, 94, 128–30 *see also* defence and
 national security; nuclear weapons
Mind Blowing Films 176
Mirza Ghulam Ahmad (prophet) 184
missionaries 187
mixed economy 65, 75
Modern Food Industries 69
Modi, Narendra
 ambitions for India of 5–6
 and APEC 91
 and CHOGM 113
 and cricket 104, 106
 on defence 128
 on democracy 127
 and the diaspora 161–2, 163
 and the economy 125
 election of 36
 and foreign policy 93
 and Malcolm Turnbull 37
 popularity of 126, 161–2
 and the Quad 132
 and religion 126
 and Scott Morrison 37–8
 vision for Delhi of 4–5
 visit to Australia of 3, 16–17, 36, 39, 198
Mohammed, Prophet 184
Momozz restaurant 107
Mookhey, Daniel 154

Moorabbin 183
Morrison, Scott 37–9, 156, 164
mosques 184
Mount Druitt 193
Mughal Empire 52–3, 55, 60, 129
multiculturalism 3, 10, 127, 140–1, 178, 186, 191, 201 *see also* cultural diversity
Murshidabad 53
Murugan temple 182
music 174–6, 185, 190
Musk, Elon 51
Mutual Defence Agreement 86
Myanmar 92
Myrdal, Gunnar 123

Nadella, Satya 149
names, anglicising of 139–40
Nandkeolyar, Sheba 146
National Defence College (India) 134
national security *see* defence and national security
nationalisation of industries 71
NATO (North Atlantic Treaty Organization) 131
Navratri 181
Nehru, Jawaharlal 73, 121
    and Australia 23–7, 29
    and bureaucracy 75
    and the Commonwealth 111
    and the diaspora 161
    and the economy 61–6, 70–1
    and foreign policy 82
    on Indian diversity 201
    and Indian independence 15
    life and principles of 64–5
    and non-alignment 81–2
Nelson, Brendan 131–2
Nepal 89, 92, 144
New Delhi, creation of 3–5
New Imperialism 58
New Industrial Policy (1991) 115
New Zealand 3, 19, 83, 90
Newcrest 149
newspapers 169–71
Nigeria 63
Nilgiri Mountains (in South India) 6
Nithiyendran, Ramesh Mario 178
Non-Aligned Movement (NAM) 9, 25, 81–4, 94
nonviolence 82, 182

Nooyi, Indra 149
North Vietnam 84
Nuclear Non-Proliferation Treaty 35
nuclear weapons 5, 31–2, 34–5, 44–6, 88, 170

Observer Research Foundation 94
occupations and professions 145–6, 185, 202
One Nation (political party) 156–7
Optus 118
Orica 149
outsourcing of jobs 118–20
outward-looking model of economic growth 61–2
overqualification 147–9
Overseas Friends of BJP (OFBJP) 162

'pagoda tree' 56
painting 177–8
Pakistan
    and Australia 26, 31, 45–6, 86–7
    and China 85, 91
    and conflict with India 45, 85–8, 93
    and defence 45–6, 84, 89–90
    emigration from 183–4
    and nuclear weapons 46
    and partition 149
    and USA 84–7
Pandey, Sameer 154
Pandit, Vikram 149
Papua New Guinea 28, 199
Parker, Andrew 151
Parliamentary Friends of India ix, x
Parramatta 1–2, 109–10, 143, 154, 181
Parthasarathy, Gopalaswami 46, 167, 170
partition of India 85, 149
Patel, Ketan 166
Peacock throne 54
Pepsi 70, 149
Peres da Costa, Suneeta 176–7
'Permit Raj' 117
Perry, Alex 139
Pertsinidis, Alexandros 139
Peru 91
Philippines 84, 90
Pichai, Sundar 149
Pierce, Mark 16
Pietsch, Juliet 148
Pillamarri, Sreeni 154
Pink Sari Project 190
political dissidence 125–6

political representation 153–5
Ponting, Ricky 103
population
　of China 10
　of England 53
　of India x, 5, 53, 125
populism 122
portraiture 177–8
post-colonialism 80, 128, 197 *see also* decolonisation
poverty 61, 65, 79, 116, 125, 127
Pratt, Richard 139
Pravasi Bharatiya Divas (Overseas Indian Day) 161
Prebisch, Raúl 62
privatisation 71
protectionism 49, 50, 76, 79, 122
　see also tariffs
Proth, Mar 187
Przecicki family 139
public sector 71, 75, 115 *see also* bureaucracy
Punjabi culture 185
PwC 151

Qatar 160
Quadrilateral Security Dialogue (the Quad) 93, 113, 130–3, 198
qualifications, recognition of 147–9

Raby, Geoff 132
race and racial attitudes 25–7, 40–4, 140, 168, 186–7 *see also* violence against Indian students; White Australia policy
Racial Discrimination Act (in Australia) 28
Radhe supermarkets 166
Rajagopalan, Rajeswari Pillai 94
Rajasthan Royals 104
'Rajiv Doctrine' 89
Ramadan 183
Rao, P.V. Narasimha 115, 124
Rasika Dance Academy 175
Ray, Robert 45
red tape 67–8, 70, 75, 117 *see also* bureaucracy
Redd, Alan 7
Reddy, Sandy 154
religion 44, 45, 126, 157–8, 179–88
remittances 161
representative organisations 158–60
Rishikesan, Rishi 182
Riverside Theatre (Parramatta) 174

Riyaz-us-Salatin 55
RMIT University 167
Rudd, Kevin 33–4, 41, 132
rum 8
rupee 70
Ruse, James 2, 3
Rushdie, Salman 69
Russia 91, 93–4, 199 *see also* USSR

Sabor, Mar 187
Saha, Suman 154
Salaam Namaste (film) 176
Salah 183
Sangha, Jason 105
sanitation 125
Santal hounds 7
Saravanaa Bhavan (restaurant) 109–10
Sari Bair 8
Sarkar, Paean 178
SEATO (Southeast Asia Treaty Organization) 83, 86, 90
security *see* defence and national security
Seelan, Sithamparapillai Thava 193
self-reliance 66–71, 79 *see also* Swadeshi
Selvaraj, Kirthana 177–8
Shah, Ashish 150, 182
Shah, Parag 150
Shah Alam, Emperor 55
Shah Jahan, Emperor 55
Shanghai Cooperation Organisation 199
Shann, Keith 24
Sharma, Dave 155
Sharma, Minu and Rajesh 170
Sharma, Priya 177
Sharma, Rashmi 110
Sharma, Sourabh 40
Shaw, George Bernard 64
Shaw, Patrick 28, 91
sheep 8, 38
Shell 70
Shivaji I, King 129
Shri Ghanshyam Maharaj 180
Sierra Leone 184
Sikh Youth Australia (SYA) 186
Sikhism 180, 184–6
Sikka Bhatnagar, Mehak 147
Singapore 61, 63, 84, 131, 144, 160, 199
Singh, Amar 173, 186–7
Singh, Baljinder 40, 139
Singh, Bill 139

Singh, Gurmesh 153
Singh, Gurnam 105
Singh, Harbhajan 44, 102–3, 113
Singh, Harman Preet 191
Singh, Hawker 184
Singh, Lisa 147, 151, 153
Singh, Maninder 191
Singh, Manmohan 34, 41, 115, 124, 130, 131
Singh, Moninder 154, 181
Singh, Narayan 54
Singh, Yadu 157
Slater, Michael 38
slavery 4
small business 150, 157
Smar, Saurabh 164
Smith, Adam 58
Smith, Stephen 33
Smith, Steve 103
socialism 64, 66, 71, 73, 114
Society for Human Resource Management 119
South Africa 16, 25, 31, 160, 199
South America 62 *see also* Brazil
South Korea 72, 93, 139
  economy of 61–3, 67
  investment in 79
  trade with 19–20, 35, 66, 92, 117
  and USA 84
Southeast Asia Treaty Organization (SEATO) 83, 86, 90
Soviet Union *see* USSR
Spence, Michael 200
Sri Guru Singh Sabha (Craigieburn, Melbourne) 185
Sri Lanka 89, 92, 113
Sri Om Care 189–90
Sthalekar, Lisa 104
Stockland 149
stone tools 7
Stoneking, Mark 6
Strathfield Community Centre (Homebush, Sydney) 190
Strathfield Council 154
students *see also* education
  exploitation of 168
  international (in Australia) 36, 40–2, 112, 117, 142, 158, 163–8
  violence against 40–2, 164–5, 168, 171
superpower, India as x, 5, 50–3, 198–200

Swachh Bharat Abhiyan 125
Swadeshi (self-reliance) 64, 68–9, 70, 114
Swaminarayan Akshardham temple 36–7
swaraj (self-rule) 64
Sydney Kannada Sangha 159
Sydney Malayalee Association 159
Sydney Tamil Manram 159
Sydney Tamil Sangam 159
Sydney Writers' Festival 177
Symonds, Andrew 44

Tae Hong Kim 139
Taiwan 61, 63, 72, 84, 93, 200
Taj Mahal 52, 114, 183
Tamil Arts and Cultural Association (TACA) 175–6
Tamil culture 175–6, 181–2
Tamil Seniors Association 190
Tange, Arthur ix, 84
Tangra 107
Tanzania 63
tariffs 61
  in Australia 59
  in Britain 58–9
  in India 60, 65–7, 75, 92, 99, 115
Tarneit 143
Tata Consultancy Services (TCS) 119
Tata Motors 49
taxation 55–7, 59, 166
taxi drivers 148
Taylor Jr, Johnny C. 119–20
Telstra 118, 200
Telugu Association of Australia 159
temples 179–80, 182–3
Tendulkar, Sachin 103
terra nullius 80
terrorism 32, 34, 42–4, 112, 113, 133
textile industry 53–4, 56, 60, 64
Thailand 72, 84, 90, 92
Thiruvizha festival 182
Thomas, Tim 150
'three C's': Commonwealth, curry and cricket 10, 76, 101
Tibet 85
'Tiger' economies 50, 79
Tingyou, Leslie John 139
Tiretta Bazaar 107
Tonka (restaurant) 110
Toongabbie Legal Centre 190–1
trade between Australia and Asia 63

trade between India and Australia 77
   in 18th–19th century 8, 59–61
   in 20th century 9, 37, 49–50, 75–6
   in 21st century 19–20, 76, 117–18
trade between India and Britain 54–8
trade protection 66–7 *see also* tariffs
transport 48–9, 92 *see also*
   automotive industry
Trilateral Strategic Dialogue (Australia, USA and Japan) 131
Trinidad and Tobago 160
Trump, Donald 132
Turbans 4 Australia 186–7
Turnbull, Malcolm 36–7

Ukraine 93–4
underemployment 147–9
United Indian Associations 159
United Nations 23, 38, 85, 88, 90
United States of America 73, 199
   Australian investment and trade with 19, 20, 76
   Australians' feelings towards 17–18
   and defence 22, 25, 27, 46, 82–6, 90
   (*See also* nuclear weapons)
universities 166–7, 200, 201 *see also* education; students
Universities Australia 164
University of Melbourne 166
University of Wollongong 167
uranium 34–5 *see also* nuclear weapons
Urban Tadka (restaurant) 110
Urdu 183
USSR *see also* Russia
   and Asian alliances 84
   and Australia 16
   dissolution of 9, 33, 92, 99, 115, 197
   economic influence on India of 62–3, 65
   military alignment with India 82, 84, 86, 89, 92, 129
   and Nehru, J. 65

Vaisakhi 185
Vajpayee, Atal Bihari 161, 169
Varghese, Peter 34, 37, 201, 202
Vedas 178

vegetarianism 109, 110, 180, 182, 189
Velji, Harish and Harry 189
Venkat, Sagarika 174–5
Vietnam 79, 83, 91, 92
Vietnam War 16, 84, 86
Vijayanagara Empire 52
INS *Vikrant* (aircraft carrier) 128–9
violence against Indian students 40–2, 164–5, 168, 171
visual art 177–8
Viswanath, Manjula 174–5
volunteering 179, 186–7, 191, 193

Wade, Matt 42
Walia, Harmohan Singh 139–40, 145
Walker, David 25
Ward, Barbara 154
Warne, Shane 102, 103, 104
Waters, Larissa 164
Watson, Shane 104
Watt, Alan 24
Watts, Tim ix
Waugh, Steve 102, 104
Webb, Beatrice and Sidney 64
Wells, H.G. 64
Wesfarmers 200
White Australia policy 26, 28, 44, 142, 186
   see also race and racial attitudes
Whitlam, Gough 16, 27–9, 45, 90–1
William of Orange 52
Wong, Penny 126, 132
workforce planning 147
working from home 119–20
World Bank 124, 149
World Press Freedom Index 126
World Wars I and II 8, 184
writers festivals 177
Wyndham City Council 154

Yadav, Leena 176
Yasmeen, Samina 87
yoga 178

Zakat 183
Zinta, Preity 176

www.ingramcontent.com/pod-product-compliance
Lightning Source LLC
Chambersburg PA
CBHW020227170426
43201CB00007B/347